America...A Golden Journey

A Sentimentally Long and Committing Road of a Thai Immigrant

Patcharin Sato, M.S.

iUniverse, Inc.
New York   Bloomington

America...A Golden Journey
A Sentimentally Long and Committing Road of a Thai Immigrant

iUniverse books may be ordered through booksellers or by contacting:

iUniverse
1663 Liberty Drive
Bloomington, IN 47403
www.iuniverse.com
1-800-Authors (1-800-288-4677)

ISBN: 978-1-4401-1450-2 (pbk)
ISBN: 978-1-4401-1451-9 (ebk)

Printed in the United States of America

iUniverse rev. date: 3/9/2009

For The Marchbanks, The Udomsilps, and The Satos

Table of Contents

Foreword

I am honored that Ms. Sato has asked me to write this brief foreword. The account of her life in Thailand, her immigration to the United States, the family that sponsored her, her education, and her journey to the North Texas Job Corps is interesting and informative. The account of her travels, tears, and successes is one more example of the triumph of the human spirit and one more example of how a person can overcome adversity and succeed.

As Vocational Manager for North Texas Job Corps, I am responsible for the overall training of students (650) in fourteen different vocations. Another of my responsibilities includes staffing and staff development.

In March 1999, the Instructor for Desktop Publishing accepted another position outside of Job Corps. After advertising for the position and interviewing several candidates, in walked this very petite, well dressed "China Doll." Because of her size and background (she was from Thailand), I initially thought the students would take advantage of her. However, her education, poise, and matter-of-fact attitude impressed me. She did very well on the interview, and I decided to hire her for the job. Her name was Patcharin (Pat) Marchbanks.

On May 10, 1999, Ms. Marchbanks reported to work and immediately took control of her class. Her firm, but fair approach made her an immediate success. She has continued to perform in this capacity. Her classroom controls, knowledge of the subject, caring attitude, and overall business attitude have made her an outstanding employee. I am pleased to have her as a part of my organization.

Warren Bassham, M.Ed.
Health Care Administrator
Former Vocational Manager

Albert Einstein once said "Weakness of attitude becomes weakness of character." Going through what Pat has experienced, we find how she has developed her strong character and has become a beloved friend to her peers and a caring teacher to her students. This journal documents an admirable example of overcoming adversities and staying true to one's values during a journey to reach the goals one set for oneself. It inspires you to dream more, do more, and become more!

Dr. John Kamthong
Arlington, Texas

I arrived at North Texas Job Corps in 1999 as a counselor, and one of my roles was to work very closely with the center staff, specifically with instructors. During my seven years at the center, I have worked with several members of the staff; however, Pat Sato is an individual that I have truly enjoyed working with! Throughout the years, I have had several students who learned the Desktop Publishing trade under Pat's leadership and they have all spoken very highly of her. Fortunately, for the past 3 - 4 years, I have assigned students to the desktop publishing trade, which gave me the opportunity to develop a great professional relationship with Pat. As a matter of fact, I was always in Pat's class learning a skill or two on Desktop Publishing. Great teacher!

Pat is a very positive individual with a great magnitude of talent. She has worked well with all students to assist them in learning the necessary skill sets to be successful. It did not matter how much work was required to assist the student, Pat was always willing to do more than her part on many occasions. This is an exceptional talent to have while working with our population of youths (ages 16 - 24).

Over the years, we have talked about ways to improve our professional careers, as well as the talents that we both share. With this being said, I truly feel that there is no limit to Pat's success in any field of human endeavor. Pat, go for that Ph.D!. Pat, you are awesome! I am honored to say that I truly admire your qualities and you have a gift from God.

Your friend,
Lantis G. Roberts, MBA
Investigator Trainee- U. S. Department of Labor –EBSA
Former Career Counselor

For the past five years, I have gotten to know Mrs. Patcharin Sato. I have worked with her on a professional basis, and we have also come to be friends. I have enjoyed working with this woman. She is a great teacher that is not only patient with her students, but is also disciplined with them. She is the type of teacher that expects a great deal from her students and will not let them fall short of her expectations, no matter what she has to do to help. She has been known to stay with students after the training day to help with projects that needed finishing, and she has counseled many students when their behavior was unacceptable. This woman is an incredible teacher and mentor to her students. I have enjoyed being a part of North Texas Job Corps, because instructors like Mrs. Sato make it all worthwhile.

Thank you,

Jennifer Duran, LVN
Former Vocational Secretary

To…..Mrs. Sato
From: Samantha Sutton, DTP student 2006

Mrs. Sato always on the go,
She's a very sweet lady,
But no one knows
That she is kind of crazy
But in a good way
She keeps the class going every single day.
She never gets loud or mad,
She is always proud, never sad.
She really knows how to teach
I just love to hear her speak.
I really like Desktop Publishing
Even though it's really not for me.
Mrs. Sato,
The best teacher I've had.
She is always good for a laugh.
Mrs. Sato I thank you
Because if you weren't in this class
I doubt if I could last.
Mrs. Sato you are a great teacher
I'll say because of you…
Your trade is a keeper.

Acknowledgements

This valuable experience of writing a book would have never happened without the kind support and contributions of the following groups of people:

The Marchbanks: "Dad" – without your love and care, I wouldn't have had a chance for anything in America. This book would never have had the chance to be born. Sandy and Michael, with your acceptance, I never feel as if I am the outsider.

My Family: My husband, Kimi – I appreciate your understanding, time and encouragement. Your kind act-of-service by making a cup of hot tea for me late at night while I was still writing my chapters was definitely awesome. My sons, Jack and Andrew -- writing on the swing while having you two playing around, in the backyard, was an amazing moment. I achieve one of my goals, by leaving my legacy to you in writing.

My Parents &My Brother: Your unconditional love, care, encouragement, and supportive conversation over the phone made me enthusiastically keep writing. Thank you for giving me a sense of having strong roots.

My Friends:
How fortunate I am to have supportive friends, as all of you are. The phone calls asking about the status of the book, the rush to get the book published, reserving some copies of the book to send to Thailand, contributing your life stories, and sharing insight on topics, made it to where I couldn't stop writing.

My Mentor:
DeWayne Owens, the author of "*How to Get Rich on Purpose*" – I never thought that I would be able to write my own biography until your visit in my office that day. Your encouragement, time, advice, and support on each step make me dream that this project is achievable.

My Editors:
Doris Owen, I am thankful for your long hours of initial editing, final proofread, and encouraging yellow post-it notes on each returned chapter. Patrick Dennis, I appreciate your editing expertise and assistance until this book is completed. Ellie Mack and Katy Karasek, thank you for your effort in editing some chapters. Dr. Pisate Kamthong, your spot editing and writing guidance are appreciated.

My Students:
I value your talents, contributions, life stories, and the opportunity to teach and work with each of you.

Preface

Many people I have known came to America for different primary reasons. Some came as the spouse of a G.I. (Government Issued Soldier) and have been living here for a few decades; some came as the fiancé or spouse of an American man or woman and are happily married living here; some initially came as an American spouse, but eventually found that the situation in marriage was worse than in their home country, and some came as an internet date. Some came to visit a boyfriend or girlfriend, to visit a son or daughter who were studying or working here, or to stay with brothers, sisters, aunts or uncles who live, work, or own businesses here. Some came as refugees, came on a vacation or a business trip, came as tourists for personal leisure with the secret intent of working and earning money, and some came as students, but also sought employment. Some truly came as students to study in the great educational system in America and to advance themselves academically; many of these people came because their situation forced them to do so, coming here being the only alternative. Some were lucky enough to win a visa lottery before planning to travel to America. I came to America for two major reasons, using a given opportunity to start a new life and utilizing the experience to achieve my dreams.

Regardless of the reasons, everyone can see, learn, and experience many useful things, and gain valuable and unforgettable memories during a stay in this great country. These experiences should be shared with newcomers or with whoever wishes to come to the United States of America to start a new life, to live better, or to just simply learn.

One day I was listening to an election campaign for a Chinese-American woman running for District Judge, which clearly stated that she is a daughter of a Chinese couple who came to America for a better life. She was the only Asian female judge running in this election. It was so amazing to see how some Asians came here to better themselves and to acquire a position in society that would otherwise not be possible in their own country. Moreover, I admire their sense of hard work and determination to achieve their dream. My hat's off to everyone who can share their life experiences, stories, suggestions, and advice from which I can learn while I am a citizen here.

Late one night, I received a phone call from a relative of mine that I had not seen for over fifteen years, asking me how to come to America to study and work. I am glad that I could suggest to her some useful websites for information and give her some advice based on my personal experience.

My primary goal in writing this book is to share with you, the reader, my learning experience in America, particularly in three main areas: personal, educational and professional. The valuable experiences of twelve years have allowed me to encounter many situations, learn many things, meet many groups of people, and to actually do something for America to return the favor by teaching, instructing, motivating and guiding its youth. What my college professors have taught me is now definitely working, and because of them I know that I am certainly able to be a good asset to the American educational system.

It is my hope that you can gain something valuable from this, as you finish reading my book. If you plan to live, study, or work in America, you will at least know how you need to prepare, what to expect, and what you might have to face while studying here. Your situation might be different, but at least you can hear about how one person succeeded. If you are educators, some practices or ways of managing the classroom might be helpful to you. If you are currently living in America and are intending to look for a job, the useful job searching techniques, and the resume and interview tips might help you out. Moreover, if you have free time to read, and you want to read about the life of an average person from Thailand, the land of smiles, having already been there on vacation, this can be something with which you can occupy your time. If you are a person who wants to improve your English reading skills, this can be an easy useful book with which to begin. Remember! I am an average person, who has used plain and simple English throughout her twelve years in America, so if you don't think your English is good, but you can still get around in America, work with Americans and get things done on a daily basis, you are doing wonderfully. If you are an average person who is familiar with many of the things I address in my book, you can feel good that you are not alone. If you are Thais who have worked in America for many decades and have moved back home to enjoy your retirement from your long effort, this book might be able to keep you informed on how the other Thais are doing here. It might remind you of the time when you first came to America and the new things you encountered when you got here. For those Americans or Thais who have at one time taken care of international students, through my book, you might come to know something of how they really feel toward all of the things you have done and have provided to help them feel welcome, while they are away from home. I am sure all of it is greatly appreciated by them.

Please enjoy the book and pick up something that can be an experience for you.

Patcharin Sato.

Chapter 1: Who's Patcharin

It was the Year of the Monkey in the Chinese zodiac. I was born that year. One member of the Chinese Culture Center of San Francisco interestingly states on his website that "people who are born in the Year of the Monkey are the erratic geniuses of the cycle. Clever, skillful, and flexible, they are remarkably inventive and original and can solve the most difficult problems with ease. There are few fields in which Monkey people wouldn't be successful, but they have a disconcerting habit of being too agreeable. They want to do things now, and if they cannot get started immediately, they become discouraged and sometimes leave their projects. Although good at making decisions, they tend to look down on others. Having common sense, Monkey people have a deep desire for knowledge and have excellent memories. Monkey people are strong willed but their anger cools quickly." (http://www.c-c-c.org/chineseculture/zodiac/Monkey.htm.) Some people say those who were born in the Year of the Monkey are very impatient and hyper. They have a desire to get things done as quickly as possible and expect to see immediate results. At heart, these groups of people are quite simple, fun, and loving. They are always cheerful and energetic.

I was born in August, 1968, in a very small rural town of the Chaiyaphum Province, in the northeastern part of Thailand. I am the daughter of Mr. Thongchai and Maliwan Udomsilp. My mother told me that she gave birth to me after three full days of off-and-on contractions. It was a difficult, dry labor. Being a mother myself, I believe that my mother must have been in very great pain. She gave birth to me naturally at home without any modern doctor, convenient equipment, or medicine. I was delivered by a midwife who was living in town. The only thing to relieve the pain was hot water, boiling with different types of medicinal herbs in a big pot in the center of the delivery room. It was a one dirt-floor room in the house that was especially prepared for delivering me. Firewood was used to boil the water, used both for drinking and bathing. The stove used was a native one that was made of clay.

My mother was in the room for seven days after I was born without going outside at all. She slept, ate, and took care of me in there. Some of the medicinal herbs used in boiling the water for her childbirth were Purpuream Rose Ginger, Cymbopogon Uintesianus Jowitt, Complezion of Citrus, Citrus leaves, Tamarind leaves, Bauhinia Retusa leaves, Acacia Concinna leaves, Nibuhria Siamensia leaves, Bark of Pomelo, Curcuma Amada, Acorus Calamusl, Bornelo, Camphor, Curcuma Zedoaria Roscoe, and Curcuma Domestica Valeton. People of Thailand traditionally believe that these herbs are capable of helping blood circulation, reducing excessive body fat, easing soreness and pain, and rejuvenating skin. Some seasoning herbs such as ginger, galangal, and lemon grass, in drinks or dishes, are believed to help reduce internal heat.

My mother often remarks that giving birth to a child these days seems to be very easy. Many choices for giving birth are available: natural, epidural, and Cesarean (C-section). My own children were delivered by C-section. She told me that in her generation, giving birth was a traumatic event in a woman's life. Delivery could result in the death of a woman in many cases due to the lack of medical necessities.

Fortunately, my mother and I survived, even though she says that I was not quite as healthy as I should have been. She also says that there were no vitamin tablets available for her to take, not even an iron pill. That might be why my mother has problems with her bones these days. I always joke with her that I hope it is not too late to buy her a big bottle of calcium pills, provide her with a lot of milk to drink, or take her to visit the best orthopedists I know. Her usual comeback is her health is much better than mine even though she gave birth without modern medicine. While I gave birth to my son with advanced equipment, medicine, and experienced American doctors, I have always had problems with my health while my mother is still going strong for a woman her age. It is really true when we compare stories about our health. I am happy that she is blessed.

I was told that after I was born, I was a small, cranky, and crying baby. I especially cried a lot in the evening. On many occasions, my parents were hardly able to eat their supper without having to worry about me. They were rarely able to enjoy their evening together in peace. I believe if the same situation happened these days, the child would be called a "colicky baby" who has great gas pains. A baby would be consistently crying, that can cause the parents to take the baby in a stroller for a long walk on the street, take a drive in the middle of the night, or make parents rock their baby in the rocking chair until they drop because of exhaustion. Back in those days, when a baby would continuously cry, they believed that the cause was a natural spirit - a thing that is imperceptible (like a ghost, I guess). My parents tried so hard to find the best traditional remedies available. They even tried to find a spiritualist. I don't know for sure what it was, but my mother told me that the traditional doctor just brewed a big jar of what was called "Holy" water for me after his long prayer, and sometimes poured it over my head. He also mashed different herbs' roots in the water for me to drink. It made me stop crying. She said it happened almost every evening. I believe it must have really been inconvenient and troublesome for my parents. My mother told me about this when I was growing up, I remember joking with her that I probably stopped crying because I was wet and cold or I was scared of the doctor's noise. I actually forgot to do the same thing with a traditional doctor when my infant son was having colic pain.

My mother told me that when I was almost two years old, my family moved from my birthplace to Loei Province to help out on my grandfather's ranch, and I was raised there. I lived there until I was twenty-four years of age. Growing up, I always had heard that my parents had such economic hardships in the small rural town in which I was born. There was no electricity and city convenience. People there lived their lives so naturally: hunting, growing rice, raising hens, planting vegetables, and farming for a living. She also told me that not many types of transportation were available for most people around town in those days, just a wagon and a bicycle. The economically well-off people would have a motorcycle. It was not convenient at all, if people wanted to go into a nearby city. They had to catch a small, old road bus very early in the morning and return home late at night. Many people walked to the city, a trip which took from sunrise until sunset. She said life was inconvenient but peaceful. People were very friendly, unselfish, and caring. The way they were living was sufficient, so they did not reach for material things. Daily living in town had no crime and no different classes of people. My mother said people were poor in terms of money, but they always had food to eat and sufficient clothing to wear. I believe they had enough of what we call "basic needs" in life; today, basic needs are growing more and more, and many people will never be able to fulfill their basic needs. That leads our society to become more materialistic and to people committing crimes. So much corruption exists, even though some groups of people have more than enough of everything. My grandmother used to say that when we were born, we did not bring anything into the world and when we are gone, we will not take anything with us either. The only thing people will remember about us is our goodness and gratefulness. I was fortunate to be taught by her. That leaves something for me to teach my own children these days. I only hope that the results for my children will be the same as when my grandmother and my mother taught me.

Since I was the first female grandchild, my grandfather gave me a very beautiful name on my original birth certificate, *Prawpran*, a name that I never recall using. Growing up knowing that my name is *Patcharin* made me wonder why I have two different names. My mother told me that when I was enrolled in elementary school, my father had changed my name from Prawpran to Patcharin, which is the name I have always used. They lost the name change documentation. I don't recall using my birth certificate for many things when I was growing up, so not having it wasn't a problem. However, these days, when children enroll in school, we need to have all documentation, such as a birth certificate, Social Security card, and immunization record. I have learned to store all of my documents in a safe place. My mother also told me that I did not have any type of vaccination when I was a baby, unlike these days -- my son has a shot or two almost every time he has a doctor's visit. Thank God I survived in those days. Maybe there were not a lot of advanced diseases back then. It seems as if the better medicines are, the higher the number of diseases found.

I did not have to worry about searching for my birth certificate, until 1994 while I was living in America. I was filing for my permanent residency status. One of the required documents was a birth certificate. Having been told by my parents over the phone that they had lost it a long time ago, I did not know what to do. My parents had to go back to that rural town for the first time in almost three decades. The town had changed over time. Now, everything seems to be more convenient. I was jokingly telling my mother that it had adapted to civilization. Luckily, throughout its adaptation, the court house still had my original birth record, which had my name as Prawpran. My parents had a major problem to match two important documentations on my name. Initially, the court house clerk said that no evidence showed that Prawpran and Patcharin are the same person. My parents asked for further help from the registration office with little hope of accomplishing anything. The answer from them was that they could do nothing, because no documentation existed of a name change. After a few days of talking, visiting, and begging between my parents and the deputy director of the court house, he finally decided to help. The deputy director issued the approval letter to assure that Prawpran is Patcharin. They are the same person.

During that period, I was anxiously and attentively waiting in America for the necessary birth certificate. Actually, it is an approval letter. I acknowledged that my parents were working really hard on it. Later on, I was told that a large sum of money flowed under the table to get a signature on that approval paper. I just realized that even my unimportant name documentation still had to be involved with corruption. What about the documentation for the wealthy or so called important people?

I grew up in a lower middle class family. I am the eldest and only daughter of three children. My youngest brother passed away in 1996. My mother is a housewife; I grew up seeing her work hard on the farm and selling food at the market to supplement the family's income. Her little savings went either to reducing my father's debt or our school allowances. She never wanted to spend the savings on herself. She worked very hard to support the family and raised three children. My father was in the civil service, and I grew up seeing him struggle financially from month to month on a small monthly salary. His face-saving attitude and trust in the wrong kinds of friends had led our family into a serious financial crisis, one that had changed my life completely. However, as parents, they raised me well. They gave the opportunity to become the best I could be on my own level of ability, one step at a time on a long and unstable ladder. Remembering my mother's teaching, "You could not choose to be born, but you could always choose to be the best in your life with dignity and determination," is something that drives my living each day to the best of my ability.

As a young woman, I struggled financially through a four-year college in a city nearby my hometown. I attended Udonthani Teacher College. Growing up hearing about my parents' financial problems, I didn't want to bother them for any costs or fees regarding school. I strived to get an education because I believed that it could help me to become who I wanted to be and do what I wanted to do. A Thai proverb, "The strongest life foundation is an education," helped me to find different ways to earn a college degree. While attending college, I took a part-time job in a small store doing bookkeeping. I took homemade candies, snacks, and desserts to sell at the college before class started. I sold clothing at a boutique for a small commission. I sold cosmetics from a catalog, earning 15% from the total sale balance. I was also responsible for helping my mother sell food in the morning market to support our family. That was how I supported myself through college. With difficult circumstances, I could not afford to have any extra activities outside of the family. Seeing my friends getting a monthly allowance from their parents made me feel sorry for myself. Fortunately, I never gave up on the situation. Looking back at how difficult my situation was helped me to be more prepared to provide educational opportunities for my own children. I now have a portion of my monthly salary contributed to the Texas States' Educational Fund for my son's college plan and have the other portion of the fund saved in a financial institution. The entire amount has been paid for. I hope that my children don't have to struggle as I did. College fees in America are so expensive and will probably continue to increase.

With many hardships in my life and my financial disadvantage, studying in my own country was hard enough. The opportunity to study, work, and live in America was out of reach and beyond my wildest dreams.

In July 1993, a few weeks before my twenty-fifth birthday, a generous American family made my dream comes true and my hopes come alive. Without their sponsorship, kindness, guidance, suggestions, and directions, the new way of life, a better way of living, an opportunity to study, and a valuable learning experience would not have happened in my life. They provided me with both financial and moral support. Most of all, in terms of necessities, they provided a safe roof over my head while I was under their care. They also gave me the best treasure, which was an education. It is a treasure that I can use in America to make a living to support myself, my family, and my parents back home. I would have not been personally, academically, and professionally successful in life for the past twelve years without them. Also, my valuable life experience would have not been possible in America without their generosity. I remember being jokingly told after my college graduation that, "I gave you wings and they are strong enough to fly." I want to say," Yes, I can fly; wherever I go, I know that I will always have a safe nest to come back to." I thank you so much, my American family. My success today could not have been without you.

Four-year-old Pat

Pat with relatives in Thailand

Texas summer in the backyard

The Udomsilps - in Thailand

Chapter 2: A New Beginning

"Dare to Dream!" This phrase never entered my mind in those days, because I never thought I would be able to have a better opportunity in life. I had learned to accept that the life I was given was the best I could have. Today, working with many American students, I realize I was once their age; they are seeking a second chance in life, just as I once did. It makes me strive to find different ways to help them make good choices to maximize their chances in life. It gives me the opportunity to let all of them know that, "We can always have a new beginning; only we can make it happen for ourselves when we have appropriate help and direction."

It was early in 1993 when I made a big decision in my life, a decision for which I received full support from my parents. It changed my life, and it also eventually affected the lives of others in my family. It was a decision to hope to be better in life and to be able to support myself, family, and my newly born son, for whom my parents accepted care. I planned and agreed to provide full financial support while I searched for a new beginning in my own life. I had no idea how I would do it, but I said I would, and I eventually did it. I remember hearing my mother mention to some of her friends and relatives that, "if my daughter says she will do something, she will get it done." These days, that statement has been acknowledged by many people around me. It was nice to learn that my words are trustworthy. My family's culture called for a daughter to be obedient, respectful, and grateful for everything the parents say, and I mean everything! Everything had to be within a boundary. I vividly remembered my mother's teaching that being a bad girl would bring embarrassment and sin to the family. It would be like having a filthy toilet in front of the house. I lived my teen life in the way they wanted me to live it, did what they told me to do, and followed where they led me no question asked. I didn't have many opportunities to be exposed to the world like many girls my age did. I was soft, positive, and naive. Those qualities are good, but they made me get hurt so easily. I lacked knowledge of real world experiences. I was family oriented and family supportive. Being the only daughter of the family, I was not encouraged enough to stand up for myself or to live away from parents, but instead to follow the familial situation and guidelines. I was suffering terribly from an unsuccessful arranged marriage at a young age, while many of my friends were searching for their future and enjoying their blossoming lives. I was balancing home life and student life, while others were just focusing on school. It was not easy in a relationship without love and understanding. I was struggling to stay in the relationship, just because I did not want to be seen as a woman who fails. I also did not want my parents to feel embarrassed and ashamed.

I finally walked out of the relationship when things came to an end. There was no alternative for me. That decision resulted in my having to leave everything behind and seek a second chance in life. I then had already obtained a bachelor's degree in general management from a four-year college. Ironically, I did not learn to manage my own life. Even though I had the degree, it did not help me much to obtain a stable job in the rural town. I just took some temporary little jobs that were available, such as an accounts receivable and payable or bookkeeping for a small, privately-owned business.

I remember when I asked permission from my parents to enroll in a vocational school in Bangkok after I learned about it from an educational catalog. The International Hotel & Airline School is privately owned by a flight attendant, who worked for a well-known airline. The high price of tuition delayed my parents' decision. I tried to convince them that I would find a part-time job to put myself through school without giving them any worry. I promised them that I would live my life the right way despite being alone in a new environment. Finally, they agreed to let me go to school in Bangkok. At departure, I was in tears when I told my mother that I would not let anybody down and I would behave myself. I promised them to do my best to finish school and look for a better job, so that I would be able to stand on my own feet. I got my mother's blessing to embark on a struggling journey for a better life. I was in tears while looking at my four-month-old son in my mother's arms at the bus station. I walked away accompanied by my father. I was determined to succeed.

Since I was not familiar with Bangkok, studying there seemed difficult. A little bit before that time, I had a chance to meet one of my good friends from high school, who had been successfully studying and living in Bangkok for years; a friend whom I had lost contact for many years, but the fond memory of our friendship had never faded. This friend always came to spend time with my family while we were in high school, joined our family for special events, and participated with our family in fun activities. When I was hospitalized from a car accident, I could count on my friend to be there for me. That person was the only one I was inclined to ask for assistance, suggestions, and information about living in a big city like Bangkok. We met at my home twice before I left for Bangkok. During our meeting, I was given contact information, including the address and phone number; indeed, my friend knew that I did not know many people in Bangkok. I thought

I was really affirmed a full support and help while I was trying to get a better start in life. During our conversation, he seemed to be very understanding, caring, and willing to help. I was even told that I would be picked up at the bus station when I arrived in Bangkok. If I really decided to go to Bangkok, I could just notify my friend. I was really expecting a lot out of our friendship and was confident that I would have his support to make it in the real world.

Imagine me, a naïve girl from a rural town, having recently given birth to an adorable healthy boy (The C-section wound was still sore, the stomach still bloated.), escorted by my father to the capital city, to pursue a second chance in life… **How?** I did not think anybody would have a worthy idea….

I left my hometown for Bangkok with a very limited amount of money; I had pawned a gold necklace which was given to me by my mother to pay a big portion of the tuition and save some for my living expenses while attending school. Hopefully, after the graduation, I would be lucky enough to find a job in a hotel business, because the school had advertised job placement assistance after graduation. I hoped to perform well, so a job would be guaranteed.

I was admitted to the students' housing provided by a relative of the school's director and started vocational school the next day. My routine started at 8:00 a.m. and ended at 3:30 p.m. for a few weeks. By having a limited expense allowance, I refused to go out with some of my classmates I had just met. I chose the most reasonable restaurant near the school to have lunch and supper. Some days after school, I was helping the owner of a house with some chores; I washed clothes and dishes, cleaned the house, and accompanied her to deliver small furniture that she sold. She kindly paid for my help with some good food and friendship. Of course, it was quite lonesome in the new surroundings, both the people and the environment.

The circumstances weren't always on my side. One day when I got to my room after school, I found out that my wallet, my address book, and some other small belongings were stolen from my purse while I was attending class. I really didn't know how it happened. Fortunately, I had paid the last portion of my tuition a few days before this incident. After a long search by the school personnel, no one could be blamed but me and my carelessness. Everybody at school knew I did not have any money. Some classmates offered me lunch and dinner. I was too ashamed to take from them every day. The school director generously offered me a loan of 3,000 bahts, which was about $100 at that time, so that I could continue studying at his school. I also received phone calls from my parents that my youngest brother was really sick and could not continue his studies. He went home to my parents, so they could take care of him. I had to go to his school and drop all his classes for him. The money for my son's formula, which I needed to send to my parents, was another thing that bothered me a great deal, even though they did not ask for it. It was a very frustrating time that I was fighting alone. I had no one with whom I could talk.

During my hardship, I decided to write to my old friend whom I thought I would be able to count on. After a few weeks of waiting, I got a phone call at school; I was so delighted that I would have someone to converse with; I would have someone that I could talk to, because we had been good friends for a long time. We met for lunch and had a long talk about the situation. The meeting was nice and friendly. My friend offered to help me find a job, if I still needed one after my school. For some unknown reason, I never heard from my good friend again after that visit--no phone calls, and no letters. I also had no way to contact him, because my address book was stolen. With the loss of the friendship, I was sad, confused, and disappointed. I determined not to contact him any more. I promised myself that I would have to survive without bothering my friend or anyone. I did not realize that later on in life, this incident would help me to become a person who values an old friendship. I put more value on the new good friendships I have built. It helps me to make myself available for good friends who actually need help. It also helped me to be sincere and try my best to keep my promises and words. Looking back these days, I wish I had the opportunity to meet that friend, to look at my friend and ask why he had disappeared from the face of the earth after uttering a sincere promise to help. It might be a good chance to thank my friend for motivating me to become strong and independent, to be a person who tries to stand on my own two feet. This incident reminds me of my Thai proverbs: "A friend is never known till a man has need," "A friend is best found in adversity," and "A friend is proved in distress." I thought I had a friend.

I could not stand my own situation. I decided to ask the school director for help in finding a part-time job while I attended school. I was so thankful that he understood my situation and was willing to help; he asked his friend at the Grand Siam Service Apartment to interview me for the receptionist position in the front office. It was a newly opened apartment with a friendly environment. There I had an opportunity to meet the kind owners who gave me valuable advice that completely changed my life later on that year. The couple ignited my desire to pursue the opportunity to seek my fortunes in the "land of opportunity," the land that I had never thought about in my twenty-five years of living. About this land, I was once told, "You can always strive for your own opportunity and pursue your success with good planning."

I started working at the apartment every day after school. My shift was from 5:00 p.m. until 11:00 p.m., and my class started at 8:00 a.m. the next day. During my shift when I was not busy, I volunteered to help serving food and drinks, be a hostess at the restaurant, or sometimes washing dishes in the kitchen after work. Mostly the apartment's guests were foreigners who were on a business trip or had contracted work in Thailand for a short period of time: a large group of ice skaters from London, a business man from Japan, an accountant from Singapore, a few engineers from Australia, many engineers and workers from America, just to name a few. The service apartment business was quite busy. By giving my extra time, the owner always allowed me to take food back to the house, so that I had some to eat the next day at school. A few months after giving birth to a child, I was hungry for every dish I saw. The food looked so delicious and smelled so wonderful. All I could do most of time was just swallowing my saliva. I did not buy anything to eat, but worked for it. While I was working there, I made some tips, and I sent all of them to my mother for my son's formula. Sometimes, when the guests wanted their business done, but they didn't have time to do it by themselves due to their work schedule, I offered to do it for them on my day off. Some wanted to buy Thai souvenirs to send or take home. Some wanted to send packages at the post office. Some wanted to buy fruits or even personal items. This helped me learn my way around Bangkok and to interact with people to get tasks accomplished. Especially, I learned the importance of customer service skills. The guests also gave me very good tips for doing their tasks. Some even gave more tips after learning that I was a student who had good service attitude.

I continued working there while doing my internship at The Sun Ruth Hotel. It was a business contract between the hotel and the school where I was enrolled. I was first a trainee in the hotel's restaurant and then in its front office. Everyday, I was determined to work hard. I tried to keep myself busy, so that I did not have to worry about my own situation. During this time, I had an opportunity to meet one American family that had a son and a daughter visiting while on a business trip to Bangkok. They were the **Marchbanks**. I was asked to show them around. Me? Tour them around? I didn't know much of anything, but I was allowed to do so by my supervisor who later on, I learned, had finished his MBA in Hotel Management from NYU in New York City, USA. He was the Thai owner of the service apartment in which I was given a part-time job. We called him "Freddie." His wife was also kind and gave me a lot of good advice while I was under their supervision.

Freddie graduated with a master's degree from NYU. He used to tell me that he worked hard in a Thai restaurant, while enrolled in school. He also told me that acquiring a visa to travel to the USA was not easy, even if it was a student visa. At that time, I had no interest in any type of visa and had no clue about why people wanted to obtain one. If only I had known that one day I would have a chance to acquire one, I would have paid more attention to his story and the information he shared with me.

I took two weeks off from work to travel with two Americans, Sandy and Michael. We spent a few days sightseeing in Bangkok, accompanied by their father's car driver. One day we went to the Thai Temple downtown by boat. It was so fascinating to me, and that was my first opportunity to travel in Bangkok, even though it is in my own country; I just could not afford this type of leisure. We went to Pattaya beach for two days and came back to Bangkok, then caught a flight to the North, Chaing Mai. Sandy paid for the whole trip and a package tour. We had a wonderful driver and a tour guide. We went shopping and enjoyed the night life. I really had a good time and saw different things that I never had the opportunity to see before meeting them. After our sightseeing, Sandy and Michael went to my hometown to meet my family. I was with them until they prepared to go back to America. I was offered the opportunity to visit them in their hometown of Paris, Texas, USA. **Visiting them in America? How?** I didn't even have any money to support myself. How could I afford a plane ticket?

One day before leaving Thailand from her vacation, Sandy took me to the American Embassy to get the necessary forms and information about acquiring a visitor visa. I just followed what she said without knowing much about the process. These days, having time to sit and look back, I was so lacking in experience and had such a limited knowledge of things. Remember, I was from a rural town…Sandy told me that she would send me the entire supportive document from America that showed that I was not going to be the public's responsibility; I would have a place to stay and somebody guaranteeing me during my visit.

I continued working at the Sun Ruth Hotel as a receptionist after the Marchbanks left Thailand. The Sun Ruth Hotel offered me a job after my internship with an outstanding performance. It was a confusing time in my life; whether I should focus on working as I planned, or try to acquire a visitor visa to visit the Marchbanks family in America. While I was confused, I went back to the Grand Siam Service Apartment to visit with Freddie and his wife. They advised me to try the visa process. I still remembered what Freddie said, "You have nothing to lose. Why not try? At least during the visa process you can learn a lot of things, such as what types of paperwork you must prepare and present. You will also learn how the officers conduct the interview and what questions will be asked." However, I kept in mind that a visa would not easily be granted.

Well, it was really true; whether I would obtain a visa or not, I would at least learn what the American embassy looks like inside, anyway. The advice I received was that if I did not have a lot of money, it was unlikely that I would be approved for a visa, because I would not be able to prove that I could fully support myself as a tourist in America. Well, my chance was not even 50% then, because all the money I had was only 80,000 Thai baht, which was about $3,200 at that time. The money was given to me before my American family left. If I were to be honest, I would admit that back in 1993, I had no idea what initial steps I should take. I did not know where I could gather the information. I only listened to what a few people I knew had to say. I wish I had learned how to use the Internet then, so I could have located all the information I wanted.

However, my learning throughout the process had happened in late June 1993. I had learned a lot myself, and with some good advice, I realized that if I wanted to visit the American family, I would have to acquire a visa category B: Visitors visa or people with a B1-B2 type visa. It is a visa for anyone wishing to visit the USA for a vacation or on business and who wishes to stay longer than ninety days. Type B visa is a non-immigrant visa that gives a person a right to come to America temporarily. This type of visa may be valid for a maximum of ten years. However, the one I got allowed for an entry period of only six months. The length of stay was determined by the immigration officer. The visa I got did not give me the right to work in America.

Early in the morning one day late in June 1993, I arrived at the American Embassy around 6:00 a.m. I could not believe the long line of people ahead of me waiting at the front of the embassy knowing that the door would not be opened until 8:00 a.m. Well, after seeing that I rushed to get in line, too. We were all given a number after the staff started working. It was a long waiting period with the hope of a positive outcome. I wished I had somebody with me there at that moment that I knew, so I could tell them how anxious, excited, and nervous I was. **I was alone.** When my number was called to submit all documents and then for an interview, I was extremely chilled. My hands were sweating, my heart was beating fast, and I felt like crying for no reason. I answered all of the questions truthfully. I was told by Freddie that some people even lie about many things and change their name many times just to get the visa to America.

I remembered hearing the officer say, "We will keep your passport here, and you can come back at 2:00 p.m. to get a visa." I politely replied, "Thank you very much, sir." To me it was not a miracle; it was the kindness of my American family that had a great impact. I then jokingly called this visa "A God Blessing Visa" I believe many of you reading this book right now have been through similar situations and might have felt like crying after feeling relief from the intensified moment. It was something for which I had been waiting for so long.

"I GOT IT!" I wanted to scream out loud to show my excitement and joy. My heart was jumping out of my chest. My, I wonder if people who won a big lottery have this type of feeling--the great feeling of achievement for something you have tried so hard to attain. I first called one of my American family's friends, who had a business in Thailand to ask her for some advice. She congratulated me and told me to get ready for a long trip to America. I went back to my hometown to inform my parents about the matter. They were very supportive of my decision and wanted me to learn. At least they already had the opportunity to meet the American family who sponsored me. I spent all the time I had with my son and my family before I started to travel.

Imagine me, an average Thai girl from a poor family who did not even have enough money for a plane ticket, going abroad for a sight seeing trip. I am not ashamed to say that I was in tears when I was at the airport, with only my father there with me. For poor people, a chance to see the airport was rare. That was the second time I had a chance to walk in the airport, even in my own country. The first time I went to pick up my brother who got a scholarship to study in Australia and came home to visit, and the time that I was leaving Thailand. I nervously went through customs to get my passport checked and followed all of the instructions closely. It was about a 7-hour flight from Thailand to Taiwan, 13 hours from Taiwan to Los Angeles, CA, and another 4 hours from Los Angeles to Dallas, TX. I memorized every step and stop, and learned everything I could. I remember even having a bad upset stomach throughout my long, exhausting flight from Thailand to America.

Before I arrived in America, airline personnel gave me an INS arrival/departure record card known as I-94 to complete. I was told that it is an important document, because I would be allowed to stay in America until the date stamped on my I-94. Usually, it is stapled onto the passport. Whenever I leave America, the card will be removed from the passport by the airline officer.

When I arrived in America, I first had to pass through the U.S. Public Health Immigration & Naturalization. I saw that it was divided into two sections, "US Citizens" and "All Other Passport." Of course, I made sure to follow the other Asians, because I thought it would be the best and safest way to do. I really like the way the author David Hampshire wrote about this process:

Once you enter America, you're under the jurisdiction of the INS who have dictatorial power over you, and who have been variously described as aggressive, brusque, bullying, stern, and intimidating. You should remain polite and answer any question in a direct and courteous manner. American immigration officials are trained to suspect that everyone who doesn't have the right to live and work in America is a potential illegal immigrant. Immigration officers have the task of deciding whether you're permitted to enter America and have the necessary documentation, including a visa if necessary, even with a visa, you don't have the right to enter America; only the immigration officer can make that decision (Hampshire 507).

My intention was clean and clear; my documentation was in order. I stepped into the line to be questioned by the officer with a high level of nervousness. Yes, he was stern, and I was extremely nervous. I recall that he asked whether this was my first time visiting America; of course, I thought he knew but asked anyway. He also asked where I was going to stay, how long I planned to stay, what my relationship was with Sandy Marchbanks, and how much money I brought with me. I truthfully answered all of his questions. Fortunately, I did not have any problem. I was able to pass through the whole process successfully. Later on, while living in America, I learned that if immigration officers suspected the person, they can reject their entry and send that person back to their country of origin. If the person cannot speak English, the officer will find someone in the area to translate.

I also learned that U.S. Customs is another area I had to go through after arrival. I was given a customs declaration form on the plane to complete. I did not have anything to declare, because I only had one suitcase of clothing and a small number of personal belongings. If people bring food items, the suitcase can be searched. Sometimes food items can be thrown away by the officer.

I could not believe that I actually was in America, until I walked out of the airline gate and saw Mr. Marchbanks and Michael standing and looking at me with a big, warm, welcoming smile. I was crying when they gave me a welcome hug at DFW Airport in Dallas, Texas, in July 1993. Sandy was in college in another city and could not come to pick me up. My feeling then was indescribable. Mr. Marchbanks placed his hand on my head lightly shaking and said, "Silly girl, why are you crying? Let's go home. We have a long drive to make." Michael was helping me claim the brand new suitcase I bought the day before I traveled. It was only one suitcase on my first day in America. He also asked me about my first long flight. "It was wonderful and it will be my unforgettable one," I responded and got ready to face my life journey in America.

B.A. Graduation in Thailand

Pat and family in Thailand

Chapter 3: A New Life Giver

Neither providing the opportunity for one person to have a new start in life, nor taking a chance on caring for a twenty-five year old woman who is from Thailand, is an easy task. This task is especially daunting, when the best start for that person would be a good education, an education in America, which is quite costly. The Marchbanks family took a big step in helping me get started on a new journey under their roof in Paris, Texas. They willingly and generously provided everything for me. With every step, I walked on my new beginning, I felt that one person was watching, caring, and willing to help me and pull me up when I fail. He had paved a strong road for my success, which I would have not been able to do on my own. He is a person who has provided me with memorable and valuable life experiences in this land of opportunity, which has been said, "turns people's dreams to reality." This land has created and provided good helping hands to many nations; it is a land where its people think nothing is impossible, a land that I would have not known from the other side of the beautiful image that is the world, if I had not come to experience it. He also had helped me to become who I am today. He is Mr. Clovis Marchbanks.

Mr. Marchbanks has gained valuable life experiences over many decades. While in the Navy, he served in World War II and in Korea. During World War II, he was at the Guadalcanal, Guam, the Philippine

Islands, and Okinawa invasions. He spent 20 years in the Navy and retired on June 2, 1962, as a Chief Electronics Technician. After retiring from the Navy, he worked in the Nuclear Medicine Instrumentation and diagnostic Ultrasound systems, and worked mostly in sales of this equipment to hospitals and universities. In 1978, he retired again, and in 1980 he entered the Directional Drilling field putting pipelines under rivers.

He worked as an engineer in this field for the next 20 years. This job involved designing the crossings and guiding the drill bits to the desired exit spot on the far side of the river. In addition to working all over the United States, he worked in Mexico, Canada, Venezuela, Bolivia, Thailand, Bangladesh, Holland, Italy, Spain, and the Ivory Coast. In the year 2000, he retired again and has not worked since then, while living at his home in Paris, TX. He has a 35-year-old daughter, Sandy, and a 31-year-old son, Michael, along with five grandchildren: Jack, Andrew, Emmett, Elena, and Luke. Two of the grandchildren are my sons, Jack and Andrew. These grandchildren keep him pretty busy, when they visit with him. They also cost him a lot during their birthdays and the Christmas season. His hobbies consist primarily of horse racing and going to the gambling casinos, along with reading technical literature, world news, and cosmology literature. Cosmology is especially interesting, because the evolution and vastness of the universe has always intrigued him.

Michael is also in the directional drilling field working as a driller on the drill rigs. He has also worked all over the world and has been working in Thailand for the last year and a half. Michael is friendly and optimistic. He is easy to get along with and fun to be around. He is a bachelor who still enjoys traveling, working, and experiencing diversity. Having to work all the time in many places, it is difficult for him to settle down as a family man. Recently, I had the opportunity to meet Michael while my family and I visited Mr. Marchbanks on the weekend. He came back from a vacation for only two weeks. He is next planning to work in Indonesia. He came back to the United States without telling us. It was a big surprise when he showed up at home. It was pretty strange that Michael told me about things and people in my country, while he is living in my country and I am living here.

Sandy is married to Doug Parkerson and has been living in Lexington, MA, for the last two years, where her husband recently received his master's degree in international development. They are the parents of 3 ½-year-old twins Emmett and Elena, and 2-year-old Luke. Doug has accepted a job with an international development company in Boston area.

For my twenty-fifth birthday, Sandy kindly made me a birthday cake. It was my first birthday cake in America. She also helped guiding me how to study and live here. She provided me with good advice, while I was trying to get into college. She was afraid that I would be homesick while most of the time I was living alone in Paris, TX. She asked Mr. Marchbanks to buy me a dog. His name is Pancho. He is the cutest dog that I have ever had, and having him gave me an opportunity to experience why Americans are so crazy about their pets. The drawback was that I also got to learn that veterinarian's services are pretty pricy. Pancho was my great companion.

Sandy is a good example of being conservative with money. I remember Mr. Marchbanks gave her a credit card to spend on personal and school matters when she was in college. He never had any problem with Sandy's overspending. She also did well in college, eventually graduating from Texas A&M University. Mr. Marchbanks has always been very proud of her for being very smart and athletic. She is also an outgoing person, who loves all the outdoor activities such as biking, rock climbing, jogging and running. When I started writing this book, Sandy was raising fund for cancer patients by competing in the Boston Marathon. Sandy and her family have moved to Bolivia, where she and her husband can provide their children the best environment for studying Spanish. Bolivia is also the developing country where her husband chose to use his knowledge after his graduate degree.

Even though Mr. Marchbanks, the person who gave me such a great opportunity, is a renowned engineer, he lives his life simply. While I was under his care, I always saw that things happened around the house and in my life with good and careful planning. I learned that living and spending conservatively was the way of life in my American family's home. Although, I was provided sufficient funds for daily living and studying, I was taught to spend money with care. The many things I have been taught have become very helpful to my daily living with my own family. They also provide me with things to teach my own children while they are growing up in America.

In the twelve years with Mr. Marchbanks' leading, providing, protecting, and teaching me, I learned a great deal about cultural diversity, living conditions, lifestyles, and practicing necessary skills for living successfully in America.

Some people have had opportunities to visit a foreign country without knowing anything of that country's culture. Some people, before traveling to another country, learn and prepare themselves for the difference in cultures; however, they sometimes still encounter many difficulties. If somebody has ever been in a community, which has ways of acting, dressing, eating, and living that are completely different from his/her own community's way, that experience will be an unforgettable memory.

Culture is not something that should be overlooked. It has been transmitted from generation to generation among groups of people or communities. Generally, different communities have different cultures. People in each community certainly believe that their culture is the best. Unfortunately, nothing can determine that one culture is better than another, because each culture might be impacted by many factors. Those factors might be geography, religion, and different belief systems. One community's culture might not be suitable for some, but each community should respect cultures other than their own.

Within twelve years, I have absolutely found a big difference between American culture and my own culture. For instance, in my country, Thailand, the traditional form of greeting is not a handshake as it is in America; it is a *wai*. According to the Thai cultural resource, a wai (pronounce *wye*), is the raising of the hands, palms joined and placed in a position lightly touching the body somewhere between the chest and the forehead. Our Thai wai is also interestingly described as "This is an important social custom that reinforces both social structure and religious observance. This elegant gesture is a combination of a greeting, a display of respect, and a statement of a person's rank in the social hierarchy. The Thai wai is not just "hello." Who wais whom, who wais first, and exactly how one places the hands in relation to the other person are all involved in the act of wai-ing. When Thais are driving and passing the Shrine or temple, located anywhere, they will usually take both hands off the steering wheel or stand straight to wai the image of Buddha housed there. At a very young age, we were taught to wai older people. A Buddhist monk never wais a layman, not even the King. It is known that the lower the inclination of the head over the joined hands, the greater the amount of respect shown. Those of lower status always initiate the wai, and the gesture may or may not be returned by the person of higher status. People of the same social status will wai each other, and it is age that counts, not gender. Thais normally see a younger man wai an older woman first, if she is of the same social status. We consider it inappropriate for an older person to wai a younger person first. It has been said that "some people believe that such an action is supposed to take seven years off the younger person's life." When we make a wai, the shape formed by the hands is similar to the closed lotus bud, which is often offered to the Lord Buddha as a symbol of purity."

While the basic greeting in English is "Hi," or "Hello, how are you?" some Thais who don't know English will often greet foreigners as "Hey, you!" They don't mean to be rude, but they simply translate from the respectful word *Khun* in Thai language, which refers to *Mr. or Mrs.* In English. The common way of greeting someone in Thai is not "How are you?" but "Where are you going?" I have not yet heard Americans greet me by saying" Where are you going?" when we first meet. It is quite amazing to see that some Americans greet each other on the walking track, in the stores, on the bus, even though they don't know each other. They simply say, "Hi," "Good Morning," or "How are you?" Sometimes, they don't even wait for a response. It is interesting to learn the differences between cultures.

Most of the time, I feel uncomfortable with my students' touching my head in a friendly fashion, because Thais believe that the head is the most sacred part of the body. We avoid touching people, especially an adult, on the head, even as a friendly gesture. It is best to be aware of the feet. They are considered the lowest and dirtiest part of the body. Thais will be sure to apologize if they accidentally step on someone's foot or touch their head. Thais don't rest their feet or put their shoes on a table, and don't stretch out their feet in anyone's direction. Thais don't point their feet at a Buddha image or a monk. Thais do not wear shoes in the house. They usually take their shoes off in front of the door before entering a house. Some houses even prepare a container of water where visitors can rinse their feet before walking into the house. Sometimes, where I now work, seeing some Americans sit on the chair and place their feet on the table while talking to each other, I still feel a little bit strange and uncomfortable. Putting their feet on the chair or table, however, is to them a quite common thing. Students might find my not letting them practice that behavior in class difficult, because they are used to it; however, that is my class expectation that they are to follow.

My American family thought I was strange when I took off my shoes and walked barefoot on their carpeted floor. They taught me that in their house having shoes on was fine. They walked with shoes on everywhere in the house and took them off just before they went to bed. Since they always saw me taking off my shoes in the house, they stopped bothering to tell me to put my shoes on anymore. It is something to which I have not yet gotten accustomed. I just feel so uncomfortable about it.

Growing up being taken to the temple and being encouraged to practice praying regularly, I have also learned that Thais feel very strongly about their religion, so they have never worn their beach clothes, shorts, or tank tops to a temple. Both women and men cover their legs and their shoulders. They don't allow children to climb over Buddha images or be disrespectful to the monks. Thais are aware of their words, behaviors, and actions in the temple. I recall that Sandy, Michael, and I went sightseeing at a beautiful temple in Thailand. She was wearing shorts. Since she learned that shorts were not appropriate, she was willing to change her outfit. I admired her for being respectful.

The other thing I found different is the displays of affection between the sexes in public; this way of acting is not common in Thailand. Touching, hugging, and kissing should be a private matter and should be behind closed doors. Parents usually do not allow children to see their affection in the house. These days, holding hands with the opposite sex in public is considered inappropriate. Members of the same sex holding hands, especially females, are considered friendship, while in America it is considered otherwise. It is, however, quite a rare occurrence to see males hold each other's hands. Normally, we do not see people kissing or hugging each other in public, even displays of friendship, such as a kiss on the cheek or forehead.

Thais are a more conservative people than Americans; we seldom express hospitality, unless it is to our family or friends. In Thailand, it is not really normal to say "hi or hello" to someone walking by or to strangers. Thais are also shy to say "Love" or "I love you" to people or even to a family member; we just give the greatest care we can; we show our hospitality by our actions, not by our words. Most Thais live with their parents before they get married. Here, it seems that eighteen-year-old Americans want to get out of their parents' home as soon as they can, and they think they are grown up. The parents are also very ready for them to be out. Thirty-year-old, unmarried children living in the house with their parents is a common thing back home.

Americans are more open than Thais. They speak their minds. They point out wrong or unreasonable things directly, but most of us just keep silent or mumble in our mind. The best thing we can do is just imply that we don't like something. Americans appear to be aggressive, while Thais are quite submissive in daily routines or circumstances.

Thais give great importance to personal hygiene and cleanliness. Thais generally bathe at least twice a day and tend to dress very politely;

long shorts and sleeves in hot climates are the norm for most tourists. Some of my American friends told me that they prefer to take a shower only in the morning. When I was in Thailand, I had never seen Thais sunbathing, because Thais do not sunbathe topless and do not wear a small piece of clothing that shows a lot of bare skin. Thais are quite friendly and respectful of Westerners. When they ask questions about age, salary and marital status, they don't mean to be rude or intrude; these are common questions in Thai culture. Here in America, however, these questions are considered inappropriate, and whoever asks these types of questions might get responses such as, "It is not your business," or "I do not have to tell you." So do not feel hurt.

Without an understanding of cultural diversity, many people could face a major culture shock. I was no exception. America is such a big country. I have learned this not only by looking on a map or reading in a book, but I was also given the opportunity to travel a lot while I was living with my American family. Five months of continuous traveling on the road from place to place in many states has given me a chance to see and to learn. I have acknowledged that America is the land of many groups from different ethnic backgrounds. These groups of people make American culture so diverse. It is interesting to see mixed racial groups, mixed cultures, and mixed minds. It is amazing to see these groups of people living separately in their own group, having their own church, participating in their own group's activities, visiting their own club, shopping in their own area, eating in their group's restaurant, and supporting their own people, etc.

The idea of a "**Melting Pot**" was not really clear to me until I came to live here and experienced it. Since each culture has both weaknesses and strengths, it is an honor to have a choice to learn and to choose to experience a good one.

To learn about Americans, the Marchbanks family members not only allowed me to experience being in their family, but they also gave me the opportunity to meet a new group of people outside the home. I remember that during my initial visit, Mr. Marchbanks' sister and her husband, Mr. and Mrs. Chapman, kindly came to pick me up early in the morning to take me to church with them, to see people, and to learn how they exercise their faith and pursue their spiritual goal. After church, I was allowed to accompany them to a Sunday brunch at a local restaurant. There, I was introduced to their friends to learn social manners and to observe how they interact with each other during mealtime. I still remember the kindness of Mr. Marchbanks' best friend; Judge Thomson's girlfriend guided and showed me different kinds of American food and American social customs, when they hosted a big Christmas party at their home and allowed to be help and participate. I happened to be the only Asian in the party. Going to the horse race and the casino boat in Arkansas and Louisiana with Judge Thomson and his girlfriend, was quite an experience. Thoroughly cleaning an entire American home, being exhausted all day, eating sandwiches, chips, and drinking soda for lunch were all part of my first step to earn an American dollar. Babysitting a seven-year-old son of my good next door neighbor gave me the first opportunity to hold a baseball bat and throw the ball. When I could not do it, he thought he was telling me the right way to do it. I was even called a "silly girl." A seven year old saying that word to a twenty-five year old in my country would have gotten a spanking. Here, I was surprised that spanking is not the appropriate way to punish or discipline children. Instead of being corrected, he was told, "Be nice to Pat." Interacting and associating with the Marchbanks family's good friend and neighbor, Mr. House and attorney Bill Flanary, was a good way to see how another American family works, lives, and handles business, especially Mr. House, who kindly gave me a chance to work part-time in his store and learn to put skills to work in an American business.

Living in an American family, being taken care of by Americans, associating with them, enjoying their friendship, studying with them, being taught by them, working with them, being given an "Outstanding Employee Award" by them, and now teaching them daily has helped me to gain more understanding about how they really are as Americans. Prior knowledge of the only great and wonderful American image would have still been there if I had not been given a chance to see another side. I found it interesting, and I certainly love the way the author, David Hampshire, describes Americans in general. He stated that,

The typical American is brash, friendly, competitive, industrious, rude, forthright, impatient, spontaneous, loud, optimistic, musical, conscientious, litigious, patriotic, naïve, wealthy, serious, demonstrative, ignorant, unworldly, fun-loving, racist, corrupt, huge, altruistic, a shopaholic, effusive, parochial, dynamic, outrageous, efficient, excessive, virile, garrulous, intense, a religious zealot, ambivalent, helpful, crude, boastful, demanding, an exhibitionist, individualistic, selfish, ebullient, gluttonous, aggressive, a hustler ambitious, proud, extrovert, flashy, compulsive, humorous, insecure, enthusiastic, greedy, uninhibited, decisive, arrogant, insincere, fickle, innovative, extravagant, pragmatic, vulgar, puritanical, artificial, unsophisticated, kind, shallow, materialistic, laid-back, entrepreneurial, tasteless, thrusting, insular, energetic, honest, hard-living, a bubble-gum blower, unethical, accessible, bigoted, warm, sporting, determined, abrasive, stressed, paranoid, ruthless, polite, conservative, generous, egotistical, vain ostentatious, promiscuous, neurotic, narcissistic, approachable, prudish, exuberant, compassionate, violent, intransigent, blunt, dramatic, hyperbolic, brusque, superficial, predatory, and a baseball fan (Hampshire 507).

No matter how Americans are in general, many gave me a chance to value and enjoy our differences, learn from our differences, and now even allow me to make a difference in their life. It is truly a great life opportunity to live in America and learn to accept, appreciate, and respect people for who they are, without criticizing and judging them.

Besides learning the difference of cultures among Americans, seeing the living conditions in America is also fascinating. I have never thought that I would see a living area so totally different from my own. I had never imagined that I would be able to see Americans living in brown paper boxes at the subway stations or under the bridges along busy highways; Americans are asking for food beside the roads and some Americans are living in the area that is considered, "below the poverty level." It is interesting when one of my American co-workers told me, "Pat, you have not seen anything yet. I will have to drive you to a place that is worse than what you saw today. But we have to go during the day. It is not quite safe in that area." "I don't want to see. It makes me feel sad," I told her. That one evening, she and I visited a crowded apartment complex area. After that day, I appreciate more of what I have and what was provided to me by my American family.

The living condition in my American home was the first thing to which I had to adjust, with the great supportive manner of a kind owner, on the first day I arrived. Coming from a lower middle class family, unaccustomed to all the luxurious furniture, less convenient living conditions, adjusting to a 3,300 square feet, well- furnished, electronically-equipped, and comfortable home, was not easy. I was worried that I would always do something wrong--hit or break something or press a button that I was not supposed to do.

When I walked into my American family's home, I was so fascinated with the big modern gray brick home, which had high ceilings. All rooms, except for the kitchen and the laundry room were carpeted. There were separate living, dining, kitchen, bar, and laundry rooms. Each of the four big bedrooms had a built-in closet. The master bedroom had an attached bathroom and shower. I learned that Americans prefer to shower than to take baths.. For the three separate bathrooms, each had its own bathtub and separate shower. A two-car garage was in the back of the house. There was a large front and backyard, with a well-maintained lawn. It was located in a nice and quiet neighborhood, which was known as an upscale area in town. A separate storage building was behind the house.

Everything in the house looked so nice, clean, and organized. Growing up in a solid concrete floor home, seeing a nice carpeted floor in almost the whole house was amazing. A big screen television and record player over a big wooden speaker were amazing, too. The exercise room that consisted of different types of workout equipment such as a treadmill, a rowing machine, and a small weight lifter, was interesting. It shows that my American family likes to stay in shape and gives importance to exercise and their health. The home office is conveniently equipped with the electronic devices such as a computer, a printer, a scanner, a fax machine, a copy machine, a phone, and a large electronic radio system. Everything seems to be handy for a business. In my country, when I wanted to make one copy, I had to ride a motorcycle almost 20 minutes to a very small shop in the nearby city. A cordless phone was in almost every room in the house; that was also very convenient to carry into the bathroom and outside of the house.

The big kitchen area was so attractive. It had eating and dining areas with beautiful built-in oak cabinets and abundant counter space. I was so excited when they showed me the dishwasher. I asked if it meant that they did not have to wash dishes by hand. They were laughing when they saw me so anxious to know about it. Of course, I was amazed to see how it worked because that was the first time in my life I had heard of a dishwasher. That was a big surprise to be presented with that smart kitchen. I recalled Michael was laughing so hard when he saw my reaction, and he told me, "Pat, it does not only have the capability to wash, but also to dry those washed dishes." I was wondering if it could put those clean dishes in the cabinets as well. Then I learned that I had to put all of the clean ones neatly in the wooden cabinets. I paid very close attention when Mr. Marchbanks showed me how to use it, in the second day of my living with them. I still remember jokingly telling my own mother over the phone when I called her in Thailand that my hands would not be rough any more, because the machine would do all the dishwashing for me. How convenient it is!

Central heating and an air conditioning unit were installed in the house. These provided cool air during the summer and warm heat in the winter. A hot water boiler provided warm water all year round. However, I learned that all these conveniences came with a service cost and maintenance fee. Within six years, my American family gave me the opportunity not only to enjoy that environment but also to work, save, and write a check to pay bills.

When looking at the laundry room connected to the kitchen, I saw that a washer and dryer handled a large load of laundry every few days. There are cabinets over them in which you can store different types of laundry detergents and softening products. A good-size empty area in that laundry room later on was a place for another refrigerator that stored all my Thai foods and Asian groceries. They took me to buy in the Asian market in Dallas when I was not able to drive. Every time we went there, we bought a lot of things, so that we didn't have to go often because it is quite far. I also learned that Americans store a lot of frozen food in the freezer.

The two-car garage is able to accommodate their big GM truck and a very nice car. The amazing thing that I learned later on was that those vehicles were paid for in cash. Not only that, the house that I was so excited about was paid off. I was so overwhelmed with an excitement and eagerness to learn how people can have this type of life. It is so much different than where I am from. I am so grateful to the Marchbanks family for giving me the opportunity to see how they live. I was fortunate to live in that secure and comfortable home for six years before I was able to buy my own home in America in 1999 after a half year of working here. Of course, I was successful in buying a new home with the good advice, support, and involvement of Mr. Marchbanks. With his suggestion and teaching, I have not yet missed any note payments or bills. Yes, it is an American home with a comfortable arrangement, with Asian culture in the house, and some of my American friends kindly take off their shoes, when they come to visit me at home.

Another thing that I have experienced in my twelve years of living here is an exciting American lifestyle. America has been known as a "world information highway" society, which creates such a lifestyle that can be called, "**If not the American way, it is no way.**" They also have a high-speed way of living, acting, and doing things. Observing them daily, I find it educational and interesting. I learned that some Americans don't mind telling me about their own lifestyle when I ask them. They are willing to share the information and teach me. Talking with them makes me acknowledge that being an attentive listener can gain a lot of good information. In some aspects, I don't have to do the trial by error method to get things done right in the appropriate way.

The first morning in my American family's home, after a long international flight, I woke up with jet lag, and I was introduced to the first American breakfast in America. I still remember clearly what I had: toast, bacon, and scrambled eggs, with a big cold glass of milk. It was delicious. But, with jet lag, an upset stomach on the flight, and adjusting to new foods, it was too much for my stomach to tolerate. The result of this was that I needed bed rest for the rest of the first two days. I was missing my Thai breakfast so much: a hot big bowl of pork, chicken, or shrimp rice soup or a big plate of fried rice, topped with at least two sunny-side-up eggs. Actually, Thais do not have different foods for different meals of the day. I grew up having three meals a day with no snack time between meals. Many people just prefer a light meal in the morning; rice soup seems to be the popular one in many families. My family back home, when talking about American breakfasts, foods, and meals--we had no idea.

During my first week, I was introduced to a variety of foods. After five full months of traveling around America with my American family, I experienced all kinds of foods at every meal, every day. I also had the opportunity to stay in different hotels such as the Best Western Inn, Holiday Inn, Marriott, Comfort Suite, LaQuinta Inn, Hampton Inn, Super 8 Motel, and Motel 6 and enjoy their free breakfast, too. While I was experiencing an American breakfast, I was also able to experience a continental breakfast as well, while staying there. I learned that a typical American breakfast usually consists of any or all of the following: eggs, bacon, ham, sausages, cereal, waffles, pancakes, syrup, toast, grits, juice, milk, and a lot of coffee. They are served pot after pot at each table in the morning time. On the table during breakfast time, there usually was butter and different types of jam. My favorite one was peach preserves. Americans also prefer things they call, "Homemade."

That includes homemade jam. Eating breakfast out often made me learn that usually breakfast costs less than the other meals.

Besides adjusting to foods, learning about American meals—breakfast, brunch, lunch, supper, and dinner—is interesting. Breakfast is usually served from as early as 6:00 a.m. until 10:00 to 11:00 a.m. Brunch is a combination of breakfast and lunch. It usually is served between 11:00 a.m. and 3:00 p.m. Many Americans like to go have brunch after church on Sunday. Lunch is served between 11:00 a.m. to 2:30 p.m. Dinner is served from around 5:30 p.m. to 11:00 p.m. It is considered the main meal of the day for most Americans. It also cost more than the other meals. These days, many restaurants and cafeterias serve these three American meals in the form of a **buffet** or **super buffet**. It is also known as all-you-can-eat style. It has been said that Americans are big eaters; they just love it. Some do not care how long they have to wait to be seated; as long as they can enjoy the buffet, they will wait in a long line of customers. In some non-buffet and decent restaurants, the customers might have to wait as long as 45 minutes to be seated at the table and have to wait 15 minutes to have their order taken, and another 30 minutes to enjoy the meal. I sometimes had lost my appetite before having a chance to taste my actual meal. Tips are expected in the restaurant and most services in America. In a restaurant, at least 15% gratuity of the meal's total is supposed to be put on the table or on the bill. Tips should be a return for good provided services.

Besides enjoying a buffet-style restaurant for food, because of their busy lifestyle, tight schedule, and overwhelming daily activities that make them not have much time to cook, most Americans prefer **fast food**. Fast foods are easy, fast, and fatty. However, they are somewhat nutritious--freshly cooked when you order, and worth the money. They are served at your convenience even at the convenience store and gas station. Since America is a fast food inventor that has its market all over the world, people have different fast food chains from which to choose: International House of Pancakes (IHOP), Waffle House, Wendy's, McDonalds, Kentucky Fried Chicken (KFC), Church's Chicken, Golden Chick, Chicken Express, Burger King, Pizza Hut, Pizza Inn, Taco Bell, What-a-Burger, Long John Silver's, and Braum's, etc. Most Americans like to have fast food for lunch and even for their three meals. Many fast food places provide a drive-thru service, which allows customers to place the order without having to see some unpleasant and rude employees. After paying and picking up the order at the window, they can even eat while they are driving. If they decide to eat in the fast food place, after placing the order, they are provided unlimited refill soft drinks in different sized cups; a super big size is the size I normally see. However, knowing that a super size, double size, and triple size hamburger or cheeseburger is quite normal, I am still able to see that a junior burger without cheese available or even with cheese requires a higher cost.

Initially, I embarrassed myself by walking into the fast food chains to order a hamburger before 11:00 o'clock. I surely did not know that I could not order it. I made a mistake not only on the time to order food, but also on the names of the food, so I just simply pointed to the number on the menu, instead of pronouncing it. I had made mistakes many times, but I still could have fast food to eat.

Since I am a very easy eater, adjusting to American foods was not a big deal. I consider myself quite fortunate that I easily adjust to things, including foods. Even though initially cheese and I did not get along well, eating pizza and cheese sauce these days is no problem. Some

Thais who just come here, including my parents and my brother, have such a hard time with American foods.

Learning that a majority of Americans love food, I still see petite Americans around me. While seeing Americans enjoy a tasty steak for dinner, I still see some enjoy just a lunch meat or peanut butter sandwich. Instead of eating a good meal for dinner, American children prefer frozen dinner meals. Sometimes, it is nice to see some American children trying to learn how to use chopsticks, instead of using a fork, knife, and soup spoon on the table. They just want to explore another's eating culture. Overall, a $0.99 junior burger with unlimited soda refills is still amazing.

Recently, my friend took me out for dinner in a decent restaurant; the food was good and the environment was pleasant. Of course, the cost of that dinner can empty my pockets if I keep eating like that every day. However, I was telling her that these days eating a variety of American food is affordable. Unlike in Thailand, I felt that American meals cost too much because I did not have money to buy them. She was telling me that she could afford only KFC at least a few times a year in her country, too.

I recall my experience while being a trainee in a coffee shop in my first week of an internship while studying in the Hotel School in Bangkok. I was assigned to work at a bakery shop, which displayed a variety of cakes, pies, and fresh rolls. They smelled so wonderfully and looked so delicious. I sold many of them to the hotel's customers. I also really wanted to eat some of those goodies, especially those fresh butter rolls. Unfortunately, I could not afford them. I remember it was then 45 bahts a roll. That 45 bahts was being saved to pay rent. When I was with my American family, I was able to eat butter rolls as much as I wanted. Mr. Marchbanks once joked with me, "Now, Pat, you can buy the whole truck of the butter rolls."

An interesting American lifestyle is also indicated by the clothing Americans wear. The Americans I have known have a lot of clothes in their closet. They have a huge walk-in closets in their homes. Some clothes have been hanging in there for quite some time and have never been worn. They have clothing for different occasions. The Sunday best clothing that they wear to Church seems to be the most decent. Their daily clothing is very relaxed and casual. They certainly focus on how comfortable it is. Blue jean shorts and a T-shirt are common for a relaxing day. The tennis shoe is popular for footwear and for informal occasions. In some American work places, however, a dress code is clearly described in the employee's handbook. The dress code can be both formal and casual. In some work places, Friday seems to be more casual than the other days of the week. Some places allow shorts, a T-shirt, and blue jeans on Friday.

Since some Americans think a lot about a comfortable and relaxing lifestyle, their clothing appears to be very open, short, tight, and quite revealing. Some workers can be sent home to change clothes, if their clothing is inappropriate. It was interesting to hear one of my co-workers say to me one day during our lunch that "you have a lot of cute work clothes and beautiful outfits. They are very decent, but I don't think I can wear them. They look too conservative, and the skirt is too long and covers too much." It is common to see some Americans wearing clothing that shows cleavages, lower bottoms, and legs. Sunbathing topless or two-piece swimsuits for some show they are not concerned about appropriateness.

I was laughing so hard when my young Thai male friend came to visit my family after his summer vacation, during his school summer break. He went to Florida and enjoyed things that a tourist state has to offer, including a private beach where he saw people sunbathing topless and half naked. "Aunt Pat, I wish I could see the young American girls there, instead, I saw many half naked, retired American men and women. That makes me not want to get old." He told me with a shy face. That is something we jokingly talk about when we meet occasionally.

These days, in my current position at work, correcting and confronting young Americans on their dress code and personal daily wear is challenging. Young females with small, tight, and too revealing outfits do not look decent. Young males with sagging and bagging pants irritate me. Obvious body modification such as tattoos and piercings that show their personal memory and preferences can be somewhat scary and unpleasant. Some designs do not appear to be appropriate for employment, so they have to cover themselves with long sleeves at all times in the workplace. These American youth are so influenced by their country's celebrities; the group that appears to be very relaxed, and having risqué clothing shows their lack of morality and decency. Is this country losing its modesty? Nobody really can tell. Modesty makes me aware of what I wear and how I present myself. Exercising "Dress for Success" is what I focus on while living and seeing some Americans' clothing.

I was told that these days, young people in America do not have to ask permission of the parents to date their daughter. Some start dating as young as fifteen years old. American guys also certainly do not need to ask permission from her parents to marry the girl. They do not even have to prepare the dowry or a bride price, as is the case in my country. Some don't have to start their marriage out with a big debt of a large amount to give to the bride's parents. Single people can date in any stage of their life. Some divorced Americans enjoy their time dating in a "Singles Club," where they can still enjoy dating in their 40s and 50s, and having their date with them at the grandchildren's football game. Divorce and remarriage are very common here; some are divorced four times, and remarried four times. Their attitude toward sex is open, while in my culture, talking about sex is taboo and shameful. According to one of my American friends, some parents even allow their children to have their girlfriend or boyfriend sleep in the house. In the case of sexually active young girls, their parents have to accompany them to visit the gynecologist's office at an early age, before having to be unwilling grandparents. The "Condoms to Go," "Adult Videos and Toys," and "Lifestyle Accessories" shops are commonly seen here. The phrase, "One-Night Stand" was never in my dictionary, before one of my American coworkers shared the information on her date. I was jokingly informed that, "Oh, Ms. Pat, we kiss on the first date and some Americans do something else." And then she just laughed and told me that, "in a sexual relationship, American women can initiate, return, and exchange." I have learned a lot of useful information from my straight-forward talking American coworkers and friends.

Typical Americans work a lot in their life and don't want to retire early. Saving for retirement seems to be everyone's goal; however, those who decide to retire and volunteer their time in the community remain active. The majority of Americans enjoy traveling and taking a vacation when they can. They are active groups of people with a "Can do" mentality. Some workaholic Americans think about reaching for bigger and better things; bigger car and bigger homes seem to mean better living conditions for some. For this reason, it is quite common to see many stressed and depressed Americans in the work place.

Besides giving me the opportunity to absorb daily living skills within their family, to gain knowledge and skills in an educational setting, to acquire new ideas and learn different ways from friends, classmates, and colleagues, the Marchbanks family generously provided me a chance to put the skills to practice in a small business, "The Rent House Business." With that business, Mr. Marchbanks recently provided me some additional funds to add into my retirement account. As I have been taught by him, "before you pay all your money to Uncle Sam (taxes for the government), you need to pay yourself by paving your way to a good retirement plan," I have carefully established the plan. I am continuously contributing to my old age financial goal, expecting that when I become eligible to retire and am blessed to enjoy it. I can travel and spend time doing what I enjoy, visiting my children, and settling in a small, peaceful, hilly home, that has a lot of trees in a safe and quiet community.

I have never in my life thought about the opportunity to become a landlord. I did not even have that type of dream in Thailand, because I knew I could not afford to dream, based on my family's financial situation. At the age of twenty-seven, in America, I had my first rent house to manage. This opportunity would have not happened if Mr. Marchbanks had not talked to me one day after I came back from school. I was excited when he mentioned that he would buy a rent house and let me take care of it while he was out of town working. He would help with a down payment, and I had to make a note payment to the bank for the monthly rent. That was the first time he taught me to deal with the bank about the mortgage loan. The second step was when he helped me to establish my credit history, in addition to adding my name on his credit card account. I, then, learned the importance of **credit** in America. As I have read, "Credit is a way of life in America, and not to have any debts is un-American and to be condemned," In my American family, I saw the opposite side of most Americans. Yes, I was taught that having good credit is wonderful, but having to pay interest and being unable to pay debt are discouraged in my home. I observed that my family did not have any debts. Mr. Marchbanks carries only one credit card and does not like to charge on it even though his credit line is as high as $30,000.

I also have learned that many Americans carry as many credit cards as possible to maximize their buying power. Some even charge over their credit limit on each card. After a lot of charges, some can not pay when the balances are due. They have to pay a large amount of interest, an over-limit charge, and sometimes a late fee. I was taught not to go crazy with my credit card, since it was a new type of money, plastic money, to me. I was also told that I needed to keep a good and clean credit record while living in America; since everything I do regarding my financial status and my credit history can always be checked. I had no idea that the teaching I received was useful, until I was living on my own and learned that I could not successfully receive a new credit card, rent an apartment, buy a new car, or even buy my new house, without my initial credit established for me by Mr. Marchbanks. A rent house mortgage and loan were my valuable lesson on credit.

I remember there were so many processes to getting the loan for the first rent house. I certainly learned each step with my full attention and interest. On the closing date, I was so excited: my heart was pounding and my hands were sweating while walking into a beautiful office at the biggest title company in town. Inside, I was in tears, while I was presented all the paper work, and my name was on a title along with Mr. Marchbanks' name, because I could not buy a house alone because of my lack of a good credit history, job, and stable income. I was so thankful that Mr. Marchbanks gave me a sense of ownership and let me be involved with the process that helped me learn to deal with American people in a business setting.

The first rent house was a white frame house with two bedrooms, one bath, living room, a kitchen, a carport, and a good size lot and backyard. It was a cute little house for which we paid about $21,500, and I expected to rent it for $275 per month. Over half of the rent would go to the mortgage, and the rest of the rent each month was saved in case of maintenance needs. Fortunately, Mr. Marchbanks decided to pay off that rent house in the following five months, because he intended to avoid paying a lot of interest, and he could not stand having debt with the bank.

Mr. Marchbanks allowed me to start working on getting it for rent after closing. I started to pay a guy to mow the lawn outside, a painter to paint the whole house, both inside and out, and to repair the inside of the house where it was needed. I cleaned up each area in the house after school. After everything was ready, I placed a small advertisement in a local daily newspaper. It did not take a long at all to receive many phone calls, both on my cell phone and at home, asking, "Is your house on 19th St. still for rent?" "We want to see inside of your rent house on 19th St. We have seen the outside. When would be a good time for you to show us?" "How much is the cleaning deposit on your rent house?" "Do you charge an application fee?" "Do you require a deposit or references?" "Can you show us this evening?" Some phone calls were requesting additional information of the house. It was a wonderful experience to use my communication skills in English, and I learned to do business with Americans.

After a few house shows, I finally found my first house renter. They were a couple with a three-year-old daughter. They just moved to town because of the husband's employment. They were good renters. I had them living in my rent house for two years before they moved out of town again. In the two years, if they had to be a little bit late on their rent, they would notify me. I didn't have any problem with them. However, I wish I could have that type of renter with one of my four rent houses.

In the following years, Mr. Marchbanks bought three additional rent houses for me to take care of. We had to do some work on every one of them. One out of three houses was especially not in good shape; we had to pay a carpenter to fix it up and remodel it before we were able to rent it out. With these three houses, I went through the same process of getting the houses ready. Two of my renters left me with quite an unpleasant memory as a landlord. One was a nurse who paid good rent only the first few months and after that always came up with excuses for being late. I remember collecting late fees a few times from her, because of our rental contract. Finally, I had to let her move out. Another renter moved out without notifying us at all; besides not paying their last month's rent, they left such a big mess in the house, causing us to spend a few days cleaning up before having the house available for the next renter. These days, when I mention buying a rent house again in the city l am living in, Mr. Marchbanks still reminds me of the mess we had to clean up, and discourages me from having the headache of a rent house; he suggested that I take another path for investment.

Since I was still in school and worked part time at Wal-Mart, managing a rent house was an additional responsibility that helped me learn to balance my schedule and tasks. I was learning business and having fun doing it. Studying, working, and managing the rent houses kept me busy all the time. One of my Thai friends, who has been in America for more than 30 years, joked with me that, "These things keep you out of trouble and help you stay focused on learning in different parts of this country. When you start out good at a young age, you can accomplish more."

In the rent house business, I have learned many valuable things such as using my computer skills learned from school to create an application, rent deposit and reference forms, a rent house contract, keep track of data on a spreadsheet, and most importantly work with people. As a landlord, I also learned to be patient, fair, and able to provide good customer service. I recall driving to different houses and giving each of the renters a ham or a turkey a week before Thanksgiving and a few days before Christmas holiday. A few times, I stopped by to see how they were doing in my rent house. That sometimes gave me the opportunity to see what needed to be fixed before it got worse. When I learned that there was something that needed to be repaired, I acted quickly and got it done in a timely manner for their convenience.

I found that communication and interaction with people is significant, because I had to deal with a carpenter, an electrician, and a plumber many times for those four houses. The experience would have been very difficult if I did not receive kind assistance and good support from Mr. John House, my American family's best friend, who is a well known and respected businessman in Paris, TX. Mr. Marchbanks was out of town a lot for his engineering work. Mr. House owned at least 75 rent houses and a motel in Paris. He certainly knows good and reasonable contract experts who could be good hands. He suggested what to do when problems related to my rent houses occurred. He even sometimes sent a carpenter who was working on his projects to help me out.

Mr. House has always been a good friend of my American family, and his friendship and kindness has extended to me and my own family.

Last Christmas holiday, we got a chance to stay in his newly built motel while visiting my American family during the holiday season. He is a very successful businessman; his success demonstrates the benefit of hard work, smart work, well managed plans, and the ability of working with people.

The rent house business also helped me to learn about some Americans who were my tenants. Some were clean and maintained the house well by themselves. They took time to mow the lawn and planted flowers, after their busy work day. They really did not call for little things that they could handle. On the other hand, some people called me about everything and did not take care of their own business. One time they called me that their trash was not picked up by the city. I wondered why they did not call the city directly. Realizing that it was my house, I called to get their trash picked up before it would offend their neighbor. They also wanted me to send someone to maintain the outside of the house, though it is their responsibility as stated in the contract.

I also learned to be friendly to my rent house next door neighbors, instead of telling her straight away to stay out of my business. One lady by the name of Shirley called me a few times complaining about one of my renters, a nurse working on a night shift at a nursing home, who came home late and had her company with her. They enjoyed their late party and had loud music. Another time, a bad thunderstorm caused a broken tree limb from the tree in my house's backyard to go over her fence. She called me right after the rain to tell me that it needed it to be taken care of.

Dealing with many issues while managing the rent houses, attending graduate school full time, and having two part-time jobs, was not always fun. However, it helped me to become a multitasking person who tried to solve problems one at a time. If I felt it was too much to handle, I learned to seek people who could give me advice. I always kept in mind that I am not an American, and local people have more experience dealing with many issues. Mr. House was my wonderful source of help. After I received help, I showed my appreciation by simply sending a "Thank You" card, or I would mention it when I got a chance. I have learned that Americans are not different from people from other parts of the world, in that they appreciate when you recognize the importance of them, their time, and their help.

While I was under the Marchbanks' roof, I was taught many good things and was given the opportunity to learn to better myself in different ways. I was guided to adjust to a cultural change in life, which happened in a variety of areas. Learning to combine my culture with American culture helps me to successfully and effectively enjoy living in America without having to only focus on working, saving, and dying for American dollars. I would like to extend my sincere gratitude to the Marchbanks family for giving me the opportunity to walk into a house with my shoes on, to warmly cuddle Pancho on a big comfortable couch in front of a big TV, to have a cup of hot chocolate while it was snowing outside, to stay in top-notch American hotels while traveling for a sightseeing trip, to eat a world renowned tasty hamburger, to let me know it is okay to shave legs, to allow me to still be polite and conservative among outspoken people, to attend a Buddhist temple regularly, to let me know it is okay to kiss on the first date and remarry, to teach me how to drive on the right side of the road, to calculate my mileage in the American system instead of Metric systems, to teach me to be thrifty so I can have some dollars left, to show me how to balance my check book and pay my bills, to energize me to plan for my old age, and to guide me to dream that everything is possible. I am trying to use all I have been taught. I, however, still refuse to sunbathe topless on a private beach, to enjoy myself on a nude beach or in a nudist camp, or to visit the "Hippie Hollow."

Doug, Sandy, Mr. Marchbanks, Pat, and Kimi

Chapter 4: "I DO" — "I Am Doing"

"Chains do not hold a marriage together. It is threads, hundreds of tiny threads which sew people together through the years." -Simone Signoret

When I was a teenager, I used to hear people talk about "The wedding gate." It was once said that "The wedding gate is a gate that the outsiders want to get in and the insiders want to get out." I am not really sure whether it is true. In my opinion, it depends on what we really find behind that gate or what we really aim to make happen after deciding to walk through that gate. For some standing in front of the gate, it might look beautiful and sound wonderful like heaven, but after living inside the gate for a while, it becomes like a hell on earth. On the other hand, some people might unwillingly approach that gate, but luckily find out that they can live happily for many years, and some can even be happy forever. "The wedding gate" is the gate of marriage.

Some people say that marriage is a risky step in life, a risk where the outcome is uncertain. Some say that it is our biggest investment and commitment to spend the rest of our life with the person that we choose; some make the choice according to love and a warm fuzzy feeling that says "I can't live without you," but many might make the choice because it is appropriate or the timing is right. It is absolutely an investment in which we place our whole heart; it is a high volume of equity on which we don't expect a big lump sum of profit return at once. The unlimited time of capital gain indicates a person's success in a relationship and commitment with another for life, and it does not present itself in the form of numeric data or the number of vested years, but rather provides the opportunity for emotional and personal growth as a mature human being. While closely and attentively watching the graph of stock trading on a computer screen every second for a financial investment, the investment of being inside the wedding gate also needs close and wise attention to every significant second to achieve one outcome: success within the wedding gate. Having a good, happy, and successful marriage is just a blessing, and it might be the dream of every woman, including me, while living here in America.

I was blessed by being given the opportunity to walk into the gate in my late thirties. That gate was opened by strong and supportive hands, with great encouragement for my success from my American family. Actually, I was not really looking forward to any new relationship. I was busy enough to not think about anything else, but striving to do the best in what I was planning to do; studying and working were my main focus. However, I realized later that the gate that my American family let me walk into is a wonderful gate to have a life learning experience. It provided me the opportunity not only to experience a real marriage life that Dr. Gary Chapman, a marriage counselor, interestingly describes as, "the real world of marriage, where hairs are always on the sink and little white spots cover the mirror, where arguments center on which way the toilet paper comes off and whether the lid should be up or down. It is a world where shoes do not walk to the closet and drawers do not close themselves, where coats do not like hangers and socks go AWOL during laundry. In this world, a look can hurt and a word can crush. Intimate lovers can become enemies and marriage a battlefield."(Chapman 203). This experience also allows for an excellent opportunity to adjust to a third culture, a Japanese culture, and to develop the ability to live effectively with the other person as a couple.

I am a Thai woman who was raised closely in a conservative Thai culture for twenty-five years and I still learn from time to time. I have also been taught to adjust to American culture for the past twelve years by my American family, friends, and colleagues. Now I am living side-by-side and working hand-in-hand with a conservative Japanese man, or I would say a typical Japanese man, to reach our common goal. It might sound interesting for some people that, based on the many questions I have been asked, I was invited to share my personal experience in a graduate class at the university on interracial marriage. For us, however, it was absolutely challenging when we decided to hold hands walking into the gate, and while we are in it, we have to hold hands ever tighter to work through many challenges and differences.

One day, one of my co-workers came by my office, saw my wedding picture, and offered me a compliment, "You two look good together as a couple." I replied, "Thank you, do we look alike or different?" Then, he interestingly replied, "Don't worry about being different, my wife and I do not only look different, but we are so different and don't have much in common; the only things we have in common are children and a mortgage." That was a good joke from a man who has been inside the wedding gate for over twenty years. I consider myself a novice, and I still have a lot more to learn, develop, improve, and grow as a married woman. My way of advancing is to read in a trial-and-error way, observe others' successes and failures, learn from the experiences of others, and most importantly work closely with my husband who has a 100 percent right to help me grow in our marriage.

Fortunately, besides our full effort and willingness to work on our marriage, we are pursuing the same common goal, a happy marriage and family. I have been so blessed that God and Lord Buddha gave me the opportunity to exercise the learning of being myself and playing my role in a tri-cultural environment. Yes, it is not easy, but I can learn and benefit from a lot of things. The article written by Gregg Hall interestingly emphasizes that, "a happy marriage is not guaranteed no matter how much the partners love each other. There are so many variables that can have an effect on the happiness and success of the marriage. It is important that both partners realize that they must continuously work on all of these aspects if they want their marriage to remain a happy and healthy relationship."(Hall).

This opportunity to learn might not have happened if one the members of my American family, Mr. Marchbanks, didn't sit down with me one day a few years back, after I was passing my thirtieth year. I still remember him telling me that he didn't want me to waste my time by not starting a family. He told me straightforwardly, "I want you to enjoy a real married life and learn about a normal relationship for a girl your age. You need to have someone who can enjoy doing the same things and able to take you to places you want to go." He insisted that now my life had gotten better; I had finished a good education, found a job, worked in the field that I loved, and was financially secure, I ought to be married and provide him some grandchildren. It was suggested that I should give myself the opportunity by opening the door to look for a good man who I could care for, and receive care in return, and be able to expect to spend time with him "for the rest of my life." He talked to me many times whenever he had the chance at home while he was off from work. He sometimes called me to talk to me about the same thing when he was on a job. He told me to start thinking about a complete family and living life happily before I got too old to enjoy it. I later realized that he was really worried about my being an "old maid." He was afraid that I would not have anybody to take care of me when I become sick or am in need of someone around, because all of my family is mostly not around. He told me that even though I have my own family, I can still visit them any time.

I remember interrupting his conversation to tell him that I was satisfied with my life. I was able to support myself by having a few good friends around me. He persuaded me to take a good look and consider one of my good male friends who had been around helping him with computer-related problems. My male friend was a smart classmate, hard working, and single. I didn't learn that Mr. Marchbanks really liked my classmate until one day he talked to me that he had asked my male friend to take me out for lunch. A few months later, I was informed that he trusted my classmate, who always carried himself well and was very knowledgeable in his field of learning, that he was a good man who could be a very good marriage partner. My classmate was one of three male friends who were always allowed and invited to join our family's activities. I was encouraged to start dating.

I didn't know that a few years from that day, I would have to go to the registration office in the American city hall to request a marriage license. A few days later, I stood in front of a judge of the peace and said, "**I DO**," taking my marriage vow among many of my good friends and witnesses. It was a happy day and a very positive one for a new beginning as a married woman, even though none of our family members from back home were participating, because we told them not to worry about coming across the world for a short ceremony. A few weeks later, we received a lot of presents from Japan.

My husband, Kimi and I first met in a library, not knowing that we were in the same class. We were studying in the same graduate school, but in different fields of study. I was studying in the College of Education, while he was studying in the College of Science and Technology. He was majoring in computer science. His undergraduate background is in Architecture from a university in Tokyo. He attended a graduate school in America, after resigning from his position as a system engineer for the company in Tokyo, Japan. He is a Japanese man, a man that Mr. Marchbanks suggested would be a good husband. I remember one day Mr. Marchbanks told me, "Before your wedding, Kimi asked my permission if he could marry you, while you were doing laundry when you both came to visit me." "What did you tell him?" I asked. He was smiling and let me know what he told my husband: "Did you talk to her and ask her if she would marry you?" Then Kimi responded, "No, I have not asked her yet. I need to let you know my intention before I tell her."

"Well, Kimi, this is America. You need to ask the girl first if she will marry you. What if I give you my permission to marry her, but she doesn't want to marry you? What are you going to do?" I was laughing when Mr. Marchbanks told me about this. That reminded me of one of the differences between our cultures —a man doesn't have to ask permission from the woman's guardian to marry her. Mr. Marchbanks was so pleased with what my husband did that day. It is nice to learn that the decency of one culture can make people in another culture happy, even sometimes without a true understanding of it. I am so pleased that I have the opportunity to again share with you the information about my life in this chapter, because it brings back a wonderful memory of the person who I never thought I would meet when I came to America. These days, while living in our non-native country, we still share and talk about our own roots, practice our good cultures, and appreciate the new things we learn each day.

Back in those days, as international students and friends, my husband and I didn't see each other much at the university, because we both definitely took our graduate study seriously and looked forward to our graduation. We also worked in our department's computer lab part-time. The only time we met was during the International Students Association's meetings or activities, or when my American family wanted their computer and network problems fixed in our home, including all of the computers I used for my private training at home. He did such an excellent job keeping all of them running and working smoothly. Also, he helped some of my students who I taught at their house keep their computers working properly. He always received a little extra money for his services, his time, and his expertise.

My husband talks less and thinks a lot, so he has been hired to think daily as a senior software engineer by an American software and network company, right after his graduation from a graduate school. He has been working for them for almost eight years, and he has no intention to pursue further education. He is from an upper middle class family on the North Island of Japan, with a family background in a fishing ship rental business. After graduation, he decided to experience life in America. It was an honor to be invited to share that experience with him.

We both share the same interest in living in a different culture and have the same common goal of building a family here in America. We started a family after we passed the age of thirty-three, which is considered quite late by some people. We have created a tri-cultural family, in which I am unable to speak Japanese and he is unable to speak Thai. We communicate in English all the time, in which I think we are quite fluent. I thought I quite easily adapted to my second culture; unfortunately, adapting to a third one has not been as easy as I thought.

Of course, it is more than I expected, because I needed to learn and understand so many aspects of Japanese culture. To me, being married is just like being in college all over again; it is not only a college of education, but it is a challenging college of married life education; I never know how each semester will turn out, because each subject is so complicated and needs a lot of effort and study time. Every day, every step, and all of the time, involves learning, both about myself and my partner to utilize all of the necessary skills to make the marriage work effectively and successfully.

As some people have said, "Marriage in general is hard work," and it needs a lot of skills and willingness to work during all of the ups and downs in the marriage. Having been through a relationship, I thought I was mature enough, experienced enough, and strong enough to handle the challenges of marriage. Since I started my marriage late, I thought wisdom about marriage would have also been acquired. I was absolutely wrong and overestimated myself. But when we just think about all beautiful things before the wedding bell rings, such as "falling in love," "being in love," a beautiful wedding grown, a handsome tuxedo, the joyful and smiling faces of family members and guests, a friendly reception, a wonderful, tasty cake and champagne, and of course, an awesome honeymoon period everything looks so beautiful, we have no time to start thinking about any mistake in our great marriage dream.

In my culture, some have never considered that they have to spend their life together for many years to pay off the debts related to their big and beautiful wedding or dowry. I used to hear that for some people, after the birth of their first child, they are still paying the debt on their wedding reception, yet we might never think that there would be one day in the future when we would have to look at our partner and ask ourselves if we really know the person we have married. Many find answers for themselves, but for some they just could not seem to find the answers and still keep searching. For many, after ten years of living together, they find out that their partner is not "the right one." For some, after being married for over thirty years, they have to go their separate ways to seek another partner. I admire and congratulate all people who have been living inside the wedding gate for years and are still keep all beautiful things inside that gate going. I realized that they must have been working so hard and effectively practicing those significant skills as a couple. They must have still been focusing on the same goal. They must have been blessed for their goodness.

In my culture back home, those couples who have been successfully married for many years have always been asked to give the blessing, make up the bed, and prepare the honeymoon room for the bride and the groom during the wedding ceremony. We believe that it is a sign of good luck and a good example for the start of the new couple. The blessing will be something like wishing the wedding couple to have a happy marriage and live happily ever after so they will have many children and grandchildren. It is a very beautiful ceremony before the new couple is sent into the gate, and they start working as a couple.

I once read that, "If being married to someone from your own culture is hard work, then being married to someone from another culture is harder work." I would not have experienced that fact, if I had not been in that situation. However, by realizing the fact, I know my starting point, and the direction I am heading is a "work in progress," working step by step, day by day, year by year, staying focused, and carefully using tools that I have picked up along the way; consequently, reaching the destination shouldn't be too difficult.

As a marriage novice, I have acquired many necessary skills along the way. These useful tools will help me to become an efficient builder, my own marriage builder. Since I am still a beginner, seeking and learning from experienced people is a good way to learn. They have been through many of marriage's peaks and valleys, so they are efficient and able to teach and share their own strategies in reaching the ultimate goal of marriage.. I am then provided a helpful way to apply what is appropriate and suitable in my own marriage. Throughout my reading, listening to experienced married couples, observing people, and seeking the guidance of a professional marriage counselor, I have learned useful skills and am able to consciously utilize them in my marriage. Some of these significant skills are value and care, a positive attitude, understanding and accepting each other's goals, respect and acceptance, communication, golden words, responsibility, and the importance of quality time.

Value and Care

I have learned that living with someone day in and day out for a few years would be quite terrible, if we live without value and care for the person. That person must be someone we think is the best; that is why we choose to share with them our time, our belongings, our house space, and our sleeping and waking moments with every day. Many situations and challenges in the marriage allow me to value Kimi's personal skills and talents. Our strengths and weaknesses allow me the opportunity to value our differences, which help me value Kimi as a human being to whom I have committed my life. No one is perfect; no one is mistake free; no one is so knowledgeable that they cannot learn some new things, especially new complicated lessons in a marriage. Having to believe in human imperfection allows me the opportunity to value the new ways and mistakes I learned from Kimi, even though it was initially difficult. When my mother visited me, she used to jokingly mention that I have never told her any bad things about my husband. Sometimes she has disagreed with things that he has done; I had to let her know that it is a good chance to value the different ways people do things. I remember what my grandmother taught me a long time ago: "Being a married girl, talking badly about your own husband is just like talking badly about yourself. Not to value your husband would be like not valuing yourself. Nobody lives every day and every night with that person except you. If that person is so bad, why did you choose him in the first place?" By valuing each other, it has helped us to live together with care. I do care how his day is: his physical and emotional well-being, what he thinks and feels. Each year when our wedding anniversary comes, I value and appreciate his care and thoughtfulness of giving me a small bouquet of flowers, a card, and gifts, to acknowledge that we both have made it through another successful year of marriage. More important than any tangible things, his saying "Thank you for marrying me" was the most unforgettable gift I received from him.

Value and care for each other helps us to be cautious in our words and actions toward each other. This sense of value and care helps me to strive to search for effective ways to close the gap between culture and language. More than anything else, I value Kimi's great sense of hard work, dependability, and high responsibility. He is the family's great provider who removes worry from me and the children. His good culture, strong character, high patience, and good family background allow me the opportunity to experience the great pride he takes in caring for our family. His integrity and honesty allow me the opportunity to value the person who always keeps his words and promises, and it leaves me no doubt that my American family has led me to a man with good personal character.

A Positive Attitude

As it is so important in many aspects of life, a positive attitude plays such a key role in my marriage. It has a lot to do daily with how we think, act, and speak toward each other as a couple. Initially, it wasn't easy to keep being positive all the time, because we are still human beings, but I have learned this skill by observing a good friend of mine who has been married for almost forty years. As a couple, they seem to be very positive and compromise on things they do together. I was told by her that," being positive is easier than being negative; it makes you feel better, and it brings better results in your marriage. You have no control over how your husband acts or thinks, but you can control what you do. If you start practicing your own attitude in a positive way, he eventually will learn that acting in such a negative way won't work with you." That reminds me of what has been said, "A positive attitude is contagious." You do not need to wait for the other people to be positive; start today to deal with people effectively in a positive way, including relating to your own marriage partner. Once the positive attitude has been exercised, the way we respond in any situation in the marriage will happen in a nice and calm way. I used to ask Kimi to let me know if I become negative, though I watch my own attitude closely, so I can work harder on myself. These days it seems to be easier and easier for me to practice; it sometimes is even easier to take negative comments in a positive way. I have learned that, as a partner, when I take control of my own attitude, I can even provide help to my husband, if it is requested. We agreed to help each other. I realized that when I think about things in a positive way in the marriage, the words I speak will be kind and caring, the tone of voice will be soft and warm, the attention won't be hurtful and harmful to Kimi, my behavior will be passive instead of aggressive, and our home environment will be friendly, peaceful, and warm, instead of hostile. Especially these days,

Kimi and I work even harder on keeping a positive attitude toward each other, because we have children and we want to lead by example. We do not want to teach our children in a negative environment.

I have also learned to practice a positive attitude from my good friend and colleague who is so soft, polite, and kind. She takes things so positively, even the worst situations at work or in her own life; she is even able to handle her divorce and the loss of her mother in a positive way. The positive attitude that I practice in my marriage has such a great impact on my personal life, my work, and my friendships with others. I hardly let little things at work bother me. I realize the importance of this attitude from one of my favorite inspirational readings written by Charles Swindoll. He interestingly states:

> The longer I live, the more I realize the impact of attitude on life. Attitude, to me, is more important than facts. It is more important than the past, than education, than money, than circumstances, than failures, than successes, than what other people think or say or do. It is more important than appearance, giftedness or skill. It will make or break a company...a church...a home. The remarkable thing is we have a choice every day regarding the attitude we will embrace for that day. We can not change our past...we can not change the fact that people will act in a certain way. We can not change the inevitable. The only thing we can do is play on the one string we have, and that is our **attitude**. I am convinced that life is 10% what happens to me and 90% how I react to it, and so it is with you. We are in charge of our **attitudes**. (Swindoll)

Personally, I found it very factual.

Understanding and accepting each other's goals

Besides learning to understand and accept Kimi as a very significant marriage team member, I have had to learn to accept that we have different opinions and views on things, and we definitely have different personal goals. As life-long team members, we have teamed up to focus on one goal in marriage, a family goal. I realize that it is very difficult to achieve my personal and professional goals and our goals without understanding his goals. The time that I have invested in my marriage has allowed me to learn to sacrifice and reset my own goals to satisfy our goals, and I know he is doing the same thing.

One time there was an opening at work that provided the opportunity for advancement and career growth, and I had a strong interest in pursuing it. Kimi disagreed with this decision and reasoned that our sons are growing up and have many activities that require me to be there for them. More responsibility and long hours at work would prevent me from participating regularly, and I would miss out on many activities. As much as I would like to go forward, I had to take time to listen and refocus on our goals instead of my own goals. Of course, our goals are of primary importance.

One late night, after I finished baking cupcakes for my students in class and finished cleaning up the kitchen, Kimi asked me, "Pat, can we sit down and talk for a little while. I have something that I need to talk to you about." After I sat down at the dinner table, he started with something like, "This year we have accomplished many big things." He named goals, all of which I certainly agreed with, that really are good accomplishment for immigrants in America. He then let me know that he had been bothered by his own thinking that at this moment he was no longer certain about the purpose or goals in life. He was thinking about setting new goals. I understand that Kimi is a thinker and a person who likes challenges. Since his routine seemed to be too simple and not challenging to him any more--not even a career in software engineering, which used to always involve changing projects for his clients, not even major household projects--he was getting to feel bored.

It seemed as if he had less interest in what he was doing. On the other hand, I am still satisfied with what I am doing. I am still having fun doing my job. However, that night I did not bother to let him know my thinking, but listened to his plan and his goals. We talked about them for almost two hours. Kimi didn't seem to be any happier.

The following day, what we discussed was bothering me. I was wondering how I would be able to help him. One of my co-workers suggested that I seek for professional advice because, as a wife, when I talk and listen to Kimi's feelings, I would be biased and try to fix what I think is a problem with my personal emotion involved. A well-trained professional can work better in guiding the way for him to stay focused and to fine tune his changing goals.

I remember sitting down separately with Kimi listing the family goals, while we were seeking professional help. It was funny that when Kimi and I presented our family goals from a personal perspective, we had the same common goal for our family, and it was the first item on our list: "a happy family." It seems that the rest of the items on the list can happen very easily if we actually focus on the first one. That practice helps us to clearly focus on our goal, along with each other's goals. Once we understand and are able to accept that, it is easy for us to listen to each other and to help each other, when we learn it is needed.

Respect and Acceptance

As a human being, one of the important basic needs in our life is to be recognized, to be important to people close to us, and to be respected. Respect, however, is a give-and-take practice. We can't expect and demand someone to respect us without focusing on giving it in return. This reminds me of what people have said about a golden rule of living:

"Treat people the way you want to be treated." and "Accept people for who they are." Once you feel respect, your actions in different situations will automatically appear to be more respectful. Before you are able to respect one person, you have to be open-minded and learn to accept the way that person is. Unfortunately, you won't be able to change that person unless he wants to change himself; it has been said that "the only person you can change is yourself." Of course, in life, change happens all the time. What we can do is to open our window widely for it, so that we won't get hit us by surprise. I have learned that once we accept and respect ourselves, the ability to respect other people forms easily.

In my marriage, respect and acceptance play such an important role. I was taught that before I am able to accept and respect Kimi for his role in our marriage, I first must be able to accept him for who he is; then accepting him in a husband role will not be difficult. The most important thing that I learned to accept is our big differences. I would be lying, if I said that, "My, it is easy. There is no problem." In fact, we have challenges that we carefully work on each day: working on ourselves, working on our tasks, and working on our roles.

Kimi and I are so different. We are not only different as people from different cultures, but we are also different individuals who come from different family backgrounds and environments. While I am the oldest child in my family, Kimi is the only child of his family. I am from a lower middle class family, while he is from an upper class family. While I struggled financially through a four-year college, Kimi had no problem pursuing his architecture degree in a well-known private university in Tokyo. Our personalities are quite opposite; while I am quite outgoing, Kimi loves privacy. While I am able to laugh out loud to the world, Kimi simply says I am just crazy laughing. I am quite easy-going and linear on many things; in contrast, Kimi is quite structural and thoughtful. While I have carelessly locked my car keys in the trunk many times, Kimi has had to drive almost an hour to get me home, wrote a check for a locksmith service, or patiently wait for my phone call while I was having my co-worker try to unlock my car manually. I believe that our professions have a lot to do with our personality. As a teacher, I must talk and interact with people most of the time, while Kimi's engineering profession requires a lot of thinking and carrying out of accuracy; while my actions can be flexible, Kimi's appear to be structural and certain. While my desire for affection should be sweet and romantic, his action of caring (without words) should be good enough for showing affection. This reminds me of what my American family taught both of us—that we need to learn to show affection to each other and to our children. Kimi was even taught to hug and kiss our son. Yet I hardly see that type of acting. I later on had to accept and respect that "showing affection" is not for him and not in his culture. Togetherness in our marriage teaches me to accept and respect our differences and to balance what I want and what Kimi can offer. I still remember when my marriage counselor asked me in one session, "Pat, do you want to be right or be happy?" Of course, my answer was to be happy. Then she went on talking to me about how I can make myself happy without disrespecting Kimi and his role, by accepting compromise.

Communication

As it is a very important key in any business organization, I have found that it is also the most significant practice and tool in the realm of marriage and in the land that is called "Home." Based upon our differences, it is impossible for Kimi and I to work out and manage our family goals without effective communication. Some friends used to ask me, "Do you two argue a lot?" I wish I could say, "Oh…No…never…" Sometimes, I wonder whether the other couples have had arguments, as we did initially in our marriage. However, I am quite lucky that we can't speak each other's language; it limits our chance to argue. The only language we verbally use in our communication is English; it makes us learn fewer bad words to harm each other in what some have called, "the battlefield of marriage." Using only English actually helps us to openly express our feelings and thoughts, since in our language something can just to be implied. While a few years dating time for many is the happiest time, Kimi and I spent those years arguing on things that result from our differences. Years passed, and we have bonded and learned about each other. These days it is much better than before; we use productive communication and talk with an open heart on different things. Most of the time, when we have disagreements or conflicts, we normally say, "Let's talk about it," or "Let's sit down and discuss it." Our current disagreements are always solved without an argument; instead we talk, about it productively. And certainly, we have no arguments in front of our sons. That is something we both agree on. Our long discussions should be just between the two of us.

Reading the book of Dr. Ed Wheat, *Love Life for Every Married Couple*, I found some interesting suggestions of five basic rules for using effective communication in the marriage:

1. Never repeat to anyone else the things your husband shares with you privately.
2. Give your husband your total enthusiastic attention and listen with interest while he becomes more comfortable in expressing himself.
3. Do not interrupt him or jump to conclusions about what he is saying.

4. Acknowledge that you understand even if you disagree, and repeat his thoughts and feelings back to him so that he is sure you understand. Do not let your disagreement sound like disapproval.

5. When you are sharing your thoughts, be careful never to sound as if you are heaping blame on him. When either of you goes on the defensive, your communication goes, too. The rapport must be reestablished. (Wheat 251)

We set aside time to talk to each other about many things after our exhausting days; we talk about our day at work, about our children, about the current book or article that we are reading, and we confide about our own feelings. Kimi does not let our problems escalate in our conflicts.

Golden Words: "Please", "Thank you", and "I am Sorry"

I have learned that these words are worth more than gold in my marriage. They work well with every situation, requesting his assistance, showing my appreciation, asking for his forgiveness on my wrongdoing, and asking for the opportunity to do things right. These words bring a wonderful feeling, especially when they are said sincerely and with a meaningful attitude to one another. They are magic words that make each other feel good and valuable. They are words which express a request instead of a demand. They also help to increase each other's self-esteem. I have learned that individual pride, most of the time, has to be forgotten in a marriage for it to work in a positive way. I don't remember exactly where I read this, but I found it so interesting, and I have learned the importance of these precise and powerful words in my own marriage. It is called, "The Most Important Words,"

The six most important words are "**I admit I made a mistake**."

The five most important words are "**You did a good job.**"

The four most important words are "**What is your opinion?**"

The three most important words are "**If you please.**"

The two most important words are "**Thank you.**"

The *least* important word is "**I**." (*The Suburban*, Canada)

Responsibility

As team members in our marriage, Kimi and I acknowledge our responsibilities, to ourselves, to each other, to our children, and outside the home. We take and share financial responsibility and inform each other on financial situations. We also talk to each other on any big purchases for our household. We were guided to create a monthly personal fund to manage our monthly personal expenses without having to worry about each other's spending. Fortunately, both of us work and earn a stable income; there are not a lot of financial issues in our marriage. We financially manage our retirement plan without hurting our family's financial needs. Other people used to ask me about Kimi's earnings, and that made me remember that I have never asked Kimi about his paycheck. I trust and value his responsibility, and I am certain about his wise spending. On the other hand, Kimi regularly shares with me about his earnings and merit increases. I still remember my American family's teaching that, "when you feel secure in your situations, personally or financially, you don't have to look over your spouse's shoulders on everything he does. When you feel sufficient, you don't have to worry about his money all the time. That will give you peace of mind and give him his space to be himself and, as the household's primary earner, to manage a family financial plan."

Besides sharing financial responsibility, we also share the household chores and the responsibility for our children's activities. He always helps with the household work load after a long work day, such as cooking, cleaning, buying groceries and household items, taking care of children, and doing laundry. I am quite lucky that I don't have to feel burdened with all the things that need to get done. I frequently appreciate Kimi's contributions, after his learning that my day is really exhausting. The kind words, "Pat, you can go into the sauna, take a shower, and go to sleep early. I will take care of everything for the kids," or "Today, I will cook a Japanese dish. You don't have to prepare anything for our supper," are still unforgettable and more appreciated than the greeting at the door, while getting out of a car, after a long tiring day, "Pat, what are we going to have for dinner today?"

These days, I am so thankful and appreciate his responsibility when I daily see how Kimi is patiently teaching my youngest son piano, in addition to taking him to attend a weekly class, after his long work day. His enthusiasm and involvement with the children's after-school and weekend activities make us so happy and shows me what a good example of fatherhood he demonstrates.

Quality Time

Full-time employment, a busy schedule, many children's activities, daily responsibilities, sometimes make us forget to spend enough time with each other as a couple. A few times when I talked about taking a vacation together, just the two of us, Kimi thought I was not serious about it. These days, we realize the importance of our couple time away from the children. We plan our vacation together. We spend time all day going to different places and doing things we like to do, such as watching movies, picnicking, walking on the track, exercising in the fitness center, shopping in the mall, visiting the bookstore or computer store, drinking coffee and talking about different things in a coffee shop, eating out and experiencing a variety of foods, meeting Kimi for lunch on my day off, helping each other cook and clean, and sometimes simply running errands together. We certainly let our children know that we sometimes need time together, so they won't be surprised when we enroll them in the YMCA parent's night out program.

Besides making time for each other and spending time as a couple, we make personal time for ourselves. I was quite lucky that Kimi understands when I need to be alone, be away from him, my children, and my work. I was also thankful for some of my friends who offer to keep my children while I am resting and spending time doing what I like. I sometimes take a day off from work (when my vacation time allows) to pamper myself in the salon, nail and spa shop, to go window shopping, to walk in the mall, to read books and to drink my favorite coffee in a quiet corner of the coffee shop or the bookstore. Or often, I just take a walk on the track around the neighborhood or listen to my favorite music at home alone.

As a couple, Kimi and I give each other enough "space" and "room for breathing." Our couple's mission is not to be together all the time, to go everywhere together, or to do the same things all the time. I acknowledge that Kimi has his personal interests and hobbies and needs time for himself, so I keep my children or take them somewhere with me to give Kimi enough time to do what he enjoys. Many times, I ask Kimi to visit Japan without us, so he can enjoy his personal time with his parents and relatives. I still remember a few times I went to visit my family in Thailand without his accompanying me. His reason was that I could have time by myself to enjoy activities in Thailand and spend time alone with my parents.

Many things, many words, and many practices were not part of my personal perception of Kimi in our initial years of marriage. I expected Kimi to be the way I thought he should be. When he wasn't, I became disappointed, sad, and regretted being married; my thought was even that I had made a mistake. After taking time to learn and follow useful guidance, I trained myself to change my perspective on Kimi and came to realize and accept the fact that Kimi is a person who has his own rights, opinions, and goals, just like me. I still remember my counselor explaining that "you have to learn to accept that Kimi is one unique individual before you think about his role in your marriage." Then, I learned that Kimi and I are a team of two unique individuals who have different points of view on things. Learning to accept and respect each other can help us form a stronger team. Knowing our tasks and being able to communicate in the same language with the willingness to achieve the same common goal, helps us to effectively play our role and to become a good team member. Spending time practicing all of our important tasks, including raising our children, using words of appreciation and willingly offering a sincere apology when we make mistakes provides us a chance to love, laugh, and grow together.

Having lived in America for the past twelve years, seeing and learning that American society has a lot of people who like to change partners as many times as they change clothes, getting married is apparently very convenient. Many drive-thru services exist in Las Vegas, a fantasy place for many couples to become engaged or to get married. The wedding drive-thru service is still an awesome experience for some. The American marriage and divorce rate is on the top of any type of graph, even though the legal fees for divorce are high. However, many American couples celebrate their 30th , 40th , 50th and even 60th marriage anniversary -- retired married couples often spend their quality time holding hands, walking on the track, participating in city activities, taking their great grandchildren to ice cream shops, traveling together in their recreational vehicle, or riding the bus to a casino. There is still the opportunity to meet men and women who are able to tell stories about how they have been married to the same person for the past 38 or 50 years.

As a marriage beginner here in America, there are good and useful books and articles on different important topics in marriage to read, learn, and follow. Professional and effective marriage counselors are available who have been or are married and successfully guide many couples. Some people might think that it is embarrassing to meet with a counselor to tell them about our problems, but to me it is a wonderful learning experience that offers useful guidance that helps me to learn little effective things that I didn't even think of. It is better than complaining about marriage without seeking help. Some might wonder if counseling is costly. Yes, it is, but for some it is really worth it. Some free marriage counselors are provided by government agencies. However, please keep in mind that nothing is really free in America; not even good guidance to save your marriage, if you do not seriously work on it. I have learned that besides working hard daily to make a living, working on a successful marriage is also a top priority while living here in America.

Pat & Kimi

Pat and Family

Pat with Sato family in Japan

Chapter 5: Seed of the Future

"In the United States today, there is a pervasive tendency to treat children as adults, and adults as children. The options of children are thus steadily expanded, while those of adults are progressively constricted. The result is unruly children and childish adults." ~Thomas Szasz

"My Sons, Jack and Andrew, you are my love, my hope, my future, and you are everything that I can ask for as a mother, not only here, in America, but everywhere you might choose to be in the world. You are my vision that only the future can tell. My prayer will always be with you, and I strongly hope that you are good persons, productive members of society, and citizens who make wise choices. And thank you for giving me the opportunity to be a mother. Raising you two in America, to the best I know how to do it, is my significant life priority."

Before I write any further, I would like to express my sincere gratitude and heartfelt appreciation to my parents for raising me and giving me a life to live until today, to experience what I am going to write about in this chapter. I appreciate their unconditional love, unlimited care and kindness, encouragement, continuous support, positive and negative motivation, their unselfishness in bringing me up, their push and pull to get me into the right track of life, their punishment and forgiveness of my mistakes in the loop of life. I value their words and spankings when I misbehaved, continuously teaching, coaching, molding, and shaping me every chance they got. I am grateful for their laughs and tears on my successes and failures in life. I am thankful for their example of handling success and failure with any life challenges, as a couple and as parents. Everything I was given from them was my lifelong appreciation of learning. And more than anything else, they have provided me with the opportunity for me to call them "**father**" and "**mother,**" which also gives me a sense of having "**roots**." Without them, there would have not been any possibility for me to share my own life experiences with you. The most valuable thing is that what I say and what I teach my children these days is based on the foundation they have given me, combined with the chance given to me to learn, a chance that has been nurtured, and has grown for the past thirty-eight years. I always remember what my mother said to me when I misbehaved in many situations, "You won't know how much we love you and care for you until you have your own children." She was absolutely right, and it was not really clear in my mind until I began raising my sons. I still remember when my mother visited me here at home last year; my sons and I sat down on the floor in front of her, our heads down at her two feet while she was sitting on the sofa, asked for her blessing and forgiveness on our verbal and physical misconduct toward her in the past. She was in tears and told us that she forgave us. She also told me that, "As a mother, nine months of carrying your unborn child, a few years of raising your children, it has not been yet a beginning. You still have a long way to go, and it is going to for the rest of your life to give them your love and care. It shouldn't be only eighteen years, as some people do in the culture that you are currently living in. No matter how grown they are, you will still worry about them, just as I am here, halfway across the world to be with you, even for a short time." I couldn't hold back my tears, and my sons, of course, wouldn't understand what their grandmother meant. They might have to wait until they have their own children. Then, they will find that the parents' teaching is a life treasure.

These days, when I talk to my mother via an international call every other weekend, I am so thankful that I still have the opportunity to share my motherhood experience with my own mother and to thank her for helping me to be a mother today. Last weekend, when I was at the Thai temple in Dallas, Texas, and while my youngest son was asking me for a dollar to buy a snow cone, with a mixed conversation in Thai and English, one lady said that, "He is so cute. How many children do you have?" After I told her that I have two sons, she interestingly said that, "I don't have any kids, but I have four cats. I am quite lucky that I don't have any children because raising them these days is so difficult. There are so many negative influences in society." After she stopped, I didn't know how to respond, because I really never thought whether I am lucky or unlucky to be a mother. I just think I am blessed to have my two sons, and it is an honor to have them, especially since I had the second one when I was close to thirty-five years of age. They are ten years apart. I envy some American mothers I meet. After their children have grown, they still have time to enjoy doing things for themselves, and they certainly look young for being grandmothers. They also had the opportunity to participate and to be involved in their children's activities when they were young and full of energy. However, one certain thing I want to tell the lady at the temple is that she will never have the opportunity to appreciate the great pride, as many women in this world, including myself, that is the experience of the greatest female duty and responsibility: being a mother.

I consider myself a beginner in world of motherhood. I, however, have learned many significant things and have tried my best to gain and obtain more information and experience every chance I get, by speaking to other mothers who are in the same situation, by seeking good advice from successful mothers, by reading from different resources, by observing other people's mother and children relationship, and by practicing everyday responsibilities, with love, care, and pride. Even though there are many useful and informative resources available to read about parenting, I still remember what my godmother taught me: "You need to use your own judgment on raising and disciplining your children. You might ask other women, but no one really knows your kids better than you do. The way that works for them might not work for you. The most important thing is that you need to take time to learn about your own kids and find the proper ways that will work for them. Remember one thing: that you are also growing with them as parents." Many times, I learn parenting skills by trial and error. I also remember a time that I joked with my children when they misbehaved: "I am so sad that you can't follow what I asked you to do, even a very simple thing. Can I resign from my job as a mother?" My son, Jack, who is now fourteen years old, said, "No, mom, it is too late to resign or to divorce from us. We won't approve your resignation." Well, that might be a returned joke, but I take it seriously that I will have to continue to do the best I can in my duty as a mother. I concentrate and strictly focus on four major areas of duty, with hope and vision, while currently working full time, twenty-four hours a day, seven days a week, without any vacation, but with one great benefit called "achievement," on a very honorable, wonderful, and challenging job that I am titled, **"mother."**

The four areas in which I work with my children and hope to leave something good with them for the rest of their lives are raising them in a good home, giving them the best possible education, leading them by the best possible example, and sharing with them the best family values.

The first area in a mother's duty is to raise them in a safe, positive, and productive environment; in a society, that is called "family" and "home." A good home, in my opinion, is not necessarily a big and beautiful house, but a clean, warm loving and caring house where everyone living there can feel safe, secure, comfortable, and able to express themselves in a positive and acceptable way. I recall when my husband and I first decided to buy a house in America. One of the many factors involved in our first home buying experience was to buy a house in a good, quiet neighborhood. I also considered a good school district for my children, even though at the time I did not have them with me yet. I even studied the crime rate in that city. Since my husband and I have a tri-cultural home, I encouraged my children to learn and practice the best of each and to be proud of themselves, even though sometimes we have to sit down and discuss the conflicts of each culture. At times we have to help each other to get through the challenges of three different cultures. They are at least able to speak more than one language and absorb more than one good thing in each culture. That opportunity allows us to support, bond, and grow. Fortunately, my children have friends who have an interest in our culture; that can make them have no hesitation on sharing our traditions and goodness.

To make a good home, besides striving to provide love and understanding to everybody in a house, I also accentuate spending positive time and positive communication with my children. As a working mother, I am unfortunate that I can't spend all my time with them as much as I want to. However, I make sure that I give them enough quality time to substitute for the time I have lost, especially my time with Jack, who is getting into his teenage years, a critical period in his life, and I didn't have time to nurture him for over a decade.

Jack and I have been reunited in America for two years. He was raised by my parents while I was studying, trying to better myself, and settling down. I strongly hoped to petition for him to immigrate to America when I was stable enough. Fortunately, I was able to start the process in 2002 and completed everything in early 2005. He has been my greatest motivation in the many things I have strived to do and to be in the past twelve years in America. Unlike many mothers who have a good opportunity to closely raise their children every day, I have missed out on good bonding time while he was growing up. In contrast, Jack has gotten all the love, care, and attention from his grandparents. Visiting him every two years and talking with him over the phone every month was never enough. We both are blessed that we still have the opportunity to bond and live together as a family through the many challenges that we have encountered. That also gives me a chance to learn that raising a child is not only concentrating on his physical growth but also mental and emotional growth. The latter should be the primary focus.

I recall one night Jack and I were cooking and talking in the kitchen. He told me that he was enjoying himself spending time like this with me. I told him that I loved him so much, and I was happy to do the same. I got a chance to ask him, "Do you feel regret that you haven't spent time with me everyday for twelve years?" His reply was the most appreciative thing I received that night, "No, mom, I don't regret it. I think if you brought me with you when I was little, you might not have been able to finish school and work, because you would have been worried about me, and wanted to raise me, and to take care of me. Then we might not have a house and everything we have now. We might not have time like tonight." I thanked him for being so understanding; at least he was as understanding as he could be.

We then talked about different things, including his describing and asking about his American friends, who are also thirteen or fourteen years old. They have a girlfriend or a boyfriend at school, and they hug and kiss each other in public. He told me that it looked funny. I asked if he would do like they were doing when he had a girlfriend. "Oh, no, Mom." I had the chance to tell him that day that he will have the feeling of liking someone, and I hope that he remains concerned about the appropriateness of showing affection to the girl he likes. He asked, "Mom, why are American kids not shy about doing that?" I recalled sharing with him that, "In American culture, showing affection is a wonderful thing and is not something to be shy about because it shows love, closeness, and bonding. However, when it shows too much in the improper or inappropriate way, and that affection is expressed in a disrespectful manner to oneself, at a given place and time, it decreases the decency of the individual. That also indicates the lack of self-discipline of a person." And we talked about using judgment of whether it is appropriate or not. The conclusion of our conversation was, "If we feel so uncomfortable when we see other people doing it, it might not really be the appropriate thing to do." I just told Jack that most of the time, we must use our judgment and observation in different situations to carry out our actions. One of many questions I received that night was: "Mom, why are a lot of songs always about love?" I don't recall whether I used to ask my mother such a question. If I have, I would have found a better way to answer Jack's question. I remember being too shy to talk to my mother about love, dating, and relationships when I was Jack's age. Actually, we had no opportunity to talk about dating. Dating while in school was considered inappropriate. Her main focus in teaching me was on my concentrating on schooling and on helping the family. Part of that was our close, conservative culture and views in the family. However, I got a chance to go out with one guy, and it is nice to have a chance to share the experience with my son. Back then, I wasn't quite sure whether it was called a date; our going out seemed to be approved by both families. I remember that his mother came over to visit with my mother, when she learned that her son often rode a bicycle to my house on the weekend and spent time helping me do the work around the house. He was the only boy I went out with in my teen years. If that was called a date, we did it for five years. I told Jack that when I was on a date, his grandmother always accompanied me because she didn't want people to talk about me in a bad way. Sixteen or seventeen years old in those days was considered still very young and dependent. I was taught to carry myself well, respect my date, and treat him nicely and appropriately. During our date, we never hugged or kissed; we also didn't walk holding hands. We always kept a slight distance while walking. The funny thing was that our mothers were walking and talking to each other behind us. When I look back on those days, having both mothers riding a motorcycle with each of us on a date was really a unique dating experience, and that might not be found in today's society.

These days, to see my Thai friends handling and approving their children's dating, it is interesting and educational for personal learning. I am looking forward to learning how I will do when my turn comes. I remember my own response to Jack's question about love was, "I am not quite sure how to put it, but let me try. Love is a basic life principle, and it is a good feeling when you are in love. People like to carry out their feelings in the form of song and music. For some people who don't believe in love, feel hurt from it, or have any bad experience with it, they can also carry out that feeling through the songs as well." "Have you gotten a girlfriend at school yet?" I asked Jack. "No, mom, I just have a friend." After that we got a chance to talk more about dating and having a girlfriend in America. "Some young Americans start dating as young as 16 or 17, some people said; dating is a social engagement between two persons, normally in the romantic way, so you can learn to interact with a person and you will have an opportunity to learn and understand a person better." I let him know that I really don't mind who he will be dating, as long as both of them are responsible and mature enough for the appropriate actions and have a good feeling for each other. My responsibility will be to observe the readiness and allow Jack to learn when he is ready. I recall some of my Thai friends still think that they want their sons and daughters dating our own ethic group. They became so stressed out when that didn't happen. "Mom, I am not going to get married early. I will be stable before starting a family." I can recall Jack told me that night. My opinion on this matter during our conversation was, "Jack, girlfriend and wife are different; it might not be difficult to date and have a girlfriend, but you might need to spend time and take consideration when you choose to marry someone. However, when you are mature enough, you will understand more about what we are talking about. Right now I ask you to concentrate on schooling and on enjoying the activities that are appropriate for your age, so you will not regret anything later on in life." It was a nice conversation that Jack and I had for almost two hours that night.

Frequently, we talk about our day. I try to ask more than, "How is your day?" because I know the answer will be, "Good, mom." I expect my children to tell me more about their day to give me a chance to have an open door of communication with them. These days, my husband and I are planning to talk to Jack more on what we call, "a sensitive topic," that will help our son not to feel embarrassed and shameful when he sees such topics on the news or hears about them from his friends. It was not surprising when one day Jack asked me about how girls have menstruation and become pregnant. I am so glad that schools in America start teaching their students about sex education at this age; at least it gives them some informative ideas on men's and women's body structures.

I surely have not yet had any problems discussing teenage topics with Andrew, because he is still young. He is currently in an American preschool, starting his pre-kindergarten. My wish is that after talking, working, and learning some parenting strategies with Jack, working and dealing with Andrew shouldn't be too difficult. I might be wrong, because different children have different learning styles, personality, and development. I might just have to wait and see what is really going to happen with him. These days, while Andrew is the "baby" of the house, he is a center of attention in our home. That starts with his innocent comment, mocking, pretending, and acting up to get attention from all of us. Andrew is sometimes a good indicator for us, who makes us aware of sending out good and appropriate messages. He also always runs around the house and checks on everybody: whether Jack is playing video games or studying; his mom is cooking, reading a magazine, writing, sleeping, or doing laundry; his dad is working on a computer, reading a book, or watching movie. He is good in helping us to always have a conversation going in our home.

Andrew was born on American soil, with two cowlicks; that has been said as to be a sign of stubbornness and flattery. Others say that it is a sign of intelligence. In fact, his personality is very pleasant to be around. He shows affection with friendly hugging and kissing (just as Americans do), which is worth waiting for after a long tiring day of work. As a toddler, his hyperactivity, jumping and moving around without concern for anything, makes me want to have a vacation far away from him for a while. I recall when we went to Japan to visit my husband's parents; his father took us out shopping and out to eat; Andrew was about 18 months old, but he was very active and ran around a lot; my father-in-law said, "This Texas boy is very active compared to Japanese boys." Some people in the store looked at him and might have wondered, "What's going on in this boy?" However, he is a very quick learner of languages, both of Thai and Japanese. Jack used to say, "It is so nice seeing Andrew speaking three languages and he can teach me, too." That benefits Jack when he wants to know some words in Japanese, in English, or in Thai - he can ask Andrew. When they both are watching a Japanese movie in Japanese, Andrew is the interpreter. It is also an enjoying time for us to listen to his daily conversations in Japanese with his father, who is trying very hard to speak only Japanese with Andrew. His intention is to leave the heritage of Japanese language with Andrew at a very young age.

Andrew and I talk to each other a lot during our driving time from home to his preschool. We talk about different things. Sometimes he proudly tells me, "Mom, today I don't get a bad note, but a good one," since he used to have two "bad notes" from his preschool. One of those notes said, "I got an office time out at school today, because I pulled my pants and underwear down in front of my class." I got the incident report when I walked by the lobby to pick him up at school. He told me that he did was because his friends did it. Of course, that incident made us sit down at the dinner table and talk about this inappropriate behavior with Andrew, and we were not smiling. He never knew that my husband and I talked and laughed about it after he went to sleep.

These days, I have been thinking about asking Andrew new questions, so that he doesn't prepare a handy answer about his incident reports and his lunch. That way, I can encourage him to converse with me more. He is an interesting little guy with his own little opinions and preferences. If I notice, for instance, that he is sometimes moody or not himself, I take time to ask why and try to find out what's going on or what's not working for him. With a little voice, he told me, "Mom, you don't listen!" when he didn't want to wear his warm jacket in a cold winter, and I was trying to put it on him. That makes me work harder on my listening skills and find more effective ways to deal with him. I certainly don't want to hear the words, "Mom, you don't listen!" again when he is eighteen, even though what I was trying to do was for his well-being. Recently, he even told me that I needed to put one of my hands back on the steering wheel while I was trying to reach for something on a passenger seat, "Mom, don't let go your hand, it might happen the accident." That let me know that his little mind has absorbed something good. Sometimes, we sing while we are in the car; "Twinkle, Twinkle Little Star," is our favorite song and we take turns singing. Once, when I finished singing, he said, "Mom, that's not the way to sing. You don't know how to sing. You need to learn from my teacher at school." Well, I was wondering if I really have to go back to a preschool at the age of thirty- eight to learn the American kids' song. I just told Andrew that I would practice some more to be a better singer. Andrew and I have had a good time singing, by having me repeat after him. Observing him daily helps me learn that children these days are developing fast, and they are really being influenced by the other children surrounding them.

The recent news I received from my old friend in Thailand about her son, who is seventeen years old, dropping out of school, and running away from home breaks my heart. My friend's sadness and her worrying about her child are very emotional. I wish I could help by more than listening and talking to her over the phone and e-mail. As a mother, I understand that she must be in a lot of pain from worrying about her son's well-being. This incident pushes me to strive harder to learn my parenting skills and putting them into practice. I had never realized that while raising my children here, understanding and practicing parenting skills became my priority, and I emphasize them when learning and searching for effective methods.

Another thing that I do to provide a good home is to give my children enough privacy, so they feel comfortable, secure, and respected. For Jack, who is now fourteen years old, I understand that it is quite important that he can have his own space and time alone in his room. I respect his privacy by knocking on his closed door before entering his room, and I ask him to do the same for me. Most of the time, it is my trust that makes him feel comfortable and allows me to develop an awareness of his actions. Besides giving him privacy at home, I sometimes allow him to go to his friends' houses; I have acknowledged these friends to be acceptable, after learning about them for a while and meeting with their parents for a period of time. I also allow Jack's friends to come over to our house, participating in our family activities, seeing our culture at the Thai temple, and sometimes spending the night. When his friends come over, I make sure Jack has enough space in playing the good host and feels comfortable being himself around his friends.

I keep in mind that a good home also should feel respectful, both between the parents and between parents and children. I remember to ask their permission before I start to use their belongings, even though I was the one who bought that stuff. But that approach gives them a sense of ownership and shows respectful for their privacy. It allows me to create a friendly and respectful environment for them, besides respecting their opinions and ideas. That also helps me to indirectly teach them manners, which is a significant job I must do.

Along with bringing them up as well as I can be in a good home, giving them the best education is a priority. Shaping their minds with the love of knowledge is a goal. Helping them to gain knowledge and obtain useful information that will help them to be productive is also a must-do job. I strongly believe that my children's education begins at home, and that makes me highly responsible for the role as their first teacher in life. The foundation that I teach in our home will pave the way for their learning in other areas. I strongly believe that without manners and discipline, academic accomplishment might not happen easily. Besides giving them an education in an American public school and later on in a university, the daily teaching on manners, morality, and discipline at home is my priority. I don't solely leave this part of education to their teachers. My goal is that in setting expectations for my children, I am starting in my own home.

In terms of education, I try my best not to tell them what I want them to be in any profession. My basic philosophy in their education is to give them skills and tools for them to be responsible, secure, and enjoy what they love to do. Yet, they are still minors in regard to making that decision about their careers; they still need a lot of information and directions. What I do is expose them to many useful resources to search for what fields they might want to be in; providing information is all I can do at the moment. One thing I never want to do is make my children to be in the path that some people called, "A super-achiever," in every subject area. All I am asking and motivating them to do is to put full effort in the things they do; they might not necessarily be the best; I don't compare them with anybody else's children, not even their friends. My husband and I work with them individually on their strengths and weaknesses and support them in any area of education. It is refreshing to see Jack's good report card from his middle school, even though he has been here for only a little over a year. I strongly hope to see a good one later on as well.

Besides teaching them at home, providing the opportunity to learn from knowledgeable teachers at school, giving them a chance to interact with people and peers, protecting them from any type of controllable hurt and harm, my husband and I allow them to exercise their ability and talent in different activities related to their personality and physical ability. Jack is very athletic and has a love for sports and stunts. We enrolled Jack in a Tae Kwon Do class and he plays on a soccer team. He has been doing wonderfully, and we are proud of him and enjoy time watching him kick and break the wooden block, and performing different forms. His willingness to do his best and be a responsible team member on a soccer field each game makes my exhausting day from work worthwhile, as I enjoy being among many American parents watching him and their children around the field. I acknowledge that as a player, he always wants to win the game. I remember before the game he always asks, "Mom, am I going to win today?" My response is, "Yes, you will win; however, if you do not, it is still okay as long as you are doing your best. Besides striving to win the game, I certainly want you to enjoy yourself by showing the best sportsmanship you can; learn to accept that in all games there are two chances, lose or win either one is wonderful as long as we put in full effort and play the game fairly."

Andrew is enrolled in a piano class, taught by the knowledgeable Suzuki method teacher. He is actively progressing for a boy his age. His concentration and hyperactivity are still challenging for his father and his teacher. I enjoy myself sitting with a cup of tea and listening to him practice daily. Of course, he is now able to play his favorite song, "Twinkle, Twinkle Little Star," on his own piano. Seeing his father patiently and closely work with him on the lesson every night around 9:00 p.m., is the greatest evidence of what Dr. Suzuki says: "Talent is not in born."

By looking to his older brother as an example, Andrew asked me to enroll him on a soccer team and in a Tae-Kwon-Do class. That's what I am thinking about doing next year, to give him the opportunity to be exposed to different things. However, my husband and I try not to overwhelm our children with too many activities. One thing we often do is that with every activity we let our children join, one of us will be there participating. I recall the time that I had to run around on a soccer field with Jack, his teammates, and their parents, when the parents played against their children. It was tiring and fun, even though I had no idea how to play soccer.

Part of my children's education at home is being taught manners. Since I have been here, I have seen many things different from my culture. One important thing I see in American children, who will be the future of their country, is their manners. When I was back home, I was taught and was able to see children in Thailand taught to be polite, to have etiquette, and to respect people. The children always listen to their parents, and relationships with parents are deep and close; the children were not allowed to talk back, while they were guided or corrected about their negative behavior. They were trained to have good manners when they were young. Most parents in Thailand have never been embarrassed by their children. In contrast, some children in America disrespect people, even their parents. I have learned that some children even curse their parents. They have too much freedom, which makes them think that they are independent, and it is therefore hard to train them. However, I think that if most of the people in today's society had good manners, the society would not have been disordered like today. I certainly hope that I don't see that happen with my own children.

Sometimes, I confer with my American co-workers during my lunch time about children's mannerisms. One of them interestingly said, "With your good Asian heritage, which makes all family members very close, you shouldn't have many problems with your children." Remember, good home helps children to excel academically and personally. So, we have many important little things to talk about in our home, such as getting along with people, respecting others' feelings, respecting others' privacy, listening and talking to others, doing things in certain way, sharing, treating people appropriately, having correct social, table, and telephone manners, and most importantly using common sense while interacting with other people.

Besides working with my children on manners, discipline is also part of their home education. Understanding that no one in this world is perfect and always does everything right, I try very hard to let Andrew and Jack know that in our house there is always room for mistakes and for improvement, but they are encouraged to learn from their mistakes, and try not to repeat the same mistake over and over again. Discipline in our home is setting of expectations and accepting of the consequences. I am trying to do my part to cooperate with their teachers to make their job easier in terms of discipline. A few times, my American co-workers talked to me and said that I am too hard on my son, Jack, when he gets in trouble at school. They remind me that Jack is a growing boy. Sometimes, the trouble that he is in is part of growing up; it is not what he intends to do, so they suggest that I just take it easy on him. I initially had a hard time accepting it. However, when I remember that we all make mistakes in our life, but mistakes provide something for us to learn from; that helps me to easily work with Jack. The incident at school allowed Jack to learn to accept the consequences for his actions. We regularly assign age-appropriate tasks to Jack and Andrew in the house to teach responsibility. We set standards and expectations for them to excel in terms of self-discipline. As part of discipline, many times I feel badly that I am unable to give toys, games, and electronic devices to my children as often as they ask for them, but I explain to them that, "About toys, you will never always get what you asked for. It is not because I can't buy it for you, but I don't want to create the habit that you will always get what you want, or get everything your way. Life is not like that. The definite thing in life is that you will never always get things that you want, as you want it to be. I don't want you to be spoiled and not value things. It is just like when you are hungry all foods and meals taste extremely good and are appreciated, but if you are full, regardless of how tasty the food is in front of you, you might not appreciate it and not value how the food was prepared or provided." On special occasions, though, they know they will get something good from us. I like the way author Wayne Parker said, "A personal investment in your children is much more important to them than any toy, video game, or electronic gadget." He encourages giving children our quality time and suggests many activities we can do as a family.

According to a Parent Education Workshop, I have learned that there are "3 F's" of effective parenting in discipline: firm, fair, and friendly. Parents should clearly state expectations and consequences and adhere to them when inappropriate behavior occurs. Parents can be fair by giving appropriate punishment that fits the crime. Also, in the case of recurring behavior, consequences should be stated in advance, so the children know what to expect. It is not necessary to give harsh punishment. Time Out can be effective when it is consistently used every time the behavior occurs. Use a friendly but firm communication style when letting children know they have behaved inappropriately and let them know they will receive the "agreed upon" consequence. Parents should encourage them to try to remember what they should do instead to avoid future consequences. However, it is suggested that you work at "catching them being good" and praise them for appropriate behavior. When I teach manners and disciplining, I don't want to sound to my children as if I am nagging. They are still young, so frequent, friendly repetition and reminders on manners are essential. Actually, when I was growing up, my mother's teaching of manners seemed like nagging, but I certainly remember most of the things that she said more than twenty years ago. I hope that my sons will do the same or even better. I strongly believe that the values that we are trying to teach our children will become useful for them and eventually their family. One day when I got home, Jack was telling me that he finished folding all of the clothes I left on Andrew's bed when I was sick and did not finish; I was so proud, and I thanked him for doing that for me.

These days, observing Jack make his own bed daily, do his own laundry and iron his clothes weekly without having to be told, take out trash every trash day, do his weekly bathroom clean up, put up clean dishes in the cabinets, check mail daily, and prepare freshly cooked rice in the rice cooker for us to enjoy after we get home from work, I am so proud of him and appreciate his effort. Recently, I was honored to accompany him to school, after a long day of work, to congratulate him as a recipient of the "Rockwall I.S.D. Academic Excellence Award." Listening to Andrew say, "Jack, we don't eat on the couch or in front of the T.V. We will make a mess of it. We need to eat at the table in the kitchen," "I make a mess, I will clean it up," or "I will save this money to buy my toys" allow me to know that all of these improvements can't happen without self-discipline and the ability to follow parents' instructions. "I am on the right track, so far," I keep telling myself.

Another part of my role as parent is leading by the best possible example for my children. I am aware that my children are watching me, both my expressions and my actions. Sometimes they joke about how I act in situations. One Friday, when Andrew and I got home, he asked if we could go to the zoo on the weekend. I said, "Well, we have to wait until your father comes home and I will ask if he would take us." Andrew responded, "No, mom, you have to say like this, 'Darling, can we go to the zoo this weekend?'" He was making his funny face with a big smile while talking. For his age, I never thought he would say such a thing; however, I realized that he might hear me sometimes say this to my husband when I ask him for a favor. Also, when Jack and Andrew correct each other's actions and behavior, they say exactly the same words that my husband and I use to correct them. One night my husband and I were talking about something while Andrew was playing with his toys nearby. It seemed to me that he wasn't paying attention, but I was wrong. During the conversation, my husband likely said, "Oh, man," a quick response from Andrew was, "We don't say that word in our house." It was exactly the same thing we used to teach them. The incident made us pay close attention to what we do and what we say in front of our kids.

While children are not mature and are unable to learn life experiences enough to make their own decisions, I believe that it must be really hard for them if they are told to do one thing and the people who told them do it differently. My husband and I acknowledge that we have the challenge of being aware of what we do, so we do not create confusion in our children as their parents and their role models. We are trying our best to be positive role models; sometimes, when I start talking about negative things while our children are around, my husband stops me. We are not perfect, but we try our best in our roles. I am sure when they grow up they can choose and learn from other models. Right now, we emphasize what is appropriate and inappropriate by leading by example in our home. We treat each other and other people with respect; we show appreciation and gratitude to the help we receive; we are thankful for things we are given or provided by taking good care and not being wasteful.

One day, in my current profession as a teacher, I had a chance to talk to my class about "what they expect from their parents" after I heard one of my students complain about her parents. One of my male students interestingly shared with me that, "I want my parents to be role models in a good relationship such as how to treat women," while the others said, "Ms. Sato, I want my parents to be our parents, not our buddies. If I see my friends have spiked hair, I surely don't want to see my father do the same." Also, one female student, 20 years old, was telling me that, "I am not going back home for Thanksgiving holiday, because my daddy will be drunk again. My mother can't say anything about it. They never take time to create an environment for me to learn a good example from them." "Have you asked if you could talk to him openly?" I asked. She replied that, "He never listens to me. We always have a confrontation. He never takes time to see that I have been hurt, abused, and have learned the hard way to handle life. I don't have anybody in my family I can trust." The information they shared was educational and made me strive even more to not put my own children in the same situation.

I acknowledge that it must be difficult to understand if one is being taught to use appropriate language while one is hearing their parents cursing in the house everyday. It must be confusing if one is being told to value good work ethics if one sees the parents sit around doing nothing all day. It must be hard to distinguish between right and wrong if one is being taught not to drink and smoke, when they see their parents doing it all the time. It must be terrible for a boy to be taught to respect a girl, when he frequently sees his father verbally and physically abuse his mother at home. This role model issue reminds me of what Dr. Shinichi Suzuki says in his book -- that our children are our reflection. What you see on them is what you demonstrate for them to see on you, and it is reflected from a home environment. He states that,

> A parent who understands that children grow by adapting to their environment will think back on his own actions when he notices something in his child that is absorbed the actions of his parents. A parent who reflects in this way possesses an admirable heart. Suppose a father opens the door with his foot. The next day his child copies him and does the same thing. The mother sees the child and scolds him. The child would never have thought of opening the door with his foot by himself. He copies an adult. He absorbed the action of his father. Children do what their parents do; if the parent changes, the child also will change unconsciously. When a person reflects, he opens his eyes to truth. Parents who do not reflect in this way are merely training their children as they would farm animals. (Suzuki 96)

Dr. Kevin Ryan also states that, "Face it: human beings learn primarily through modeling. In fact, you can't avoid being an example to your children, whether good or bad. Being a good example, then, is probably your most important job" (Ryan).

Every chance I get, I will take time to share with them about the importance of family values. Being Thai, I have learned that the family is the important foundation in life and society. Our family life is very close, loving, caring, and supportive. It has also been referred to as a "very closely nested family." Every family member has a sense of family orientation. Growing up, we have always been taught to honor and respect our parents. Our parents are at the top of our family hierarchy, and they have all of the authority in the house. We have been taught that our important duty is to return gratitude to our parents and to take care of them when they become old. I believe that results in not having to hear Thai adults talking about putting their old parents in the nursing home. In the past, Thai parents usually stay with their children, when they get old, helping to raise their grandchildren and assisting with the little house chores while their children work outside of the house. In most cases, they don't accept any monetary reimbursement in return for their help. They are happy just for to be good helping hands for their children. Nowadays, this value might slightly change in the big city, but the old valuable tradition still appears to be seen in the countryside. This tradition brings warmth and closeness that transforms from one generation to the next.

Being Japanese, my husband allows our children to absorb the great family values of high responsibility, honesty, and keeping words and promises. He also emphasizes the value of thriftiness to help our children learn the value of money, property, and food. Sometimes, it is not surprising to hear my kindergarten son talking about "not wasting food" to his brother while they are eating at the table. That results from his having a "time out" when he wastes food on his plate. Providing them a piggy bank and opening their bank account allows them to start learning the saving and budgeting of their little allowances.

Courage is another value we teach our children, especially courage to do the right thing. We would like our children to have courage to interact with their classmates and peers; courage to meet a new group of people; courage to learn different cultures and try different types of foods; courage to stand up for themselves while growing up among different ethic groups; courage to dream of their own profession and follow their dream. I recall telling Jack when he had a problem with a friend mocking his accent in school to "be proud of our language and accent, but try your best to improve in English to effectively communicate in school and later on at work. You might not yet be able to speak the best English, but none of your friends are able to speak a word of your language. You traveled half way around the world to study in the same class with them, but yet they have not gone to your country to study your language. Be proud of who you are and where you are from, but be respectful to the others." These days, Andrew still needs a lot of encouragement to interact with strangers, while Jack is doing quite well with his American classmates and schoolmates. As someone said, "Letting your own fear win is not an option," Jack demonstrated his courage in the right way. One Sunday afternoon, after we came back from the temple, Jack saw a desk in usable condition at our neighbor's trash area. We were wondering whether they trashed it or kept it for a yard sale. Jack said, "Mom, I'm going to ask. I see someone is working in the backyard." A few minutes later, he came back home and stated that he was given that desk. He cleaned and polished it well before asking my husband to help him put it in his bedroom.

One day during our lunch time at work, I was asking my American co-workers about American family values. "American family values are quite broad because there are so many ethnic groups here. Each group sets family values differently," one of them responded. She interestingly asked if I had heard, "Be nice to your children because they will be the ones to pick your nursing home. For most families, by the age of eighteen, they want their children to leave the house to learn independence. Some American children, when they leave home for college, don't come back home permanently any more." This reminds me of what one male co-worker said, "When I was eighteen, my dad told me that it's time for me to get out. There will be only one man in a house." I said, "Wow, that must be tough." Then he shared that, "No, not really. I was ready to go, too. I didn't want to follow their rules anymore. I worked my way through college and came home only for special occasions."

I actually like the American value of independence, starting to work, earn money, and striving to make a living at a young age. Most of them work a lot when they are young, so that they are able to enjoy their retirement early. For some, getting out of the house early allows them to learn valuable life lessons that they encounter on their challenging road. It has been said, "There is no greater guide to success than the lessons taught by our own mistakes." I believe that the majority of them just want to get good support and helping hands when they actually need their parents. As a couple I met said, "We let our children learn on their own when they are gone to college, but we are always there if they need us. We are watching them mature with their own life experiences with a strong foundation from home."

I also was told by my American friend that, "Some parents let their children be out of control at a very young age." I hope this is not a starting point for having some unruly children who hardly show respect to their parents, who don't listen and follow any given instructions, who are very outspoken using different kinds of inappropriate language, who appear to be in charge of the house, not the parents, and who never learn to show love, care, and sharing. Some even call their parents by their first names, because their parents set no boundaries, are too friendly, and act as if they are their children's buddies. In that case, it might be hard to rule the children when they are given a lot of money, dropped off at the mall, and told, "Go find something to do; we will come back to pick you up after our party ends." Some American children are even told by the parents, "Find something to do and leave me alone; here is your allowance." I was once told that some well-off

American families' children, who "have it all" in all aspects, have no respect for and get no direction from their parents.

I acknowledge the difference in the family values that they have set for their children. Sometimes, it is really hard to determine which one is right or wrong, because we all believe differently. One experienced mother once said, "If you personally don't feel right, it might not be the right thing to do for your children while they are minors and unable to maturely make their own decisions." I thought that that was good advice.

One of my American co-workers is a very successful mother, both at home and at work. Her children are very well-educated and successful in their personal lives and careers. I used to ask her, for my personal motherhood experience, "What are the family values you taught to your children?" She kindly shared with me that, "The family values that I have taught my children are to be kind, to be polite, to be respectful toward your parents and other people, to treat other people like you want to be treated, to be kind to your sister and brother, to dress appropriately (does not always work) whatever you do, to do a good job, and to clean up behind yourselves (Sato, this does not always work either)." Her information was very helpful for me to understand that I am heading in the right direction while raising my sons here. And I believe that family values are the significant key to shaping and molding quality, character, and personality in a person.

Many times Jack and Andrew mention their brotherhood, when they ask for something such as toys, foods, or candies, from each other. Little Andrew says many times when Jack is playing roughly with him: "Don't hit me, we are brothers." "I am your little brother; you are not supposed to hurt me." "Can I have your toys? We are brothers." Jack must have been frustrated when Andrew asked for a small piece of his favorite food as he was about to eat, but the teaching is, "You are a big brother; you have to sacrifice for your little brother. If you can't sacrifice on a little thing, how can you help each other when your parents are gone?" For Andrew, the teaching is, "Even though you are a little brother, it does not mean that you have to ask for a favor all the time. You have to let your big brother enjoy what he wants to eat, too. You need to learn to give, not only want to take from your big brother." It is refreshing to hear both of them showing appreciation for each other by saying "Thank you" for things they do for each other and "Sorry" when they ask for forgiveness.

Frequently, I hear them say that something is not fair. I sometimes have to mention that most things in life are not fair and to just learn to accept and get used to that fact. Many things in life are out of our control; the only thing we have full control over is ourselves. We can't expect people to do or think the way we want them to do all the time. They might not understand what I mean now, but when they become more mature, they will see it more clearly. I used to say to my sons, "Many things I am teaching you two these days are things your grandmother taught me when I was your age. It was exactly the same way, just different things and generations. I was like you; sometimes I was against what she was teaching, and I didn't initially learn that her teaching was the most precious thing that I have inherited. When I teach you over and over, it might seem as if I am nagging you about the same thing. However, I realize that what I teach you today will be what you will teach your children in the future." As someone might say, "You teach your son today; you also teach your grandson in the future."

While living here, I really love how some Americans show their family values of "unity" or "togetherness" by having a "Family

Reunion." For some, their family reunion is hosted every year; each family just takes turns hosting it. Some families agree on doing it every few years. Their family members travel from all over the country. I was honored to attend some a few times, as a guest. That was an awesome life experience. I sometimes think that I need to do that for my family back home, or suggest someone in the family to host. Then I will travel there. Recently, I got a call from Mr. Marchbanks telling me that he was going to his family reunion. There he expected to see his first cousin whom he had never seen in his life. "How amazing," I said over the phone. I was so happy to hear how excited he was when he was showing us the pictures when we visited him last month.

Learning the value of family, I have never traced my family tree, as many people do, but my parents have. They tried to keep in touch with other family members. Every one of my family members lives far away from each other, but most of them always teach their kids to keep in touch with every generation. I was taught to contact my cousin's children when I have time, in order to stay close to our family members. Since my youth, I was told about one of my aunts who had married an American man and came over to America over 35 years ago. She has not gone back to visit in over twenty years. She only wrote letters to her mother. I have never seen my aunt, but I am happy to hear about her from the other people in the family. I got her phone number from my mother. I called her, and I will take the opportunity to visit her soon. It is nice to talk over the phone with a person that I have never seen in my life, and that I have a chance to find "The Lost" of my Thai family members while I am here in America.

American culture, in direct and straightforward communication, has given me the opportunity to easily say, "Sons, I am proud of you," "Thank you for helping me by cleaning up your bedroom," "I appreciate your help," and most importantly, it allows me to sincerely and openly tell my sons that, "I love you," in addition to admitting, "Sons, I am sorry, I made a mistake." That was what I hardly heard from my own parents, because in our conservative culture, the implications and actions are more expressive to show than to tell. These days, occasionally, Mr. Marchbanks and I still discuss our showing more affection to our children by hugging and kissing, as a loving American way. Mr. Marchbanks said many times that, "I'm hardly able to encourage Kimi to show love and affection. Even though I know that he loves his children so much, I hardly see him hug and kiss. I guess it is me that is having difficulty accepting this part of your culture." I was laughing when I saw his expression. One of many good American values that the Marchbanks family taught me, I am also teaching to my own children – that they can become effective and efficient while living and growing up in American society.

As parents, even though we have a long way to go, many things our sons demonstrate to us help us to see that we are heading in the right direction for them. Daily, we try our best to provide the best possible environment and positive framework to assist them to grow up exercising their skills and talents with our love and support.

Jack & Andrew "I Believe I Can Fly"

Andrew is ready for his piano recital

Christmas Presents from Oto San

Chapter 6: Family Fun—Quality Time

As an average person, I live my life very simply and conservatively. My daily and weekly routine is not fixed, but there are not a lot of changes either. Weekdays, I mostly work at least 8-10 hours each day. I hardly take my office work home; I try to get it all done during my work hours. When I get home, it is my family time until my children go to bed. Preparing food for dinner is routinely happens every evening, unless one evening we all have to be hurry to take my older son to his soccer practice or game or on Thursday evenings my little one has to go to his piano lesson. Since I am a working mother, spending enough time on a daily basis with my children and family is significant. As Dr. Mehrotra, a psychologist said, "A working mother who spends one hour of quality time every day with her child will probably establish a better bond with her child than one who is home nagging the child all the time." Treva Williams also defines quality time as concentrated, uninterrupted time to spend with children, spouse, and friends, with the expectation that it will be relaxed and free of conflict, and it should provide the opportunity for meaningful conversation and worthwhile things to do. In truth, in our family we certainly have our own favorite leisure activities, but together we participate in our family fun, on which everybody is always allowed to have an opinion and input. My husband and I regularly plan events and activities for our children to explore things for their own experience and to develop their social skills.

In our family, Sunday is a temple day, similar to most American families who go to their church on Sunday. Our Thai temple is in Dallas. It takes about 30-40 minutes to get there driving from our house one way. I have been going to the temple since I was a college student, living with my American family in Paris, Texas. Then it took me abut one hour and a half one way from my family's home to join Thais at the temple. Now, driving 30 minutes from our current location is nothing difficult at all. Recently, I enrolled my son, Andrew, in our Saturday Thai school, for him to learn about Thai language, culture, and music, all of which are being taught by volunteer teachers from a university in Thailand.

My family can enjoy many fun things at the temple after our morning chanting and blessing. We join many Thais to eat in a big room after all monks have finished their eating and blessing. Delicious dishes are prepared by Thai people to take to our temple on Sunday. Jokingly I told my sons that, "We can have the best Thai food buffet to eat at our temple with no cost." Sometimes Thai restaurants even brought many famous dishes to the temple for Thais to enjoy and appreciate. We help clean up dishes, the eating area, and building afterward. I also prepare at least one dish to take to the temple each Sunday. If I didn't have enough time to cook, I could buy from available food shops that sell different kinds of foods in the temple area. These food shops are open only on Sunday to service Thais and Asian people near that area. They are also the meeting point for many Thais to chat and bond with each other.

These days, I see a lot of food shops selling a variety of dishes in the temple area, unlike those days when I was in college -- there was only one noodle shop at the temple, where I could enjoy eating. At every religious ceremony at our Thai temple, we have more fun. There are fun performances by children and adults, live music and singers, games, and many food shops and restaurants that sell a variety of foods. Sometimes, a few Thai souvenir shops display all kinds of beautiful merchandise. I also enjoy seeing Thais wearing a variety of styles of Thai silk dresses during ceremonies. When we have a ceremony, we must respect the neighbors around the temple area. The sound from music and microphones on the stage needs to be toned down to an acceptable level. Americans love privacy and don't want to be bothered by our loud noise. I remember one time an American lady walked into the middle of our on-stage activities to ask a master of ceremonies to turn down the sound. Also, when we park our cars off the temple area, we must not block our neighbors' driveways. It is important to be aware of these little things since our temple is in the city, and it is quite crowded during the big event.

Big trees and beautiful flowers are at our temple for us to appreciate. Thai monks spend a lot of time besides their religious duty to beautify the temple and surrounding area. I love sitting and reading my books and magazines on a chair around a fish pond that monks have provided. It is so peaceful around that area, even though sometimes you can hear children's noise from a nearby temple playground. Many children enjoy playing in the playground, including my sons. A wide space filled with sand, a swing, and a slide are the favorite of all fun activities for the children.

During the fruit season, a lot of prunes and pears are on the trees around the temple. While they are being prepared for monks, we are also given some to eat or to take home. One of my friends likes to pick up the fruit on the ground left over from birds to take home to feed the animals on his farm.

The temple also has a library and Thai cultural center for people to learn about Thailand and enjoy Thai traditions. A lot of Thai books and magazines, donated by Thais, are available to check out with no cost. The display of Thai stuff is so outstanding. By looking at it many times, I am so homesick and miss Thailand.

My family usually leaves our temple around 1:30 p.m. After our temple time, our next family fun is grocery shopping in the Asian market, which is about a ten-minute drive from the temple. There are many kinds of Asian foods, fruits, and groceries we can buy there. We could get fresh vegetables, live fish, and meat there as well. Frozen food, dried food, and canned food are also available. I would say we could get anything just as in Thailand, if we didn't mind about the freshness on some items. The price is around three times what we would pay in Thailand. When my mother visited me from Thailand, I took her to the Asian market; she didn't want to buy anything. She said, "Everything is so expensive here." She converted and compared almost every dollar we spent to our Thai currency; currently, one dollar is equal to forty Thai bahts.

At the Asian market, everybody in my family can pick what each person likes to eat. My older son likes an instant noodle from Thailand, so he always goes to that section and selects various kinds and flavors. Noodle soup is usually his convenient dish after he gets home from school. The movies and videos section is another place in the store he likes to visit. My youngest son loves to see live fish and crabs. There is a big glass aquarium showing live fish that you could pick if you want to buy one. Several workers are available to clean and cut them for you. When I tell my American co-workers about this, they are terrified and think we are strange, buying live fish. However, this is very common in Thailand. The other section where my family likes to spend time is the snack and candy section; my husband is especially in favor of this section; there are many kinds to choose from. Most of the time, he chooses snacks made in Japan. My family loves snacks, and it is a big part of our grocery buying. We usually leave a grocery shop with many big bags to carry out to our car.

Either Saturday or Sunday afternoon, during summer time, we like to take our children to a swimming pool in the YMCA near our house. We have been a member for over three years. My older son swims quite well, while my younger one is still learning to swim. He likes to dive under the water. He has a good time in the pool with all of us. My husband spends his time around our little son teaching him to swim. Sometimes, I just read a book at the table around the pool while my older son is doing his lap swim among Americans. Many times we are all in the pool playing water activities with the other families, because there is some pool equipment we can enjoy.

It has been said that swimming is a very popular sport in America. That is probably why there are so many private pools in many Americans' homes. There are also public pools and pools in health clubs and hotels. There are even heated indoor pools that people can enjoy swimming in, while it is snowing outside the buildings. One of my friends also has a pool in her backyard. Many times she invites us for a pool party outside of her house. She has told me that it costs a lot to maintain a pool in a good condition.

The YMCA has an indoor swimming pool, and it provides swimming lessons to both adults and children. Many of them take classes during weekdays. There are also people taking lessons provided by a local outdoor pool. The fee is cheaper than in the YMCA. By many people taking swimming lessons, I think Americans really give importance to swimming as a sport. They also enjoy other pool activities such as group exercise and water aerobics. Besides swimming at the YMCA, we use available facilities and participate in activities such as the weight room, yoga, kick boxing, basketball, and volleyball. One activity we like is "A family night out" or "family fun day" that we could enjoy on some weekends for a few hours. Snacks and games are available for family members to spend enjoyable time together.

Spring and summer are times for our family to enjoy the park. A city park is near our house. It is well-landscaped and well-equipped for children to have fun and adults to spend their leisure time there. In the evening, many people talk while walking in pairs or jogging with headphone sets in their ears, listening to their favorite music while concentrating on their exercise. A city park is not too crowded and has a pond, foot or hiking trails, biking trails, a small water park, and a picnic area. My children love to go fishing in the park and also feed fish and ducks in the pond. They have a lot of fun in a water park as well. I have to prepare spare clothing for them to change every time. While my husband supervises our children, I sometimes take a walk or jog on a track around the park. The city park is free of charge for most facilities. Many people pay only a small fee to use the city pool in the park.

A playground is another facility where my children love to spend a lot of their time for enjoyment. Of all activities in the park, nothing could be as delightful as the night of the 4th of July each year. There are so many beautiful fireworks shown at the park. I remembered carrying chairs, mats, a picnic basket full of food and snacks, a cooler full of water, ice, and drinks to appreciate the event. Our family likes to find a good spot to enjoy the fireworks show when it gets dark. Some years we go to the park at five o' clock in the evening waiting to see the show, which usually starts at nine o'clock at night. There are so many people at the city park, too. The movie night and the live band in the park is another event that the whole city can enjoy. I guess this is a small portion of enjoyment that we all can benefit from, as a result of the tax money that we pay from our income.

Amusement parks are another place where my family can have fun. Many facilities have been designed to satisfy children, young adults, and adults who are young at heart. Six Flags of Texas is my oldest son's favorite roller-coaster park. Though there are so many different kinds of rides, the admission fee is quite expensive. My family goes only once a year. Normally, we go in October with some of our friends and their families. After we have paid the entrance fee, we were allowed to enjoy many of all the attractions, even though for some attractions we have to stand in line waiting for over an hour. However, we can buy a pass for a fast lane. This pass helps and gives us a shorter waiting time. After being exhausted from the rides, we have to stand in a long line waiting to buy food, which costs two or three times more than what we buy outside the park.

We also like to spend time as a family in a water park, where all rides and activities are water based. There is one in the City of Rowlett near our house called "The Wet Zone" and another one is the City of Allen, which takes us around 40 minutes to reach. My older son likes the giant tidal wave pool, a slider, a whirlpool, and a few more exciting ones for teens that I don't even know the name of; on one, I might have a heart attack if I try it, because it's so high and steep. So many people are having fun, screaming and shouting at the top of their lungs.

Shopping is actually my personal fun, but most of the times I ask my family to come along to have more fun as a family. Our shopping could be in many places: an Asian store, a local retail store, especially Wal-Mart, and the malls. When we go to the malls, everybody has time to do what they like. I spend time walking around window shopping, buying clothes, shoes, cosmetics, and sometimes jewelry. A lot of the time, I am so amazed that Americans spend a lot of their money shopping. I could see many big bags in both hands while they walk in the mall. At Christmas time, especially, they almost drag all of their bags on the floor because they have too many bags to carry. Some of them hardly have a hand available to hold their children's hand. That makes many children get lost from their parents. Some are crying, roaming around, looking for their mothers. Some people push a full shopping cart around in a retail store or supermarket. Some items drop on the floor from the cart. Some even need another shopping cart for that shopping. A customer service person helps to carry the cart out on some occasions. Computer and electronic shops are my husband's favorite places to shop. He can spend many hours there without getting bored. There are so many kinds of technologies he can explore and have fun testing. Sometimes he can get a good deal on a different piece of hardware. Most shops have advertisements sent out weekly. He keeps his eyes on what will be on sale or will have a good mail-in rebate program. We have rarely bought full price pieces. He does compare prices on hardware he buys and always obtains good information from consumer reports. My older son loves the video game shop and saves his allowance to buy what he likes, but most of the time he consults with us about the appropriateness of the game. The little one wouldn't have interest in anything other than toy shops. My husband and I have to take turns to supervise him while he is concentrating playing with the available toys.

I see a variety of imported goods to choose from in America. Qualities are competitive, but the price is cheaper than one labeled

"Made in USA." My family is a bargain buyer; as I mentioned, we compare prices and also look at different store advertisements in the newspaper for a good deal on the same merchandise. Actually, I found some Americans do the same thing. My American co-workers even share information with me about what is on sale this week and where we can get them. Wal-Mart has a "matching any advertisement" policy where we could get any store's desired products from Wal-Mart at the same advertised price. My youngest son likes Wal-Mart. He could play in the toy section for a long period of time. After finishing playing, he puts all items back neatly on shelves; after he stops playing, he does not need the toys anymore. We buy new toys for our children for only special occasions such as their birthday or Christmas. I certainly get a long list of what they would like to have for those special times.

Most toys that my children have are from the place that we all call "a family frugal fun," or a garage or yard sale or a thrift plaza. Normally, many families in the city we live in have a lot of garage sales on Saturday. My children have fun picking up all kinds of good condition toys for a cheaper price; sometimes we get a full plastic bag for one dollar. After they get home, they clean up neatly and play with those toys until they don't want them anymore; that is the time they put all those toys in the boxes and send them to the Goodwill Industry store.

We normally eat out on the weekend together. We go to different places to give our children the opportunity to explore a variety of foods and see interesting American styles of eating. This activity also provides us a chance to teach our children table and social manners. For breakfast, we sometimes go to a donut shop, IHOP, Waffle House, and McDonald's. My youngest son likes to be taken to McDonald's for its indoor playground. He doesn't really eat most of the time; he just wants to play with the other children. When he is ready to eat, his favorite order is chicken nuggets and fries, including free toys for a kid's meal. He likes a lot of ketchup on his fries. The other fast food places we like to go to experience are Sonic and Braum's. We also like to go for lunch at Chinese restaurants for the all-you-can-eat buffet. My older son stuffs himself up every time we go there, as he always says, "*to make it worth his money.*" There are different kinds of dishes available for us to enjoy at reasonable prices. Normally, we leave a 15% tip on the total amount we spend on eating. I also teach my children that tips should be based on the service they received. They have been taught to give tips, because those waiters' and waitresses' primary earning is based on tips from their customers. These days, Jack is good in observing the customer service skills of our waiter or waitress while they are servicing and taking orders. Some of his unsatisfactory comments allow us to talk about the basic skills in servicing, such as having a smile on your face and a nice tone of voice, being clean and organized, and having a friendly manner, as well as showing courtesy and politeness. These skills are needed in most careers. They are encouraged to clean up any mess they make and not to leave dirtiness for those workers. They are working hard enough. I used to ask my sons, "If you are working here, do you want people to leave a filthy table for you to clean up every time? If you don't, those workers don't want to clean your mess either, so be considerate to the other people's feelings."

Sometimes we go out to eat Mexican food. We have experienced a few places such as On the Border, Taco Bueno, Taco Delight, and Taco Cabaña, and some locally owned restaurants. My husband and I like Mexican food. He likes chips and salsa sauce; especially Taco Cabaña always provides a variety of fresh salsa sauces.

One place that we go to eat quite often is a Japanese restaurant. The arrangement of food is so beautiful. The taste of many dishes is delicious. Tempura is my sons' favorite dish, while my husband will not trade sushi for anything. We like to go eat a lunch buffet, so that we can have many options from which to choose. Dinner time is pretty expensive at a Japanese restaurant. Actually, dinner costs more than lunch at any restaurant in America that I have experienced. I assume it might be that during dinner customers have a lot of time to enjoy foods and can consume more without any rush, unlike lunch time when most of them have to go to work within an hour. Friday night seems to be the most crowded night in the restaurants. Some American parents and couples spend Friday night as a date night and pay the babysitters, so they can go out and eat together.

On Tuesday evening we often go to the city public library. It requires a library card, and we each had one made there. We check out movies, books, and magazines. Some movies allow us to return them in five days, while others allow only three days. My little boy, Andrew, likes to play children's computer games on one computer there, while the older one, Jack, likes to search the Internet and check out martial arts books.

Another family activity that everybody enjoys is our "visiting Granddad" time. That is my family visiting Mr. Marchbanks at his house in Paris, Texas. We plan our visit every month, and it has become our monthly routine. Usually, we start our trip after work on Friday. It is around 75 miles from our house to Paris. It takes us around one hour and forty-five minutes on the road one way to visit granddad. While driving, we spend time in our car listening to our children's favorite songs, such as "Aloha," a theme song from the Japanese movie Cat Return." Michael Jackson's "Billy Jean," Abba's "Thank you for the music," and the Beatles' "Across the Universe." We sing along as a family. Sometimes, the children want to take turns. While my husband is doing the duty of chauffeur, I take the duty of a D.J. to switch music at my sons' request. While in the car, we also talk about different things, including our day. My husband and I sometimes listen to our sons argue in the back seat on how to say things in Thai and Japanese. On the way to Paris, Texas, we have to pass a city named Commerce, which is the home city of Texas A&M University-Commerce, where my husband and I attended graduate school. We take the opportunity to show our children around the campus and different places near the university where we spent most of our time while we were studying. Those places are the university track and stadium, where I spent time walking after finishing my work in the computer lab before getting ready for classes in the evening; the library where I spent time reading and finding information for my projects; the family housing was the place I sometimes visited my friends and socialized with their families; my Thai friends' apartment was a good place for many kinds of Thai food I could enjoy eating before going to class. It was also a place to discuss about projects for Thai Students Association's activities. My children might not have any idea about how I really lived my college life, but this opportunity allows them to see different areas and ask questions. Jack even asked if he is coming to study here after his high school years. Besides Commerce, we also passed a few small towns, cotton fields, and flat farmlands. Seeing all of these reminds me of my daily commuting time during graduate school. It was a long drive everyday for two years from Paris to Commerce, Texas.

When we arrive at granddad's house, we usually have dinner and visit. My children just spend time around their granddad playing toys, watching movies, and eating ice cream. Andrew loves to watch granddad smoke his pipe. One time when he was at home, he got a pen in his mouth pretending that it was a pipe. I had to ask granddad to not let him to see because he copies. I used to ask if he wanted to quit smoking, because he had quit before. He would laugh and tell me,

"Pat, for my age, there are a few things that I enjoy doing, and smoking is one of them." That was the same thing he told his doctor. That makes me stay quiet and never ask him to quit any more. Andrew also loves to ride on granddad's big pickup truck, while Jack was taught to ride the lawnmower. After a while, he was able to finish mowing both the front and backyards for granddad. That reminds me of the time I also drove a lawnmower when I was living in the house. Even though I had money to pay for a yard man, I just wanted to save $25 for my personal expense.

Every time before we leave, we have breakfast and lunch with granddad. Visiting granddad is something my family loves to do, and we are happy doing it. We also visit him during a special occasion such as Father's Day, Christmas, the Thanksgiving holiday, and his birthday, as well as to get together when Sandy and her family come to visit, and when Michael comes home from overseas. We enjoy visiting with them, and our children have a good time playing together. Visiting Mr. Marchbanks with my family helps me to see his happiness, and it provides us time to talk about different topics, do things around the house together, have playing time with my children, and help on little things around the house. It is just a small thing that I can do to return his continued kindness; all my heart I know I couldn't return enough. He certainly doesn't expect anything from us but a good time with the grandkids. Visiting time is also a good bonding time between us and a time that helps him to stay active to keep up with my hyper children. Even though he sometimes gets tired of answering Andrew's many questions, or getting things out of Andrew's way, I can still see the joy on his face. One time during our visit, we talked about my possible further education. I got a chance to ask whether it was difficult for him to put Sandy, Michael, and I through school. He simply replied, "No, not really, because I had plenty of money when I was working, and you guys were doing well in school, so I didn't have to worry about it while working." Mr. Marchbanks is still teaching me many things to improve my living in America, including financial management beyond putting money in savings. That makes me try to live my life with goals and plans. I am carefully and actively working toward them.

Recently, during our visit, we got a chance to talk about preparing a living will, which my husband and I have been discussing for a short period of time. The reason that made us start thinking about creating a will is that our children are still young; if unexpected occurrences happen, we want to make sure our children will be well taken care of by their legal guardians, because our family members live so far away. "The will" is a life plan that my husband and I have agreed to do, with the experienced suggestions of Mr. Marchbanks. Sitting with the lawyer, expressing our wishes, receiving suggestions, and listing all items while having our will made was quite an experience for both of us, especially the part where we express what we want to happen after each of us die. It is a somewhat strange feeling to plan what we want to happens, though we will never see it, even including how we want our funeral to be like. However, it is a precautionary act that both of us decided to do.

It has been a week after our last visit with granddad. We just got a call from him yesterday that he is doing fine and spends time on the treadmill and a rowing machine for 30 minutes a day. I asked him not to over exercise. He told me that he needed to stay in good shape and get himself ready for our next visit, and we certainly are looking forward to visiting him in a couple more weeks.

One of our unforgettable family fun days is our quality time with my parents during their visit. Many immigrants like myself and some that I have known, dream of giving our parents the opportunity to visit us in America after we get settled. Some might dream to give their parents their first travel abroad ever. Some might give their parents a paid vacation package from their first year salary in America. A few perhaps want to invite their parents for their wedding, after deciding to establish a new family abroad. Some just enthusiastically want to invite their parents to join them during their college graduation. Some simply ask the parents for help in raising their children while having to work long hours everyday, seven days a week, to make a living among different groups of citizens. I personally invited my parents to visit me for a simple reason: to see where and how I have been living my life for the past twelve years. Fortunately, that was their first long flight traveling abroad. It was a good experience from the beginning until the end of the trip. Their first time, my parents went to the American consulate office in Bangkok to request a visitor visa, was already an overwhelming and learning experience. They had to prepare a lot of necessary documents along with my affidavit of support that I sent to them. I recall a process of financial planning and saving one large amount of money to send to my parents' account in Thailand for the visa process and for the plane tickets. It was also my proud project of saving, while knowing that my parents appreciated what I was trying to do for them: give them a chance to see the parts of the world that are different from theirs in terms of both culture and lifestyles. That happened when they were close to sixty years of age--a chance that they also had never thought of before.

One week before September 11, 2001, my parents were granted a ten-year visitor visa to America. That was a joyful permission to enter America legally. It was fantastic news when they let me know over the phone. I was happy planning their trip, which included purchasing round-trip tickets for them. My mother was talking about it costing a lot when I called her. After the terror attack in September, my mother was terrified to take a trip to visit me in America. She decided to cancel her plans to a later year. She mentioned to me that, "I might not have a chance to go to America, because I am so afraid." I remember telling her that whenever she can get rid of her terrified feeling, she could come again. I quite understood my mother because she had never been outside of her hometown for a long period of time. Coming into a new environment might be frightening for her; plus, she was also concerned about her property and house in Thailand. Besides that, she did not want me to spend a lot of money on the plane tickets.

My father finally decided to take a trip to visit me alone in October 2001. He was planning to stay three weeks, as his vacation time allowed. Of course, he was so excited and got ready to take his trip. I was so anxious and happy to see my father in my own home in America. I got my house ready and planned for activities and places to take him to visit. I wanted to take him to visit my American family and my good friends. Certainly, I wanted to take him to see my current work place, the computer lab, and the university where I worked and graduated from. I just wanted my father to see where I got shaped and molded to become a professional working Thai woman in America. I waited for his flight to land at the DFW airport with a full heart of happiness. I was excitedly watching almost everybody come through the gate after the check-in process at Customs. I was laughing with joy when I saw my father push a cart off the escalator. He was lightly in tears, while hugging me with happiness and relief. I was joking with him, "What does it feel like, Father, being a rural town man coming to America?" He was shaking his head while responding, "Oh, it is so far away and it has been such a long flight. Now, I understood why you were exhausted when you went home to visit," he said while I was driving him home.

On the way to my home, he was so fascinated with American roads, cars, homes, and buildings, especially seeing his daughter driving a nice car (in his opinion) among those people on the road. That reminded us to talk about when I was riding a bicycle, hung on the handles with many baskets and bags, to the morning market, helping my mother selling food before going to school in my teen years. I mentioned to my father that maybe the hardship and the tough time have passed. It helped me learn the value of the past, appreciate the present, and carefully move forward into the future. It also gave me the opportunity to become stronger emotionally. I was joking with him that without the lesson in the past, I might not have had enough drive to own a car and drive it here. I remember seeing him nodding his head. My father could not sleep much for the first few days. I imagined that was jet-lagged. He told me that at night while he could not sleep, he was thinking about how I have been living here without any family members nearby for so many years. He just could not see how I became so independent and able to adjust among all the strangers in a new environment.

I went to work early in the morning. Except on the weekend, my father did not see me during breakfast time. I could only spend time with him in the evening and on the weekend. This reminds me of hearing one Thai parent at the Thai temple complain that her children did not have time for her during her visit. She said her children had to work every day. She came to visit, but she just had to stay at home by herself. My parents did not mind. They had the opportunity to see how some Thais really work here. We all have to work for a living here. Many of us take our jobs so seriously. In America, without a job and income, it is so hard and difficult to live life comfortably. We have a lot of bills to pay each month for the many services we have. For some people, they still have to support a family back in their homeland. At the end of his vacation, my father had a lot of good things to share with my mother.

In July 2003, my mother could no longer give me excuses for being afraid to travel by plane, or about the big amount of money for a plane ticket, when she learned that I certainly needed help during my surgery a couple months after giving birth to Andrew. I still remember that day, one week before my surgery; I was anxiously waiting for my mother at the airport and didn't see her come out with the other passengers after a long period of time. I was really worried. I went to ask the airline staff at the counter and came back to wait. Not too long after that, there was a lady approaching me asking if I was waiting for my mother. She took me inside the Customs area in the back and told me that my mother was with the immigration officer because she could not answer anything she was asked. When my mother saw me walk into the office, she started crying and hugged me with happiness. She told me that she was scared and didn't know what to say to them. Six months after that day, I would never forget all of the quality activities we all did together as a family with my mother around. However, one thing I noticed was that my parents might have enjoyed many things we did together, but they were quite lonesome being around people who were not Thais in a new environment. They were worried about many expenses, because they always think about our Thai baht. That's including the time that I took my mother to see my family doctor without health insurance. I remember what they told me, when I asked them if they wanted me to file a petition for them to come to stay with me, "We don't think we want to live here. We prefer to live in our country, even though we will miss you and our grandchildren a lot. We don't want to be your burden, while you are working hard to support yourself and your family." So, what I get from them was a wonderful visit and a few international calls a few times a month.

Another activity that our family spends time doing together is working around the house, mowing, cleaning, cutting trees and brush, watering plants, growing a small vegetable garden, and picking weeds in the yard. My husband and Jack help each other putting soil and making a dirt bed for me to plant Thai herbs and hot peppers. Andrew and I help each other to pull a water hose around the backyard. There are four good- sized trees in the backyard, and they are strong enough for Andrew to climb, while we all are working. Those activities give me a chance to share with my sons the stories from when I was growing up about climbing up mango, star fruit, and jack fruit trees. We also help each other inside the house; while my husband vacuums the carpet, Jack does his laundry, folds or irons his clothes, and Andrew cleans up his toys. Even though, it is a work activity, it is a productive period that allows us time to communicate, to be close, to laugh, and to guide our children. Most of the time, when we don't schedule anything outside the house, we just stay in and are involved with things that our children choose to do. We help Andrew draw and color on his paper and activity book at the table, on the kitchen floor, or in the office. We participate in Andrew's band playing as a guitarist, his guitar being made of many plastic blocks, playing a drum set which was made of a few empty brown paper boxes. All members either sit on the kitchen stools or on the carpet floor doing their own task, while Michael Jackson's song or Japanese music is playing. We spend time with our children when they play computer games or surf the net. We race with them in the games that they choose to play on the T.V. in the living room. My husband is wonderful at suggesting, providing, and monitoring the appropriateness of the game activity. Occasionally, I just lay down on Jack's bed and rest, while he chooses to work on his computer, play on his PSP (Play Station Portable), and listen to his music.

Because of the distance from our house to the skating place, ice skating is a once a year activity we let our children enjoy. Sitting, drinking good coffee, waving hands, and encouraging and cheering my husband coaching the boys on the icy floor among many people is an amazing feeling. Our lunch together in the restaurant near the skating area, watching the other people, is also a wonderful moment. Besides having fun together as a family, each activity provides us a good opportunity to participate, observe, and find out about our children's strengths, talents, and weaknesses. That helps us to learn to better our parenting skills in helping and coaching them to exercise the things they are good at and improve on their weak points. We acknowledge that this moment is a precious time for our involvement, because when they get to a certain age, they will need less of our attendance and participation. The age will come when we have to let them make their own decisions and learn from the outcome. All we might have to do is to just provide our support and offer suggestions when they are asked for. More than anything else, family fun is quality time when we can show our love, caring, and support without words. The act of crawling on the carpet floor searching for missing crayons under the sofa in the living room, having a little boy jump on our back acting like he is horseback riding, laying on the tile floor cheering our racing car that never wins, because little hands always grasp it before it reaches the finish line, sitting on the recliner or laying on the teenager's bed listening to his description of how he plays his favorite games or how to convert music tracks into mp3 files, and listening to the boys' argument on what color and how the drawing by the bigger one should be completed by the little one all qualify as quality time. Quality time and family fun activities for us don't have to be something that is expensive, but they are things that hold everybody's attention and that we enjoy doing together.

Shall we dance? - Andrew & Mom

Visit Japan

Andrew & Granddad

Chapter 7: Living and Bonding

"Many people will walk in and out of your life; but only true friends will leave footprints in your heart." – Unknown --

It is quite lonesome for people living abroad, working and meeting with a new group of people, and moving into a new environment. There are no family members around. There are no relatives to help out and take care during the time of need. To get through this circumstance in life, having a good "friendship" with the new group of people we meet is significant. By definition, friendship can be defined as "a relationship between two people integrated by respect, affection, and admiration. It is an in-depth relationship that brings understanding, comfort, trust, and relaxation. It requires equality and reliability from both parties."

I consider myself a positive, caring, outgoing, and friendly person. I also put a lot of value into interpersonal skills. I indeed value the importance of a friendship with people I meet while I live, study, and work in America. I value a friendship with a few of my friends back home as well, those with whom I am still able to keep in contact after over twelve years away from my home country. I consider myself a less friend person, but I do have several good and wonderful ones. They are Thais, Americans, Chinese, and Pilipino. They are friends who I know will be there when I need them the most. Though my friendship with each one of them has helped me to value the sayings, "Actions speak louder than words," "Act before you speak, and afterwards speak according to your actions," and "Speak well of your friends, of your enemy; say nothing." I truly believe that "we will be judged by the company we keep." So, it is an honor to have them as companions. Making and keeping a friendship with them is the most important of my priorities. Each and every one of them allows me the opportunity to learn the significance of diversity, trust, love, sharing, and caring. The differences make our friendship become closer, more appreciated and stronger. Within the past twelve years, I have learned, valued, and appreciated many things these people have done for me as "**Friends**."

While in America, I have really enjoyed having friends who are older than I am. There are so many wonderful things I can learn from them. I agree that "wisdom comes with age." That is the greatest advantage of having friends who have had many years of experience and insights on different things. I especially like to learn from people who have been in America for many years longer than I have. They could share with me many circumstances they encountered and solutions for different problems and challenges they have met. I also get the opportunity to hear from someone who has experienced periods in American history that I have only read about or heard about from the world news.

Charin Clayton is the first friend who allowed me the opportunity to appreciate a wonderful friendship in America. She is more than a friend. She is like a real sister to me, because of her continuous love and care. I was in the library at Paris Junior College doing my English homework back in January 1994, when one of the American reading teachers, after learning that I was a Thai student, told me that she knows one Thai lady who married an American and is now living and raising three children in Paris. The Thai lady once attended her reading class. I was so happy after knowing that there was a Thai living in the same city, because I had not yet met any Thais, since I had been in America. The teacher told me that she still had the Thai lady's phone number and would make a phone call for me. She asked for my American family's phone number to give to the Thai lady.

The following day I received a phone call from the Thai lady introducing herself and scheduling to meet. She told me that she would come to visit me at my American family's house after asking for the address. I was so excited to hear Thai language from a person who lived near me but who I had not yet met. That was the beginning of my important twelve-year friendship with Mrs. Charin Clayton and her family. Throughout the years, she has been a very good friend. I know that if I need her, she will always be there. She always introduces me to her friends as her adopted sister. She is the most friendly, optimistic, funny, thoughtful, loving, giving, and caring friend I have ever had.

She provided me my first Thai food meal, after many months in America. We ate at her home when we first met. It was a delicious meal. We had beef curry, barbecued chicken, and Thai style carrot salad. Many times, she prepared dishes for me to keep in the refrigerator, so I could eat them after school without having to cook. I came back from school one day, opened the garage door, and backed up my car without noticing a red container filled with good food, intentionally cooked by her for me to eat after classes. I ran over the container. I lost one of the dishes prepared by her kindness. Now, it is a joke that both of us still talk about, and I still have not yet done a good job of replacing that red container.

Despite being busy taking care of her three children, especially a four-month-old baby, she spared her time to dress me up in a traditional Thai dress for the International Student Dinner Night hosted by the Paris Junior College that I attended. It was a long process of wrapping a Thai material called "Jong Kha Ben" around me and pinning it with many safety pins to prevent it from falling off while I was at the party. She patiently helped me go through that wonderful event at the college.

She took me to the Thai temple in Dallas for the first time. That allowed me the opportunity to see more Thais who lived around the Dallas area. Her introduction to the temple paved the way for me to continue to join Thais' praying and activities for the past twelve years living in America. These days, the Thai temple is also a place where my own family participates in prayer and practice, learning from monks and studying the basic teachings of our Lord Buddha to increase our own spirituality. My praying, believing, and following of some of his teachings helps me get through many of life's difficulties and brings me peace of mind when I am sad, hurt, confused, and hopeless. My faith in him guides me to be aware of my actions and practices toward things and people. It also leads me to accept the consequences of our own actions in life.

Charin transported me from one place to another, when I was unable to drive without a valid driver's license. She took me to and from the post office when I wanted to send mail and money to my family in Thailand. She took me to college for an English test before my I-20 issuance. She also drove me to buy groceries, while my American family was out of town working.

Charin has always provided me with useful and helpful guidance. She encouraged me to put full effort in my study, while I was in college. She shares with me the story of her Thai friend who finished her studies in America and went back home and is doing very well. I still remember her teaching me to be grateful to my American family, "You are lucky to have the American family support you in college; it costs a lot. Study hard and finish your studying, so you then can find a job and be able to support yourself. Later on you can bring your son from Thailand." She said that to me, while I was visiting her one day after school. She taught me to be patient during difficult situations and to stay focused on my studies, "I cannot send you to school like your American family, but you can always come and live with me. I can only provide a place to stay and food to eat." She was teaching me with care.

She allowed me to be part of her family, taking me along on the family's activities at her own expense. The activities included taking a trip out of town, shopping, buying Thai groceries, attending church, going to our Thai temple, participating in a party, inviting me to be involved in her children's school activities, visiting her friends and family members, relaxing at the lake, and fishing in the pond at her farm. These activities I would not have been able to do on my own, while attending college classes full time. Besides having fun with her, I got the opportunity to learn how to live in America from her.

I remember that one Christmas season, we went shopping in Dallas at 10:00 a.m., and we spent all day having fun. We came back to Paris at almost midnight. After our exhausting shopping day, her husband took us around to look at many beautiful Christmas light decorations in a very nice neighborhood.

She and her family joined me during my graduation from graduate school in December 1998. They congratulated me with joy. Recently, I had the opportunity to attend her son's graduation from high school. He was about six years old when his mother and I first met. Time flies; it has been twelve years.

Her friendship was not only being given to me; it was also extended to my family members. She and her family participated in my husband's graduation ceremony, our wedding, and my son's birthday party. They visited with my parents when they came over to visit me from Thailand.

Almost every year, she hosts a New Year's party at her house for us to get together, and to appreciate each other's company and friendship; it also gives us the opportunity to have fun with dancing and activities while enjoying many good foods.

I acknowledge that all the things she has done for me were based on her good heart, and her kindness, willingness, love and caring. None of those things she helped with were an obligation. Every day, her continuous friendship is still one of my greatly appreciated life experiences, and it has certainly become stronger and healthier.

There is only one phrase I want to use to describe the second Thai lady I have known while living in America. She is a "Phenomenal woman." She has such a strong character that I don't think I will ever be able to obtain. She is the woman who has had such a big impact on my life, and she was part of building the person I have become today. I will always remember what she says, "We may not think we are successful much in America, but don't forget that we came to this country with only one suitcase, along with one brain and two hands. We didn't even have money to pay for our own plane ticket. Don't compare your success with anybody else's but your own. People value success differently." I also still appreciate when she taught me that "no matter how much money you make in America, you will never have enough to support yourself and family, if you don't know how to save and value it."

For the last twelve years, her words of wisdom about living here are still deeply in my memory. Her gentle hug and soft shoulder to cry on when I am sad are still missed since she retired to Thailand. The encouraging words to overcome many obstacles in life still motivate me to move forward in life. Her unconditional guidance has helped me to find the positive solutions for many life challenges. Many of her motivational words have helped me to strive to live my life in America to the fullest.

Her financial assistance allowed me to borrow the money to finally finish up the construction of a house, my mother's dream house in Thailand, is still appreciated. I remember every exciting moment I shared with her while I was working on this big project in Thailand. She told me that she would love to build a house for her retirement in Thailand someday; that was twelve years ago. Now she has accomplished that task; she has paid for a beautiful house with a very nice yard and garden, while enjoying her life in her mother's land. I am so glad that I had a chance to return her help, while she was building her house in Thailand.

Every delicious meal provided by her not only physically helped me grow up, but also mentally molded me into a person who appreciates every single dish and every single grain of rice that comes from hard-earned money made in America. It broke my heart, when I saw people throw away food and prepared by other people.

Her sincere friendship abroad made me feel loved. The motherhood that she showed me while being away from my own mother studying, living, and working in America, is valuable and priceless. Her love and care toward me has increased my awareness of unselfish living and her ability to provide love and care to others.

Her physical, mental, and financial independence has taught me to appreciate all the help I have received from other people, especially my

American family. It also helps me to become more aware of my own financial situation. That includes avoiding bothering people financially, as well as helping others when I can, but never financially pampering them until they don't know and don't learn to help themselves. Her independent living and hard work are such a great example for me to learn from. Her forgiving mentality helps soften the heart of others who have hurt her in the past. Her great determination and patience in life are a good quality to learn that helps to reach the destination.

The useful helping hands that she provided me throughout my pregnancy, and to help care for my newborn baby would never have been seen with anyone but my own mother. It is something that is hardly returnable and forgettable. The trust that she placed in me made me aware of her every action, word, and promise.

The most important of many significant things are her magnificent life experiences from both living in Thailand, as well as from almost 40 years of living in America. Her sharing about life's lessons has allowed me to learn a good quality of living. The experience is absolutely out of this world. She is the Thai lady who I call my "Godmother."

In this section of the book, I want to go back down through my memories with her and share with you about my relationship and friendship with her. I knew my godmother through my friendship with Charin Clayton. It was exciting to hear that Charin would take me to meet another Thai lady who has lived in Paris, Texas for a long time. They have known each other for quite some time. It was a nice feeling when I met my godmother.

She was a divorced mother, living with her teenage daughter. My godmother did not finish the fourth grade in Thailand, but she had been making a living by working in an American factory for many years. By the time I met her, she had been living in America for almost 40 years. She is a very nice and soft spoken lady. She invited me for dinner in the weeks that followed. It was a delicious meal with friendly conversation. It was funny when she told me that she initially did not want to have anything to do with any international students, because she had a bad experience with a few of them, especially Thai students whom she had met. I guess I behaved myself well enough to get invited to a few more dinners and other affairs in the following months and ultimately for the past twelve years. After school, I often stopped by her house to visit before I went home. She called me to ask if I wanted to go for a walk in the evening on the track around the park. My godmother and I walked together almost every day; we walked at least three miles a day. If we missed each other during our walking time, each of us knew where to find the other. We went to the Thai temple in Dallas together on the weekend. After that, we went shopping for groceries in the Asian market.

Since I lived mostly by myself in the house because my American family worked out of town, I spent a lot of my free time after school with my godmother. Almost every day, my godmother cooked delicious food for me to eat. She sometimes left a message on my answering machine, telling me to eat supper with her when I got home from school or from my part-time jobs. I was allowed to bring left-over food home to pack for lunch to eat at school or at work. When I was sick, my godmother prepared a delicious rice soup dish for me and came to spend the night to take care of me at my American family home.

Many times when I faced problems in life, she was always there for me to talk to. She listened to me, to my problems, with an understanding attitude. She suggested ways to solve those problems and patiently encouraged me when I was so down and crying. I remember knocking on the front door in the middle of the night with tears in my eyes, when I got a call from my mother telling me about the death of my youngest brother. It was one of the many hardships from back home that I was facing while trying to concentrate on my studies. Her support, understanding, and encouragement helped me to overcome the great sadness of loss. She helped collect donations from her Thai friends and allowed me to send them to my mother for my brother's funeral back home. It was quite a large amount.

During the time I was trying to get into graduate school, she patiently listened to my whining about the long process of evaluating and testing all of the documents. Then, when I graduated and looked for a job, she still kept motivating me. She even went on a ride with me to the interview for my current position.

I was able to talk openly to my godmother about everything, because of her kindness. I felt so close to her and wanted to share with her about what is going on with me, my studies, and my job. Godmother asked her friend to help me get a part-time job at Wal-Mart, and I worked there for almost two years. While I was busy, studying full time, and working at three different part-time jobs, I did not have much time to see her, but she always called to check on me. Sometimes, after getting off work at 11:00 p.m. at night, I stopped by to see her, because I knew she was still watching television.

I enjoyed going shopping with my godmother. We went to different places, including malls. Most of the time, we did not buy anything, but we walked around spending time together, talking and eating. We loved to shop for jewelry together, especially 24 carat gold jewelry. Godmother has many beautiful kinds of jewelry. She also liked to buy good quality diamonds.

Many little things my godmother and I have done together helped to develop a connection between us. Her caring over many years built up my love and trust of her as if she were my real mother. Whenever I called my real mother in Thailand to tell her about my godmother's generosity, she told me to be grateful and show my gratitude. She encouraged me to return the respect and willingness to help my godmother on any matter she asked.

I remember one time I met a life challenge from Thailand. I could not sleep; I tossed and turned on my bed until one or two o' clock in the morning. I got up and drove to my godmother's house. She opened the door for me and allowed me to sleep on the bed with her; I realized her gentle hard-working hands placed a blanket on me, and they were so kind and warm while I was half asleep at night. I woke up in the morning in her bedroom, and the nice breeze I felt from the opened window over the bed helped heal my anger, hurt, and pain. Her kind words teaching me to offer forgiveness to my family member has softened my heart over time.

She attended my graduation from graduate school and shed joyful tears when I walked across the stage during the ceremony. I knew she was proud of me and happy to see my educational accomplishment. I remember she said, "I wish your parents could have a chance to see you on this day. I am sure they would be as happy as I am." Sometimes she mentioned, "I am so proud of you. Seeing that you try so hard to handle problems in life while focusing on your studies, I wonder how you make it." I remember replying, "I wouldn't have been able to make it without your help, Godmother."

She was actively helping me to move into my new house in Rockwall, Texas, after I lived in an apartment for six months while having a full time job. For a few days, we were so busy packing, loading, and unloading boxes. We helped each other clean the whole house before arranging my furniture. After the move was in process for a few days, she was busy taking care of me after my operation. She stayed in the hospital room with me prior to the nurses coming to take me to the operation room. She stayed with me in our new house for two weeks before going back to her own home in Paris, Texas. Every dish she prepared during my sickness was really appreciated.

She was so supportive, seeing me and my husband busy organizing our wedding without a family. Her blessing and kindness made every step run so smoothly. She attended my wedding with joy. She even bought a brand new beautiful dress to wear on my wedding day. When I became pregnant, my constant craving for spaghetti caused my godmother to cook a big pot of sauce for me to eat everyday. She spent a lot of time with me during my pregnancy, before she went back to Thailand for a few months. Her frugal shopping for my maternity dress at a garage sale was so thoughtful.

She rushed to see me at the hospital, after her long flight from Thailand. Her travel day from Thailand was the same day as my C-section. I had an operation in the morning, and my godmother arrived at 3:30 p.m. She visited me everyday, while I was in the hospital after giving birth to my youngest son, Andrew. She then started taking care of him full time at home, when he was four days old. Having my godmother with me during my first two months after having my son was absolutely outstanding. She was not only taking care of Andrew, but also taking care of me while my incision from C-section was still sore and I was unable to lift heavy things. She was awake almost every two hours at night to help me feed my son, and it was greatly appreciated. She was excited to give Andrew a bath for the first time at home. I remember she said, "I don't know whether I still remember how to do it. It has been almost thirty years since I have done this." Her rocking Andrew in the chair was unforgettable.

She had helped me raise my son, Andrew for four months, before she decided to go back to Thailand. Andrew was so attached to her. When he cried at night, he would stop crying if my godmother held him. When I got him from my godmother, he started crying again. I remember trying many ways to stop him from colicky crying -- rocking on a chair, holding and walking him around the house, singing him different songs, or dancing for a long hour. It was rough and frustrating for all of us. My godmother was patiently guiding me in what to do. She actively helped me to find a good babysitter before she left for Thailand.

My godmother is now spending her retirement in her home city in Thailand. She has come to visit us in the U.S.A. a few times and still plans to come whenever she can. I call to check on her every other week. My family and I miss her so much, and we are looking forward to visiting her next year. Every moment, I pray for my godmother to have a good time for the rest of her life in our home country. In America, she worked so hard and had been through a lot of things. She absolutely deserves the best.

Through my godmother, I was introduced to one more Thai lady named Ladda, who has been living in a nearby city for over a decade. She was married for almost 30 years and has no children. Her American husband passed away three years ago. He was an incredible man who was really friendly. When she is free from her work schedule, she likes to come spend time with us at home, but many times she is hardly able to do it, because of her love of work and the way she cherishes a good paycheck.

One Friday after work, I followed my own routine by picking up my son, Andrew, at pre-school. That day, he seemed to have a good day, because I saw him playing with his classmates. I didn't allow him to play long, because we needed to get home early that day. When I got home, my husband was cooking a Japanese chicken curry in the kitchen. We were planning to cook a few more dishes. That evening, we were expecting one of our family's long-time good friends, Ladda Wicks. She was coming for dinner and she would pick up a suitcase to take back home to Thailand for my parents. She would be leaving for Thailand for a three-week vacation a couple of days later. Being good friends, when we go back to Thailand, we can ask each other to bring some merchandise and souvenirs back. She had her boyfriend accompanying her that evening. She is one of a few close friends I have. I have known her since I was in college. I remember being introduced to her by my godmother at a get-together luncheon. She has been involved in my family's special activities, my family members' birthday parties, my graduation, and my mother's visit from Thailand. She always calls to have a little chat a few times a week after she gets home from work. She sometimes calls to share what she is eating for supper and asks what my day is like. We live in a different city; it is an almost one and a half hour drive, so calling each other seems to be the most effective way to stay in contact.

She is something of a workaholic. She works a lot of hours a week and a long hour shift; in many cases, she even works seven days a week. She usually gets home late from work. She is a very hard working lady in an American factory. Knowing her allows me to learn a hard-working skill and gives me determination to make a good living in America. She always tells me that she did not finish third grade in Thailand, but she has been working alongside American people for more than twenty years. With good financial awareness and management from her earnings, she has built up a secure plan for her retirement. She mentioned to me that she "would never be able to make this happen if I was still in Thailand." She is planning to retire in America; unlike many Thais I know who want to spend their retirement back home.

She is a widow of a very friendly American man who died of a heart attack. She has been living alone since his death. It must be hard for her having to live by herself after 29 years of marriage. This gave me the opportunity to experience a great strength in her and her excellent ability to deal with her situation. She is still doing wonderfully on her own without anybody's help. She still keeps going to work, managing her own finances and the household. She is a strong Thai lady that is a good example for many who think living in America is easy. I really admire her, because of her great ability to successfully make a quality living for her own life in America and occasionally supporting her family members back home.

Even though she did not finish elementary school in our country, she loves to read. Her ability to memorize things amazes me. She remembers almost every Thai movie star, actor and actress from reading the different types of Thai entertainment magazines that she bought from an Asian store in Dallas. When she told me about all those celebrities, I had no clue who they were and not much interest in their stories. She also remembers the directions, roads, and places in Bangkok after being here for over 30 years.

Ladda has such a great sense of humor. She always tells the story of her working as a maid in Bangkok almost 30 years ago. That includes spending all her time after work on her days off playing cards and gambling until she was unable to save money. She shared information on a girlish topic with a humble attitude. She recently started dating a wonderful and friendly American guy who is a little bit younger than she is; he can eat many kinds of our Thai spicy foods. Ladda enjoyed the food, but she could not eat a lot of the spicy ones. Her boyfriend did not make me feel uncomfortable about making any dish at all, when they came over to visit. I could even eat a Thai green papaya salad, which is a famous dish of my hometown. Some Thais refuse to eat it because of the spiciness, taste, and smell. It is nice to know he is an American who does not mind our food.

I have been allowed to call this Thai lady "Mom" and call her husband "Dad" for the last 10 years. They are parents away from my real parents in Thailand. They allow me to experience their good parenthood in raising their children, grandparenthood with their grand kids, and a good partnership as a couple. The most important thing is that they allow my children to have the opportunity to experience having grandparents nearby for family activities and important occasions such as birthdays, Thanksgiving, and Christmas. My family has always been allowed to visit them at their home in Hugo, Oklahoma. My youngest son always shows off to his friends that he has grandparents. At the temple, after we did our morning blessing, he would tell one of his playmates, "I am going to see my grandma; she is sitting over there." Then, he would run to see and hug his grandma. Every time he learned that she was coming over to the house, he looked forward to seeing her. He knew that when Grandma came over, he would get either a toy or different types of snacks.

My friendship with them started at a Wal-Mart's check-out register. I was then working part time as a cashier after school. They were at my register to be checked out. I remember being asked, "Are you Pilipino?" "No, madam, I am Thai." I responded while taking care of them. I was so happy to learn that she was also Thai. After that first meeting, they always came to see me at work, when they did their shopping in

Paris, Texas. I was also invited to visit them at their home and spend time with them on a few occasions, while I was in college. They are Mr. and Mrs. Thurman. I love to talk with them a lot. Each conversation is not only fun, but informative. There is always something to learn from them, especially a small parts of their life experience that they kindly share with me. Since their marriage is an interracial Thai and American marriage, they have done wonderfully to make their marriage successful for 38 years. By talking with them, I have gotten a lot of good advice for when I am faced with some problems in my interracial marriage as well. It was an honor to have the opportunity to learn from them about their life together. Also, it is fantastic to learn about how Mrs. Thurman's experience and adjustment to life in America.

They were married in Thailand back in 1968, while Mr. Thurman was in Thailand on his duty, which was then called, "The American G.I." He was a technician in the Air Force. After they married, they lived in Thailand for two years. Mrs. Thurman came to America in 1970, with a very little ability to speak English. She learned to communicate in English only with her husband and some of his friends. Her first trip to America was also her first time on a plane. She was then four months pregnant with their second son, and they traveled in the plane with their first son, who was one year old. That was a very long trip for her to travel alone with a child to a place that was only a dream. When I asked Mr. Thurman why he did not come with them, he told me, "I was in the Air Force. I could not travel with my family. I had to return on a military flight." "Your wife must have been scared." Mrs. Thurman used to tell me that she had mixed feelings when she was on the plane; she was scared, confused, anxious, and worried. She cried when she was at the airport in Japan, and was told by one Thai lady, who was also on the same flight, "Go ahead; finish your rice plate, because it might be your last rice meal." That made her more worried about what was ahead of her.

Mr. Thurman continued to share with me an interesting story about their journey, "My wife was met at the airport by my sister of whom she had never even seen a picture. She could not speak English enough to explain who she was, or for whom she was looking. I had written notes and letters for my wife for everything she needed at L.A. international airport, to get in contact with my sister. She met one person on the plane that was very helpful in finding my sister. My sister had a picture of my wife and our son, with the clothes they were going to be wearing; that worked quite well, as my sister recognized her when she arrived. My sister picked up my wife and took my wife to her home, which was about six hours later."

"Were you worried about them?" I asked.

"Of course, when I arrived in San Francisco, CA., I called my wife, who was scared, because she was in a strange country, where no one she met could speak her language and could communicate with her. My sister was trying to comfort her in any way she could, but it was hard since both of them did not know each other's language. After our military debriefing, I flew to L.A. to be reunited with my wife and my son who were very scared. We spent a night with my sister who was planning to travel back to Oklahoma with us for a vacation. Then, we traveled across the country from California to Oklahoma, which was quite a trip for my wife who had never seen so many different places."

"How did your family react when they learned that you were bringing back home a wife and a son?" I asked with my curiosity.

"My family at first was not really crazy about me marrying a girl from a different country, but it was not too long before my wife had won over my family's love. My wife was very polite and, as most Thais, she was very family oriented. They are very polite to their elders and go out of their way to help those who need help. I think my family thought more of her after a short time than they did me. My wife was a very beautiful person, not only on the outside, but on the inside as well."

One day, when she came to spend time with me in my own home, I had a chance to ask Mrs. Thurman a question about how she reacted to their rejection. She was kindly telling me that she understood her in-law's feelings about her coming to America with her husband. She tried very hard to do her best as a new family member. Back in those days, Thais were the same way in that parents had a lot to do with children choosing their in-laws. During our conversation, I remember she mentioned to me that "I was positive, soft, and worked hard in a house. Politeness, patience, and respect are good qualities that are always helpful when dealing with people, no matter who they are. When they are negative to you, you don't have to return their negativity. Remember one thing, Pat, you should always keep a smile on your face. You don't have to buy it; you can smile as much as you want. There are not many people who will respond to a smile with a frown." That was a very good lesson she gave me during her visit. That gave me the opportunity to ask her more about her initial experience in America.

I was told that they returned to California from Oklahoma after visiting his family. They rented a place and lived in Merced. He took his wife to buy groceries on the base. She was fascinated by the big store on the military base, because it was quite an experience for her, having been in America less than 30 days and having never been in a large food store. She had never cooked on a gas cook stove with an oven. The first time she turned on the stove, she was very lucky not to be badly burnt. She had turned on the oven, which did not have a pilot light. Then, she struck a match in it, which caused the oven to blow up after the gas had been on for a few minutes. She was slightly burnt on the arms.

Mrs. Thurman is a nice lady. It took her only a short time to find several friends who could help her out and who were very good to her. That help was included at the time of their second son's birth while they were in California. I have had the opportunity to learn about their interesting parenthood as well. Mr. Thurman was in the Air Force for five years.

They returned to his hometown in Oklahoma in 1970, and once again Mrs. Thurman had to meet a new group of people. With the kind support of her husband, she worked very hard to learn English, both in speaking and writing to effectively communicate with people. She asked Mr. Thurman to teach her to drive, and later on she was able to do it. I was told that she studied for her test and passed it successfully; even the driver examiner enjoyed her hospitality during the driving test. She took the initiative to attend a cooking class to learn how to cook American food. She became a good cook of both American and Thai foods.

When raising their three children, she was active in their school activities and helped out in anything she could. While she was a stay-at-home mom, volunteering her time at school also helped her a lot with her English. She was also there for her children when they needed her. She is blessed to have such wonderful and successful children. All three of them received college degrees and have their own families. That gives her the opportunity to be involved with her grandchildren's activities, and she helps by keeping them for their parents from time to time. She just loves it.

Long before I knew this talented woman, she was an active volunteer who was skilled in growing a lot of Thai vegetables and preparing Thai hot sauces, available weekly during the summer to purchase at the temple. Throughout our good friendship, I have not only had the opportunity to consume fresh vegetables, but also to enjoy her conversation on different topics. A few times, I was invited to visit and help her harvest her vegetables and other farm products. She is a people person; she likes to talk with many people, which has sometimes gotten her into trouble. By selling her products, she is really exercising her people skills.

She loves to work in her garden in her family's 100-acre ranch. Among the few Thais I know, she owns the biggest farm properties and animals. She lives her life on that big farm enjoying the ranch style of living that many Thais, including myself, will never experience. The lifestyle reminds me of my home country's up country side living: getting up in the morning and opening windows to enjoy a nice and cool breeze, working on the farm early in the morning, taking a nap during the day, and listening to the sound of crickets and small insects at night. She told me that back home, living life in the countryside was so simple. The difference between here and home is that everything on her farm now is so convenient. It starts with a nice and comfortably-equipped house, cars, tractors, and modern farm equipment.

She tells me that she is unable to either read or write well in both Thai and English. The amazing thing is that she is able to communicate and drive to many places by herself in America. One thing I have to remember when she asks for directions is that she could not read the names of roads. I have to take her somewhere only one time; she remembers almost everything we pass, every building in the surrounding area, and every turn I make.

She is a housewife who has successfully raised her own two children, while being good company to her supportive American husband. To take time off from her family, this year on the Fourth of July, she called me at the office to ask me if I could take her to a Laos temple nearby for an outdoor party at night. There were a lot of entertaining activities and many food shops. There was also live music on the stage and a big ground floor for people to enjoy and dance. Seeing a lot of people there and many good foods made me miss home. I took two Thai ladies to the temple that night. They wanted to enjoy themselves, but they did not want me to wait for them. After eating with them, I left them there and went back to pick them up at 2:00 a.m. on the following day. After we got to my house, we did not go to bed right away; we enjoyed each other's conversation until almost 4:00 a.m. that day. Both of them spent time with me and my family, before they left the house around noon. It was a nice visit we had.

I was introduced to another Thai lady at a house blessing party in Oklahoma back in 1999. In my opinion, she is beautiful and charming with a good figure after having three grown-up sons. She is very funny and outspoken. I was also told that she was well-off from her working hard in her family's small business here and establishing a small business in Thailand. I was so fascinated to learn about how a Thai woman has been so successful.

After that day and with my busy schedule, I did not contact her much until I was invited to attend her 10th anniversary the following year. She had been married to an American man for 10 years. It was a nice party with a lot of people and good food. She looked so beautiful in a light blue dress during that party, and I had the opportunity to visit her house for the first time after the party.

Our friendship was not really close until the middle of 2001. I got a phone call from her asking me to help her find a job in my work place. I was told that she was filing for a divorce and moving to live in Dallas. With no questions asked about the details of her personal life, I agreed to help her get a job in the campus cafeteria. Helping and seeing her going through each stage of her divorce allowed me the opportunity to exercise my friendship by listening, spending time with her, and just simply being there when she needed me. She is a strong character who can handle a situation so well. I could not see myself being able to do even half of what she was doing, if I happened to be in that situation.

She started working as a cook's helper. With her ability to cook and outstanding work skills, she got promoted to a full-time cooking position. A petite Thai woman cooking in the cafeteria along with a few American cooks to serve over 650 American youths a day was absolutely unbelievable. She has been doing such an excellent job. Her food taste delicious and it has been recognized by many. During her employment here at the center, I have gotten the chance to meet her almost everyday. Before she goes home, she stops by my classroom after she gets off work and has a little chat if I am not busy with students. I sometimes help her with different types of paper work and with translating of English. Our friendship has developed gradually and has become close.

She is another Thai woman who works so hard everyday in this country to make a living on her own as a single woman. She is always actively working in the cafeteria, among a few lazy co-workers who want to sit down waiting for each work hour to pass by. Her reputation for cooking American food is well-known. She has been telling me that "If only I could read and understanding English well, I could do much better in my field of work." Or sometimes she would mention, "I should have paid more attention in English class, when I was studying in our country."

"Why don't you attend class at night at the local college?" I used to ask.

"I don't like to study, I only like to cook." She was laughing while responding to my question.

"I think you should start reading at least one line at a time, so you can read the recipe in English." I gave another try.

"I might, but reading makes me want to go to sleep," she jokingly told me.

However, she makes me proud that her American co-worker sometimes still has to ask her what is stated in recipes and on food labels. She could tell her co-worker correctly.

"See, it is not only me who can't read English." She loudly laughed with me one day, when we were talking about studying English.

Throughout our strong friendship, I have had the opportunity to learn from this Thai lady's life experience. She came here on a tourist visa and strived to work and live legally here, so that she could save money. She is no different than many Thais I have encountered who are seeking the opportunity to become successful and financially independent by working so hard in this land of opportunity, dreaming that one day they can save enough money for a better life in their home country and to support their Thai family back home from their hard-earned money that they received from long hours of work. She has been determined to create a comfortable living environment for her family in Thailand. When she was asked, she never told many family members how hard she has to work for the amount of money that she sends. I was told that many times her family never appreciated her sacrifice. Actually, this seems to be one problem that I keep hearing from many Thais who are living here. They have been suffering emotionally from the long distance treatment by their family members back home, when they can not provide enough financial help. Those relatives might just think that people who work here make a lot of money and have a lot of savings. They never know that there are many bills and expenses associated with their earnings as well.

She is a very kind-hearted person who has helped people a lot. Some people just simply take advantage of her kindness. One time, she was going to help one Thai student who came to America to get a student visa, but he didn't really want to study. He wanted to work in the restaurant to save money. He enrolled in a language school for one semester and stopped. He asked her to rent him a room in her house, so he could pay less rent than paying for an apartment. When I learned about it, I asked her not to be involved. She can be in trouble with immigration law. Since she lives among many Thais, there is always something I hear about and am able to learn from, in terms of making a living, being involved with good activities, or having a problem with immigration status.

I have learned a lot about her determination to work hard and work smart in her field. She has gained a significant cooking skill from a few American cooks. Those skills have helped her to be able to work and live independently with a good reputation as a single Thai woman in America. She certainly devoted her time to working. Sometimes, after she finished working all day in the cafeteria, she stops by my office to take a short nap, before going to her second job in the evening. She normally finishes her work around 11:00 p.m. at night and reports to work again around 5:00 a.m. the following morning. That does not include getting up early to get ready for work. She also has to drive about 30 minutes from her home to our campus in the morning traffic. This is the routine of a strong-hearted Thai woman who strives to fight in the great expectation of a good retirement plan that working with an American company provides. She is a friend who really makes me clearly see that money surely does not grow on trees. The hard-earned money in America for many Thais has come from great sacrifice, determination, and self-discipline.

She has the ability to cook different types of food well. My favorite dishes that she makes are chicken curry, barbeque pork on a stick, and a delicious cheesecake. She prepares good food for me to enjoy on her little free time. I still remember that she always prepared a different dish for me to eat while I was pregnant. She also brought ten beautiful maternity dresses back from Thailand for me, when she came back from her vacation.

She has such strong character and a great deal of patience to deal with many challenges and problems while living in America. She is tough and fights with life. She is the type of person who is not defeated easily and who does not hesitate to reach for help when she needs it. At the same time, she is very open to learning new things in life.

Her friendship, kindness, and frequent visits in the office make many of my students think that she is my sister. When she has served food to them in the cafeteria, they have told her if I am not in class for some reason. They would ask her if I am doing better when I am out on a sick leave. Some students asked her to give me a card that they created in class, while I was out.

Many times on the job, she has become frustrated with her limited understanding of English, when she was dealing with her American co-workers. I have encouraged her to learn more by taking one small step at a time. Her long work hours on two different jobs make it difficult for her to concentrate. She always jokes with me that "When I find my Prince Charming or a rich boyfriend, I might not have to work this hard." She was laughing at her words.

Our friendship is valuable and healthy. The one thing that I know is that she will be there for me when I need her assistance, and I will certainly do the same for her.

Another good friendship I have experienced started in 2002. I want to take the opportunity to extend my sincere thanks to a person who has not only been a good friend of mine, but also a wonderful babysitter and care-giver to my youngest son. She has been like his godmother. She sensitively responds to his needs when he is in good health and when he is sick. She is a person who has offered her help at times, when I desperately needed good care for my four-month old son while getting ready to go back to teaching after my maternity leave. It was so delightful to get a *"YES"* phone call from her after my long search in many childcare centers around the city. She agreed to provide care for my son in her own home. Her daily hard work caring for my son was outstanding.

As a working mother, finding the best care for my child is significant. She has helped me to have peace of mind at work by ensuring excellent services. I did not have to worry while I was working, because she took such good care of him. I remember many times I had to pick up my son late, due to a meeting or training. She never complained or made me worry. She did not even charge a late pick-up fee. She understands things easily and is willing to help, when she feels it is needed. There was a time that she saw I had become really exhausted from work and home. She offered to keep my son on the weekend or at night, so that I could rest. Her responsibility ensured me that my son would be fed, bathed, and changed. I was lucky that I never experienced my child staying in a soiled diaper when I picked him up from a baby-sitter's home. I was told that some kids stayed dirty all day long and got cleaned up only before the parents' pick up time.

Her loving and caring for my son for over two years, day in and day out, helped to develop a good friendship between us, especially with my son. She has had such a great impact on his life. Her house is a place in which my son feels secure and is a place he wants to be. I remember times when I have picked my son up and have had to go through a big battle just to get him into the car. He was crying and whining all the way home. Before bedtime, he asked me to take him to see her and her daughter. Sometimes, it was a nightmare trying to calm him down at night. I had to pick up the phone and ask her to talk to him over the phone.

My co-worker jokingly said that she envied me when I told her that I was going to eat lunch from the box packed by my friend and baby-sitter. She loves to cook, especially sweets, cakes, and different kinds of Thai desserts. When I drop off or pick up my son, she sometimes prepares food for my lunch box or a dish to take home after an exhausting day at work. She always prepares a nice dish for special occasions such as Valentine's Day, Easter, and Halloween, to give away to her friends. With her cooking talent, she usually prepares different types of Thai desserts to sell at the temple and the Thai store.

A few times on my birthday in August, she has made phone calls to all of our friends to arrange and organize a surprise birthday party for me. I was not informed about anything, but was invited to have supper after work at one of our Thai friend's houses. I was surprised, happy, and so thankful for her thoughtfulness. When each of us wants to sit down and talk about some challenges that we encounter in life, we find time to confide in each other and to provide ways to solve the problems.

These days, even though she is not baby-sitting my son any more, because he goes to school full-day at an American pre-school, we still schedule to have lunch or dinner to allow for fun time for our children to play together. She has a five-year-old daughter who my son dearly loves. She is a cute and adorable little girl. She and my son have grown up together, since her mother started baby-sitting. They love to play with each other, both at home and at the temple. Sometimes they call to talk to each other on the phone. My friend and I laugh that they keep their conversation going as if they are adults. Many times, while my son was at his pre-school, she asks her mother to take her to pick him up and bring him home to play together. I got a call to pick him up at their house after work. Whenever I have important business to take care of, I have to ask her to keep my son in her care. It is usually some small personal business that I am unable to take care of, due to my full-time work schedule. Only she can do this for me, and she has never hesitated to help. The fact that she took the time to go to the courthouse to pay my speeding fine is still unforgettable. Her willingness to help is the thing for which I am most appreciative.

Throughout my excellent friendship with this friend, I got the opportunity to experience another good friendship with one Thai lady who has been in the US for almost fifteen years. She moved from Canada, after living there for over ten years. She is from a city in the northern part of Thailand. She has been like a sister to me. I have received a lot of good, kind, and helpful advice from her, especially her advice on raising a teenager, due to her experiencing raising two teenage children. Not only was she a wonderful host for my surprise birthday party, but she was also a host for the many good supper times for me after a long work day. She usually calls at work to invite me to a get-together meal and to swim time for our children. She prepares a lot of good northern dishes for us to enjoy, and she packs food for us to take home after a delicious supper.

She loves to work in a vegetable garden in her own backyard, planting different kinds of herbs and vegetables. She provides for us to take them back home with us when we visit her at her home. Her yard always looks nice and clean.

She is a very outgoing lady who always has parties and outside activities with her American friends. She loves and appreciates our country's Thai silk. She surely looks fabulous in her Thai silk dresses. I remember her coming to the office to try on and pick up a few Thai dresses which were made and sent from Thailand for her by my mother. These days, even though I don't see her much, once in a while she calls my office to check on me just to see if my family and I are doing fine. If I don't have a chance to answer her phone call, she always leaves a message for me to call her back. I have always appreciated her friendliness and thoughtfulness.

From the first week of my teaching career until now, her friendship has been a pleasant life experience for me. My seven years of working would have been quite difficult without my good Pilipino friend around. Even though we work in different departments, she has such a great impact on my days at work. Her advice and suggestions, as a person who has more experience in the workforce and as a good friend, make some work-related challenges easier to overcome. Our Asian heritage makes us related easily, even though we are from different countries.

Whenever we have professional and personal problems, it is easy for us to listen, understand and confer with each other. Her friendship is absolutely priceless. Her loving, caring, and sharing have always been recognized, not only by me, but also by many others working with us. Her positive attitude and outlook make her a person that everybody wants to be around. Her dependability and good helping hand with many tasks make me very confident that once I ask her, all will be done, and it has always been done awesomely. Everything is done, before I knew about it. That includes many times where she has corrected the report and my English usage, has found and bought a new pair of stockings when I was carelessly wearing a wrong color to work on a bad and rushed day. Her willingness to help with a positive attitude on any matter has always been appreciated. Her understanding makes me feel close and confident to talk openly about different things that bother me. She is very thoughtful and observant of things that I prefer. That includes my favorite foods and desserts. Her love and caring are not only given toward me, but it is also extended to my family. Cres, you are the friend who gives me more than I could ask for.

Leslie Amendariz, (You are a friend whose last name I have difficulty pronouncing.) I remember asking you if I could talk about our friendship in my book. Your reply was, "Oh…darling, you can write all you want about me. Don't forget to mention that I am your crazy American friend who doesn't eat vegetables. And make sure you leave out some really bad things I did." Then, she just laughed. Your friendliness and open laughter are amazing. Your funny jokes help me learn and understand more English and slang, too. Your correcting much of my pronunciation of English words at work helps me strive to learn more and more (I even talked to myself when I was driving); many times, it is so difficult to pronounce the "R's" and "L's." in words. I still remember what you sent to me and Cres through the e-mail: "I believe that Cres, Pat, and I were brought together for a reason. We are all so different, yet so alike. We all bring something to the table, and this binds us all together." Yes, you and I were brought together when I started working in April 1999. I still remember confiding in you after work on our challenging days, the long hours of helping each other to solve personal problems, the caring and sharing about different things and topics, the fun and friendly lunch time, and, when we were together a lot at work, how people joked that you were my shadow. Your love of my Thai hot sauce was amazing and makes me never feel hesitant to share. However, one thing that has never been accomplished with you is getting you to eat vegetables other than cucumbers and carrots. Your concern with my health when I didn't feel well at work, your time checking my blood pressure, your advice on drugs and medicine after I told you about my symptoms were all really appreciated. It is so nice and beneficial to have a good nurse as a friend.

Another friend of mine is a very decent and conservative Chinese girl from Beijing, China. She is my best friend and beloved of my family. I am so glad that I have had the opportunity to have her as a friend. She is absolutely a good-hearted type of person that is not easy to find in this world. She is a good friend that anybody would want to have. Her positive and caring attitude has always been appreciated. Our friendship began as classmates in graduate school back in 1997. Then, we worked together in the department's computer lab. She is a very smart girl who always presented creative, neat, and well-organized projects. Her work and intelligence were hardly matched by many in class. She is a very good self-motivated classmate who strives to learn new things and doesn't hesitate to share information with me. While I write this section, it brings back memories of her helping with projects that I struggled to get through and the time job-hunting after graduation. She graduated two semesters ahead of me and was able to experience trying to find a job in a professional field before I did. The experience, advice, and information she shared with me were very helpful. Her encouragement during her down time was appreciated, and that helped to drive me forward.

The way she carried herself and her ability to maintain a home life and motherhood while studying full-time were amazing. She commuted weekly between the city she lived in and the university; it was almost two hours driving one way. She then had a three-year-old son who was in a car seat during his mom's commute. She took care of him while living in a family housing apartment on weekdays attending school Monday-Thursday. She put a great deal of effort into balancing the responsibilities of raising her son, attending class, completing her homework and projects, and working part-time in the department computer lab. She gave me the opportunity to experience a good friend who has such great patience and determination; she was a friend who showed me that starting from the point zero is better than not having a chance to start at all, a wonderful friend who kept encouraging me by telling me that one day we will become successful in this country. As international students, we dreamed of having a good and secure job in America, so that we can support ourselves, our family, and our parents back home.

While working in the lab one day, I remember learning that one of our American classmates had gotten a job; we were so thrilled. While we were so excited for her, we talked to each other about whether we would have such a day on which we would be so happy for being offered a job after our graduation. We talked about expected salaries and benefits. She was the first friend who shared with me information about stock investment and a saving plan for a retirement in the future.

Even though we are both quite busy these days with our schedules and our responsibilities, we are still good friends. We do not have as much time to see each other as we had in college. At least one time a year, both of our families will get together and spend the day catching up, letting our children play together while we are visiting and drinking tea, cooking and eating, chatting and sharing our experiences throughout the year, communicating about our work, discussing our problems, and having fun with our American dream.

While I am bonding with new friends here, my old friends back home are still important and have many things I can appreciate and from which I can learn. However, due to our distance, busy schedule, loss of contact, and some life priorities, a continuous friendship is quite difficult. I was fortunate that during my visit to Thailand last year, I had the chance to see two of my good high school friends, who I haven't seen or contacted for twelve years. I truly enjoyed the very short period of time with them. While writing this section, I was reminded of a letter I sent to them after I got back from Thailand. It is my opinion that while there are so many negative things going on around the world, having a chance to acknowledge and express the appreciation of the positive things people have done in my life is a blessing, especially the good friends I don't know if I will have a chance to meet again. We really can't predict the future, but it is our choice to look for positive things that we can experience from people with whom we are in contact. I wrote this letter with joy.

Dear Friend,

I hope everything is going fine with you in Thailand. I would like to express my sincere thanks for your kindness and warm hospitality during my visit in March and early April. Thank you for picking me up at the airport late at night. It was wonderful and surprising to see you again after all these years.

I enjoyed seeing you at Khon Khean Airport before our long drive to visit Muang Loei. It was such a fantastic time to see Wangsaphung, your hometown, and your parents again. I am so grateful that they are still very kind to me. Moreover, we got the opportunity to see our old high school friend, Ubon, and my good neighbors, Aunt Dang and Uncle Ae. The dinner is Wangsaphung was delicious. The conversations were really valuable and unforgettable.

Thank you for all your driving and helping me pack my suitcases. Your driving from Bangkok to Chaiyaphum that night was appreciated. I knew it was a tiring night for you, driving many hours after a long day of work. I enjoyed your visit to my hometown very much. Also, I still remember how tasty the fresh coffee was during our trip back from Loei to Bangkok. Even though our trip back to Bangkok was long and tiring, I still enjoyed shopping at Zeer Rangsit for CDs for my friends in the States. A long check-in process at the airport helped me to have more time with my family and you. My flight departed a little late, and the flight was long hours in flight, but I got back to the U.S. safely.

Thank you for everything you have done during my visit. During your free time or your vacation from work, please allow me to have you as our guest in Texas. I will take you on a tour around Rockwall, the city I have been living in since my graduation. We'll go visit McKinney, the city where I work. My family will show you around Dallas. I will take you to visit my American family and visit some of my Thai friends' families. We will give you the opportunity to see American lifestyles, experience American culture, and eat tasty American foods. Again, thank you, and please visit me in the United States in the future.

Love always,
Your Friend.

Other than my visit with these two friends, I had the opportunity to get the contact number of one high school friend and classmate who lived with me in my parents' house for one semester. My, how time flies! I have not seen her since we graduated from high school; that was almost twenty years ago. It has been over a year since she and I have been in contact with each other through the benefit of our world advanced technology. Recently, I got the e-mail from her telling me about her graduation from graduate school. I am so proud of her and learned that she had worked so hard to get to that point. I still remember that when we graduated from high school, she was not planning to continue in school, but to start a family. Through our e-mail exchange, we share information, talk about our children, our personal and professional improvement, and we plan to visit each other when we have a chance to travel. It was nice to learn that she is doing extremely well with her life and is such a good provider to her children. Her birthday is coming soon; I might just send her a beautiful birthday card to wish her a happy birthday. One of many good things that I have learned from Americans is that sending a card to our friends and loved ones on different occasions provides us the opportunity to express our care and thoughtfulness. Her birthday card will be in the international mail, and later on my e-mail will go through cyberspace to indicate my appreciation of our friendship.

With every friendship, I have experienced a great deal of diversity. I recognize and value each friend's skills and talents. I learned to accept them for who they are, and they accept me for who I am, as we learn that nobody is perfect. We encourage each other's strength and suggest improvements on any weaknesses. I listen to each of them when I learn that they need to talk. At many times in our friendship, we don't really need our friends to help solve problems or to fix anything; we just need someone to listen. Each of us has never minded listening and offering suggestions when they are asked for. I always acknowledge that if my friends don't trust me, they will not talk to me about their problems;

they certainly will not open the door for me to talk to them about mine. Helping each other with problems and challenges helps us to bond in our friendship. If they don't love me, they won't share their time and experience; without love and care, our friendship will never grow. By talking with them when they have problems, I am not only doing my part as a friend to help find a solution, but I am also learning valuable lessons from their situations. Who knows? Some day I might encounter the same situation in my life. At least I would know what to do and how to start solving the problem. I have learned that there are many things in life we can't just learn from reading books; we also learn from listening and talking to people who have experienced it. Some educated people might not find the way to escape the circle of life, as we have known that there is a time the big lion still needs help from a little mouse.

Each one of my friendships is unique because each of us is different. Our friendship gives us the opportunity to put forth positive effort to learn from one another. As we are busy with our own schedules as daughters, mothers, wives, and for some, workers, we still find a little time to catch up in our friendship and to help each other grow as human beings. I am blessed to have such good friends.

Pat with Charin and Ubon

Godmother in Thailand

Chapter 8: My House—My Mother's Dream

If an average person's success is measured by fulfilling a mother's great dream, I can raise the flag to claim that victory. If the small thing that indicates the success of a daughter is that she can provide for her parents and give them a good home to live in when they reach their old age, after they spend all their life raising her, I have tasted that success. It was a very proud moment when I completed a big project I had worked on for three years -- three full years of hard work. It was even better after staying in it for a month during my visit to Thailand in 2002. It was another achievement of a thirty-two year-old girl who has benefited from living and working in America.

My father picked me up at the airport in Bangkok around 11:45 p.m. that night in January 2002. Then, he brought me back to our hometown without bothering to waste any time staying in Bangkok. I was anxious to see the project. It was about a six to seven hour drive after a long international flight. We got to my hometown a little after 6:30 a.m. the next day. When he made a turn into the driveway, I could see a big beautiful white brick house ahead of me.

"How is your new house?" my father asked me while he was smiling.

"It is beautiful, father, but why is it so big?" I replied.

"Looking at the plan you sent, I did not know it would be this big." I continued.

"Look!, your mother is waiting for you on the front porch." My father pointed to the front of the house. My mother was standing there and ready to show off her completed project, after a warm greeting and welcome home. It was nice to be home. It was especially nice to be home, since that time I was in a new home...I really mean it was my mother's dream home.

While I was working in a computer lab at Texas A&M University-Commerce, I saved a small amount of money from my salary and sent it to my mother to purchase a small lot of land. This lot was adjacent to the one my mother had inherited from my grandparents after they passed away. Later on, that lot was given to me by my mother. By combining two lots, it would be a good size of land on which to build a house. It was a house for my mother who asked me over the phone to build her a house when she moved back to her birthplace, after being away since she married my father. It had been almost thirty nine years. She decided to move back to live closer to her brothers, sisters, and other relatives. I assumed that she might feel quite lonesome living so far away from them and none of her children lived close by. That reminds me of several Thais I have met at the temple in America, who talk about moving back to Thailand when they reach their retirement age. Some said that they do not want to be so lonely living by themselves in this country when they get old. Sometimes, I think about what I will have to do when I reach that age -- stay here, or move back home. I still have not been able to find the answer.

I just could not refuse, when my mother told me about her reasons for moving back to her hometown. I accepted her request and gave her a green light to start the process. I recall sending another amount of money to her on the Thai mother's day in 1999. She later used that money to put up the fence around the lots. It was not a fancy looking fence, but a wire fence which could be used to separate the property from the neighbor. After the fence was completed, there was a process of getting a lot of fill dirt to level up the land and letting it settle for the construction. I was informed of every step of the process over the phone when I called my parents every other weekend. During that time, I acknowledged that my mother was really busy getting things done and preparing to start building a house. I was working hard and trying to save everything I earned.

A few months later I received two pictures of houses from my mother. In one of them, she was standing in front of the house that she likes and plans to build hers similar to it. It is a one-family house in the city near her hometown. The other picture was her brother's newly-built house. It is a nice looking house with a beautiful block concrete fence. I was given the option that if I chose this design, I would not have to pay for a house plan. I could use his. He also knew some reasonable builders I could use. I thought that was a good deal, so I could save some money, due to my limited budget. I gratefully accepted the offer and asked my uncle to help me find a good builder. He also was a wonderful help to my parents in finding some reasonable extra materials. When I did not send money in time, he was the one my mother borrowed money from to continue the construction. She returned it to him after she received the money that I sent.

During that time, I had just started working full time and did not have much savings. A big project in Thailand was really a challenging one. It was a project that helped me develop good self-control in my spending. It made me limit all types of expenses. Was I stingy? No, not really, but I had a purpose that I needed to focus on. I surely expected to see the result. I limited my budget on professional clothing. As for many women who have recently started working, clothing is quite important, because it enhances your personal appearance. Of course, I wanted to look good. However, my dresses for work mostly came from a thrift plaza, a garage sale, or a goodwill industry. I was lucky that a few of my good friends taught me how to choose clothing in good condition and of a good brand. They even suggested to me to visit different locations. After I bought clothing, I cleaned the items well and neatly pressed them. No one realized that many of them had been used; they were second-hand clothing. One day while I was teaching in my class, I overheard two female students between 19 to 21 years old talking about me. Their conversation was like, "Ms. Sato looks rich. She has so many cute outfits. I have never seen her wear the same one twice."

"She is always well-dressed," said the other student. I just pretended that I didn't hear anything. I wanted to laugh so badly and tell them that, "Ms. Sato got all of these cute dresses from an American thrift shop." When I told my close friends about my students' conversation, they were laughing and joking with me, saying that, "Clothing looks good on a nice hanger… huh." "Of course…my dear…there will be a time when I can spend money on my outfits without thinking about the hanger." I responded. That was a joke about the money I saved during my big project. Luckily, most of my new working clothes were sent from Thailand by my mother. Most of them were specially made by a dress maker. The material was real hand-woven Thai silk. I think my mother felt pity for me, because I saved too much and I didn't want to spend money to dress myself up. I was also wearing long hair simply because I didn't want to spend the money for a haircut. I packed my lunch box everyday, so I could save money by not having to eat lunch outside campus. I limited myself by not eating out on the weekend. I refused to have any kind of entertainment outside of my home, not even renting a movie from a movie rental. I watched my grocery expenses. I looked at the newspaper for special deals and extra sales each week. When I found one, I would buy a reasonably priced big package, separated it into a small portion, and stored in the freezer for individual meals. I especially could not really afford to buy shrimp and salmon often, no matter how much I would like to eat them. They were too expensive. Poor me, for everything I wanted to eat, I would think about how many bricks I could buy if I calculated into a Thai baht. That was a sacrifice that I forced myself to make.

Even though I tried to save money any way I could, the amount was still not big enough to finish a house in Thailand. I decided to talk to one Thai lady who I respect as if she were my own mother. She is my godmother, the one who inspired and motivated me while I was studying in college. She quietly observed me working on my project. One day, she told me that she was so proud of me for what I was trying to do for my parents. She did not have a chance to return to her parents, because they had passed away. She kindly offered to help to finish the house. She took me to an American bank and requested a personal loan, using her certificate of deposit as collateral. The loan process did not take a long time to get approval, because of her outstanding credit record. Credit is the way of trust and a way of life here in America. Without good credit, everything seems to be quite difficult, even renting a house, apartment, or buying a car.

She lent me a large amount of money without requesting any type of contract or collateral from me. I remember her saying that, *"I trust you, [in the] many years that I have known you, you have proved to me many things [so] that this amount of money won't ruin our friendship. I wish I could have a chance to challenge myself by doing something good for parents back home like you. Go ahead, finish it, so you won't feel regret like I do sometimes.*" I had no idea that a few years later, I would have a chance to return her favor when she was building her own house in Thailand.

I sent that amount of money to my mother, who was also working really hard continuously overseeing the construction back home. My father was also helping her, though he was busy with his work schedule. My brother traveled many hours to help out sometimes on weekends. He drove my mother to pick out some material and equipment. Everybody was doing their part and looking forward to seeing the result.

I was informed at every major step of construction: the cement truck came today; the brick truck finished unloading many rounds today; the foundation was completed; a few days ago, some worker wanted to get an advance on his labor fee, due to the sickness of his child; a builder is going to lay brick tomorrow; the roof will be finished in the next few days; tiles were selected for the floor (we hope you like the color); a carpenter came to estimate the additional need of wood work; a painter gave an estimated fee for the whole house (we chose the light green; it is nice), and also the mosquito screen needs to be installed, that would be extra. I was focusing on work, while listening to the news from back home. It was a joyous feeling to hear everything about the construction. I was so happy to see many construction pictures my father sent for me to view. He was not a good camera man, but I knew he tried his best. Even though different parts of the picture were cut off, my picture of the finished project was still beautiful in my mind.

When many printed pictures came into my hands in America, I looked and looked and looked at them many times a day. Every step on each picture was part of my victory. I even placed some pictures in my office to remind myself of what I was doing; I had to work hard, so that the construction could be completed on time.

A few phone calls from my mother informed me that construction was over budget, due to a few extra things that were not originally in the plan, and that the house could not be finished without additional money. It was a new problem I was facing. I had no more money. Every paycheck I received, I used to make the payment to the bank on the loan that my godmother kindly helped me get. "What am I going to do? A house almost....almost completed.

One day I received a letter from my credit card company. It was an offer for a 3.9% APR on a personal loan, due to my outstanding credit history that my American family created for me. I saw the offer as my new opportunity to finish up the construction, even though it would put me into more debt. I kept thinking to myself, "I just want to get it done; it is just one extra mile on a smooth road for my own racing." I took out another $5000 loan from the credit card company, transferred the money to Thailand, and waited for a phone call. Yes, my mother received the money. I knew she would utilize it to finish that last mile.

A month later, I received an excited phone call from my mother asking, "I am going to the city to buy buckets of paint. What color do you really want me to get?" She was asking me while I was here in America and had no idea about paint color.

"Mother, I like [a] light color, but I will let you make the decision since you will be living in the house. Any color will be okay with me." I recalled telling her.

"The builder and the painter said that it would take only a few more weeks to finish the work," she excitedly informed me.

"We will move in after the final inspection," she continued.

I asked, "Please send me some pictures, mother. I want to see, too." There was no picture sent from Thailand, but there were many delightful words for me when I called. I knew she was anxious to see the completed house as well.

"The new house is finished. It is so beautiful. I never thought I would have a chance to live in this type of house in my life."

My happy, poor mother could not wait for me to see her big completed project, while she was telling me about her new house blessing schedule. Then, she was telling me the total cost of our new house in Thai baht. Yes, I was surprised how I was able to do it.

Even though the new house in Thailand was finished, I still had two loans to pay off. I never once missed a payment. I continued to limit my expenses and was able to make my last payment on the loan in 2004. It took me a few years to pay off the house project. I was quite fortunate that I did not have to make a payment on a fifteen-year note like I did on my own house in America. Yes, the house in Thailand is the most beautiful house that my parents have ever had. They are very proud to live in it, with a wonderful sense of ownership. Since it was paid for, they didn't have to worry about anything. I am also responsible for the utility expenses and maintenance. According to my mother, it is the house that they, as a lower middle class family, had never dared to dream of. It is a house that I built with my salaries from the first few years of full-time employment in America. It was hard earned money. It is a house that my parents worked on so hard throughout the process. It is definitely a safe home I built for my older son to live in while he was under my parents' care.

Of course, it is the big proud project that I achieved in my early thirties. In my culture, returning our parents' kindness for raising us is not an obligation, but it is a willingness to show gratitude that we learn we must do. Having been brought up in a family which struggled financially has always made me dream of helping my parents to pursue a financial security and a debt free lifestyle. I would not have experienced that debt-free feeling if I didn't have the opportunity to be in my American family's home, seeing that everything was paid in cash and will not collect interest.

My project of building a house for my parents was finished. "**I did it!**" I recall as I was smiling with happiness while sleeping on the bed in my new bedroom with my nine-year old son during my visit to Thailand in 2002.

My House in Thailand

Chapter 9: Gateway to the Future

Some people say that the most precious gift in life is education. It has more value than money and any other types of tangible assets. Growing up, I had always been taught that the significant foundation of life is an education, which allows for the formation of knowledge. Knowledge is a significant key to success, and it is a passport to a good future. However, Les Giblin, the author of the book titled <u>Skill with People</u>, stated, "Knowledge itself is of no value. It is the use of knowledge that makes it valuable. The knowledge will do you no good until and unless you use it." I certainly like his final thought that, "life does not pay off for you on what you can do. Life pays off for you on what you do." These days, after reading the book written by Mr. Robert Kiyosaki, <u>Rich Dad, Poor Dad</u>, I am still quite sure that education is the endless treasure for one to benefit in life, even though for some it might not require study in the academic setting. I am so glad that I strive to study, even though I was once told in my native land that "Being a woman means one doesn't need to study a lot; after getting married, a husband will take care of you." I am so proud that I didn't wait for that to happen when I took the educational path that was provided for me twelve years ago. Within the academic arena, besides pursuing academic success, I was also given an opportune period to learn the important information that benefits my studies and my life living here: the competency to use language and the significance of health insurance. It has been a wonderful learning experience.

The opportunity to gain and obtain knowledge from an education within the American educational system wouldn't have happened without the full support of my American family. There was nothing that could have made me happier than being informed by my American family that they would sponsor me to study in America and would provide me all of the necessary documentation to take to the U.S. embassy in Thailand to request a student visa. The most fortunate thing I learned was that my American family values the importance of education. It all began from the day I was sent to take an English test at Paris Junior College while I was visiting the Marchbanks family on a six-month visitor visa. After I passed the test and expressed my interest in studying in the college, I was granted an I-20 by the Paris Junior College to file at the American consulate along with all of the necessary documentation to apply for a student visa. The I-20 form is a Certificate of Eligibility that is completed by the school authorities when a prospective student is accepted to study in that school. It is a very important document that an international student must have in order to obtain a student visa. Each student must be able to show that he/she can pay for their study and support themselves financially for at least one year. Even though many international students want to work, they are allowed to work on campus up to 20 hours a week while school is in session. For all types of off-campus jobs, it is required that you have permission from the Immigration and Naturalization Services office. However, finding a job and working while studying is not always as easy as many prospective students think.

In January 1994, I was granted a student visa, which I then learned is a category F for full time academic and language students. My F-1 student visa was issued for the length of five years to attend Paris Junior College in Paris, Texas. I learned that I must be accepted in college as a full-time student and continue in full-time education for my student visa to remain valid. I enrolled for the Spring semester. Since I had, by that time, already obtained a bachelor's degree from a college in Thailand, my main focus during the first semester was not clearly on any majors. I was advised by my American family to enroll in English classes, both reading and writing. They wanted me to be familiar with the educational system and be more efficient in English, while adjusting to studying and living here. Of course, there were so many things that made me feel so overwhelmed at the beginning. The first week in an American college was so different and fascinating: the buildings, the classrooms, the instructors, the classmates, the study, as well as seeing a few Asian students among the Americans. It began with a fast and organized registration process that didn't cause me any problems, because I received good assistance from the staff. They made each step run so smoothly. One important thing that made the registration day go so well was a tuition check provided by my American family. I recalled the tuition check for my first semester in an American college was $1,300 for a few English classes. That was an international student's rate. It was about three times more than the "in state" tuition fee. It was also my first opportunity to learn that American colleges and universities have a different tuition fee for different categories of students. It is quite painful for some of the international students, when it comes to the amount of tuition they have to pay, compared to the amount American students pay for the same classes and same credit hours. I remember one Philipino student saying, "Well, this is the price that we have to pay to be educated here, so study hard; it is too expensive to get a B in any class." I was so thankful to Mr. Marchbanks when he handed me that tuition check, because that was something I wouldn't have been able to do by myself. That registration day reminded me of my registration days in my Thai college, when my parents had to think about where they could find the money for my tuition each semester. I acknowledged that every semester was a big task for them.

In 1994, I thought a $1,200 check was large enough for my registration day. I never thought that a few years later I would have to hand a $3,100 tuition check to the office lady, when I registered for my first semester classes in graduate school. I still remember my pounding heart and sweating palms, before I gave the check to the registrar at the registration office in the admissions building. That check would have been the amount of 120,000 Thai baht. Some people could build a whole house with this amount, but here it was the tuition fee for one semester, excluding any other fees and books. At that moment I was thinking to myself that, "This is the biggest investment I have made in education my whole life."

That Spring semester was my first in the American educational system. There are two major semesters a year in most colleges and universities: Spring and Fall. A mini term and summer sessions, each of which is very intensive, are also available. For those students who want to complete their degree faster, they can attend college year round, if classes are offered. Many students take time off from school during the summer to work full time, save some money, and go back to school full time when the Fall semester begins. I have seen a lot of my American classmates obtain part-time employment to put themselves through college during major semesters. Some obtain student loans to finance their studies. Many of my classmates are qualified for financial aid and some types of federal grants. I have learned that America provides many possible resources to assist its citizens to pursue their education.

While taking English classes with a few students from different countries, I observed that everybody studied hard. Most of us were in the library all the time to get tutoring with our essays, homework, assignments, or simply to read English books. At the end of each semester, many of us, including myself, were on the Dean's List. Back home, I was not the smartest student in class, and I was not the brightest one in many subjects. I was an average student who made good enough grades to complete each semester without having to repeat. I hardly made any A grades in my grade report during my four years of college in Thailand. Much of my study time was set aside for a part-time job to support myself through college. I studied, but I didn't think I gave my studies enough time. Unlike studying here, without any financial worry, I devoted all my time to study and expected to learn and obtain more. One thing I realized was that my goals in education was clearer than those of the other students. That helped me to stay focused on what I was trying to achieve, and acknowledge that the opportunity to study here didn't come easily.

Besides learning English, during the following semesters at Paris Junior College, I was enrolled in more credit classes, including computer and math classes. Many of them were fun and interesting. In English class each semester, especially, I was taught to write many essays on different topics. My writing instructor was very helpful and always available for help. One of my favorite places on campus was a writing lab in the English department. I then had no idea that the foundation that I received would become a strong and important tool in assisting me to communicate successfully in my personal and professional life. The primary tool is language and being able to use it effectively. I recall being told by my American family and friends to "speak...speak English as much as possible...don't be shy...and don't be afraid that you will make mistakes....we will help to correct you." Many times, they helped me by checking my essays before I submitted them. I was encouraged to associate with American classmates and the other international students with whom I could use English in communication all the time. Moreover, I loved going to college each day without having to wear a uniform like I did when I was in my country. All the students in the class looked casual in their daily clothing. There was a well-equipped computer lab that allowed me to finish my assignments and gain experience with technology. The instructors and my American classmates were friendly and fun, even though some classmates didn't make it through college because they had to drop out and work full time. Many of them were having a family and trying to study; it was not easy for them to put themselves through college and support a family. Some didn't even have enough time to finish their homework. Some had to miss classes because their children were sick. Some worked very hard to balance home life, work life, and student life. Some of them went back to college many years after finishing high school; they had worked and raised children. They really tried hard to adjust themselves to the academic arena after those years. Being around them helped me to learn diversity, responsibility, time management, the value of money, effort, and most importantly, determination.

I took some time off during my second year of study to travel, as advised by my American family. I was also told that my traveling was the reward for my effort when I always brought a good grade report home and was on the Dean's List in most semesters. I recall a happy time when my American family showed off my grade report to their friends, saying that, "I told Pat that "C" is a passing grade, but she studied hard to make a GPA of 4.0 on this report." I was so happy for the reward they gave me. A few months on the road and many times on my visit to different states by air, allowed me to see more of America than I expected. My American family joked with me that, "Pat, you have seen more of America than some Americans who live here." I had the opportunity to visit Colorado, Utah and Wyoming during one winter break. There, I saw snow for the first time in my life. I was so excited and went crazy over it. It was so beautiful and amazing, when I saw more snow at the ski resorts. The mountain of snow and the extremely icy cold weather was an unforgettable memory.

During that trip, I didn't know that my study goal would become more intensified and my will to pursue what I had not yet dreamed of, was motivated and it became stronger. I was encouraged to pursue "**a graduate degree,**" by two Thai students who I met during my trip to Denver, Colorado. Both of them were already in their second semester in the MBA program at Colorado State University. I met the girl while I was dining in a Thai restaurant, and she was the waitress there part time on her days off from school. Since I was in Denver for three weeks, we became friends, and I got a chance to meet her boyfriend and visit them at their apartment. They studied hard and tried to earn some extra money while they were in graduate school. Then, I had the opportunity to learn how some Thai students were working, studying, and looking for ways to stay and work legally here after graduation. We kept in contact, after I came back to Texas and until they graduated and went back to Thailand. Meeting these two friends, I was motivated to visit the graduate school to inquire about the information to be admitted in the following years. Through the process, I had learned many significant things, which included two important tests and a long evaluation process of my Bachelor's Degree transcript from Thailand.

During my last two semesters in the Junior college, before I was informed that after a few more classes, I would be eligible to receive an Associate Degree of Applied Sciences, I put more effort in preparing myself for the TOEFL and GRE tests, as they are the important requirements for a graduate school admission. I received useful suggestions from my two Thai friends in Denver and the admissions counselor at Texas A&M University-Commerce. I strongly hoped to score high enough to be accepted in their graduate program. Unfortunately, my first try at taking the tests was not successful. My score was not high enough. That made me realize that I needed to put more effort and time into studying for the tests. I studied intensively for the following few months, and I passed the test with acceptable scores. I still clearly remember how I studied for the TOEFL (Test of English as a Foreign Language,) until my effort paid off. It took a lot of work, time, and practice, for an average person like me. This test is used to evaluate the proficiency of students for whom English is a second language and who wish to study in colleges or universities in which English will be the language of instruction. The test is used to measure verbal skills and understanding of spoken English, which is very important to get the full benefit from the lecture room. There are three different sections on the test: listening comprehension, structure & written expression, and vocabulary & reading comprehension. However, the required score on this test depends on each college and university.

I was once asked by my niece about how I studied for the TOEFL and spent the time to learn the language. I recalled sharing with her that, "I tried to learn English everyday, and I was quite lucky on the listening part, because I stayed with an American family, with whom I must use English on a daily basis. The conversation helped me to become familiar with accents and sounds. However, initially, the speed of our conversation initially made it difficult for me to fully understand." After I failed my first test, I didn't take it easy on preparing myself for my second attempt. I checked out the TOEFL preparation books from the college library, made a lot of copies out of a work book, purchased the cassette tapes, and started studying. Everyday I practiced taking the test; every chance I got, I listened to the tapes, and every opportunity I had, and I spoke with native English speaking people. One thing I learned about studying English is, "Don't wait…start studying as soon as possible, so you can learn more on these three important parts: listening, speaking, and writing." Some international students are good in the grammar and reading parts, but fail in the listening part. I personally found there are many ways to improve one's listening skills, besides listening to music, watching news and programs on television, watching movies and shows, listening to the radio in the car, and attending a lecture in class; simply exchanging a friendly greeting and making a basic conversation at the local stores is also essential for learning. At least you will hear a native response. Vocabulary and technical terms were the hardest part of the test for me. It was suggested that to improve this part of my language skills, I needed to read more. When I read and learned some new vocabulary, phrases, and sentences, I jotted them down in my notebook and learned to form those words into sentences; sometimes it made sense, but many times I had to ask for help. However, I realized that it was part of advancing myself. After twelve years of living here, the importance of learning and being able to communicate effectively in English still remains a priority to me. Everyday is a day to learn new things in English. I still jot things down in my small notebook, and I carry it with me most of the time.

The longer I live here, the better I understand how important language proficiency is in my daily life. Some long term immigrants whose native language is not English allow me the opportunity to learn more on this matter. It is amazing to see many people who can speak and pronounce English words and sentences clearly, but don't know how to spell them. Some struggle in their jobs, because they lack the ability to use the language. I recently met one soft-spoken Thai lady at a Thai temple. She was sharing with me that she was offered the opportunity to baby sit the American family's seven and five-year old children. She was so worried that she wouldn't be able to communicate in English and wouldn't be able to maintain her employment. I encouraged her that it was a chance to learn. She can even learn from the children she is babysitting. Some American children could help to correct our language, while others might just laugh at and mock our accent. I recall saying to her that, "Don't be shy. It is not our language. If you want to work here, you must start learning now and be open-minded when you are corrected. Don't become embarrassed when you are corrected by those two American kids." She thanked me for my little motivation.

These days, being in a marriage in which only English must be used to communicate gave me a chance to strive to be more efficient in my language usage, so I can effectively utilize one of many significant marriage tools with my husband. Since we both realized that communication is the key to working things out, the ability to express our point clearly and properly helps us to form our understanding quickly.

In my current position as a teacher in career technical education, language is a significant key to enable me to effectively perform my job. Part of my position is to assist the work base learning coordinator with placing students in a job for work experience and employment, especially a job in a training area. It is a wonderful experience every time I go out to meet prospective employers, using English in our business communications. I have a chance to meet new people and to learn about their businesses and services. Initially, I felt small and shy when meeting and talking with them about my training program and my students. I think that I just lacked confidence. These days, my professional work experience and responsibility help me gain the self-confidence to present myself, my training, and my students.

It is amazing to see myself moving from one place to another, walking in and out of different stores, offices and companies. I have found that it is very challenging, but it has given me the chance to exercise my patience. Many times I walked into companies just to receive their rejection of my students as interns or just to be told that, "we don't have time to train your students." Sometimes, the way some employees looked at me finding a job for my students made me really feel like asking them if they had ever looked for a job. But I just kept my cool and confidently presented my product -- my students. I reassured myself that at least I had tried my best to do what I am supposed to do. While many times I have successfully placed students in different jobs, I also encountered some unfortunate times. Business meetings in new companies benefit me because I can see how American people work and how their work environment looks. I don't really think negatively when I receive a "NO" for an answer for a placement. I also make a trip to visit the same company after a few months. I think I might have a chance, because management comes and goes most of the time. This time, I might not be successful in placing a student, but next time I might be lucky; I keep trying, because it just does not hurt. It might be worse than not trying anything at all. Most importantly, I have a chance to learn to better my use of the English language.

Those days while I was studying at Paris Junior College, besides realizing the usefulness of language usage, I also learned the significance of medical or health insurance, and its significance is still evident in my daily life. As an international student, I was required to have medical insurance while enrolled in college. That was the beginning of my knowledge of how important health insurance is and how much it cost in America. The premium check, written for $960 per year by my American family and given to the insurance agency twelve years ago for my medical insurance, has not been forgotten. The information on medical insurance from family and friends made me strive to take good care of myself, so that my family wouldn't have to spend more money on my medical expenses. It was not quite successful.

As the Lord Buddha teaches, sickness is one of the four life cycles that every life living on earth can not escape: being born, being old, being sick, and dying. It is unfortunate that being sick in this life cycle in out of our control, even though we are living in a country world famous for its medical facilities and well-known for its doctors. Since illness is out of my control, preventing a high cost for the treatment is something for which I must be responsible.

Medical insurance is really significant in America. Without one, living here is quite risky and may create a major burden for many people. The hospital bills can cost you a fortune, and you might have to spend your whole life working to pay the bills. "If you don't have money to pay the bills, they can take your belongings, your car or your house," I was told back in 1994. Yet, I didn't understand all about its importance until I first had to go to the doctor for my first female check-up in America. It cost about $250. Yes, it was a lot to me, since the same type of service might cost only $10 back home. Well, there was no other option for me. I also learned that some doctors here, if you don't have any medical insurance, don't even see you. Some offices don't even take any new patients, even if you have a good type of insurance. Most of the time when calling the doctor's office, you will first be asked about your medical insurance rather than if you are hurting badly right now. You might be told that the first availability for the doctor to see you is a month or two from now. I really had to become accustomed to the way Americans do business in the medical arena. Unlike back home, we can drive to the clinic or hospital without any appointment for to receive medical services. We have to just make sure about the listed service hours. I have not yet learned that many people are deep in debt from medical bills. I am not really sure about these days, though. It is good experience to learn about the differences.

I learned that there are so many immigrants, including Thais, living here without medical insurance. They try their best to take care of themselves and to not get sick. Unfortunately, sickness is so uncertain. It can happen any time, and when it happens, they usually buy over-the-counter medication to treat themselves, or they ask for help from their own native doctors who provide their services in the Dallas area. Sometimes they pay for the service in cash or create a services payment plan, which can be paid in full or in installments. I didn't realize that some Americans also suffer from the need for medical insurance.

Recently, I got a flyer hanging on my house door asking for help and encouraging me to join the community "Garage Sale" that would benefit a breast cancer patient in our neighborhood. This American family is enduring tremendous hardship. It is a family of seven members; two parents and five children. The mother, who is 33 years old, has recently been diagnosed with breast cancer, so she proceeded with the double mastectomy that was recommended by the doctors at the well-known hospital near the city in which she lives. Shortly after the surgery and after further testing, they have found that the cancer has spread into some of her bones.

Unfortunately, this family does not have any type of medical insurance. They have been approved for some assistance through a breast cancer fund that has helped with the cost of the surgery and some of the medications, but it was not enough. One of the medications she need costs about $10,000 per week. The community has pulled together to help this family offset the costs they are going to incur during this time of hardship, by holding a series of different fundraisers. A community garage sale was one of these activities. All of the proceeds would be donated to this family. Besides that, we are being asked to donate items that will help to make the garage sale a success event. We can also host our own garage sale at home and bring the proceeds as our donation. Or, we can donate cash to help this family.

When I was giving birth to my son, Andrew, by c-section, I stayed in the hospital for a week. I was in a private room, with a willingness to pay extra from my pocket, expecting good services while I was not much able to help myself. I did not realize that I did not pay enough for the nurse to help me to feed my son while he was crying in the crib, and I could not move from the bed. I certainly did not pay enough to have one of the nurses' smiles every time I requested her services. A few weeks after the hospital stay, I had to start making payments on my hospital bills for six months. It was $13,000, but I was responsible for only 20% after the other 80% of the total cost was paid by my insurance company. That didn't include the physician and surgeon's fees prior to staying in the hospital. My mother jokingly said, "The cost you pay to give birth to one child, a mother in our country can give birth to more than five children." I was laughing when I responded to her by saying, "That is why I don't plan to have any more kids, mother. Otherwise, I might be broke all of my life and working myself to death to pay off all of the medical, physician, and hospital bills."

The few surgeries I received at the hospital created many bills for me to keep paying for at least six months. Not only that, but the more I go to see the doctor, the higher my insurance premium goes up. Even though the doctors in America are well-known for their expertise, the fees associated with provided services are not low at all. For some of us who can not afford to write a big check for medical services, doctor's offices also provide payment plans; in three-month or six-month installment periods. It seems to me that every worker in America should show great concern for medical insurance benefits, when they are seeking employment. They want to make sure everybody in their family is being medically covered in times of need. They are really fortunate, if medical expenses are 100% paid by the company, because most of us have to pay some portion of the bills.

One of my most unforgettable medical experiences was calling an ambulance. I personally want to advise you to think whether it is really necessary before you call one; just don't think that dialing 911 is the most convenient way. My experience happened in January 2004, while I was driving back home from work. I unexpectedly got hit in the back of my car while I was completely stopped at a traffic light. I was so shocked and didn't know what to do when I saw the car that hit me make a quick turn and run away. My chest and stomach were very painful (that was around my third month after a big surgery), and I was not able to breathe. While I put my head down on the steering wheel, one gentleman was knocking on the driver's side window, asking me to open the locked door and to see if I was okay. I told him that I was having difficulty breathing. I realized that he had called the police, and I didn't really know for sure who had called the ambulance for me. I was taken to the hospital, while my damaged car was parked at the McDonald's parking lot near the accident location.

After a long process of checking in at the emergency section at the hospital, I found myself able to breathe better, and I had no injury on any part of my body. There was only a pain in my stomach and soreness for a few days. I then had to deal with the auto insurance company to get my Camry repaired, because the car that hit my car didn't have any insurance. This incident helped me to learn that there are uninsured vehicles on American roads. Not only that, I later got a bill from American Medical Response for the amount of $1,400. That was the cost of calling the ambulance and for the services I received at the hospital. I had to make the arrangement to pay that bill over an additional six months. My advice is to please make sure you really desperately need the ambulance before you make the phone call. If you think you can carefully drive yourself to the hospital, please do so. Otherwise, you will end up paying a big price for your medical response experience like I did.

One day, getting the bill from my female doctor at the OB/GYN office in the amount of $922 made me become more exhausted after getting home from a long day of work. The statement indicated the dates and types of services provided in the previous month. When I made the appointment to see the doctor, it reminded me of what I have read; "The doctor is your best friend." Of course, it sound really nice, but here in America, even though they know a lot about your medical condition because they have been taking care of you for a long time, it makes you think twice about how much it is going to cost you to go see your "best friend." This time the idea didn't even make me able to force a smile when I looked at the bill. There was a bright green post it arrow pointed to the amount, "Your insurance covered all but the mount shown on this statement. May we please have your remittance by return mail?" Well, if I said "NO," I would have a bad record on my credit report because I didn't pay my bill, wouldn't I? Of course, I would. Or there might be another bill with a 21% interest rate on a past due or unpaid balance. The following day, I called my current insurance company; I just wanted to ask why I didn't see any portion of this bill paid. It took me almost twenty minutes to get a chance to talk to a customer service representative. There were so many automated responses that provided many options. If I didn't pay close attention, I might get lost on my call or might have to start over and wait another twenty minutes, in case I selected the wrong options. Good listening skills in English will be very helpful in this respect.

Once I got a chance to ask the questions, the lady told me, "Please hold." Yes, it was another long period before I was told that, "We haven't yet processed the claim; we are waiting for your existing form or the letter of creditable coverage from your previous insurance company." "How can I send you all these documents, if I have none with me?" I asked. "You can call your previous insurance company to request this documentation. I will give you the fax number, so you can fax it to us. Then, we will process your claim." My coverage from the last company was terminated seven or eight months earlier. I looked through my mail to find the number to call. Again, I had to wait for a long while, with many automated options to choose from, before I talked to a customer representative. Fortunately, when I requested the letter, she told me that I should have it within a week. At least after this hassle, I hoped that I wouldn't have to pay the $922 bill out of my pocket. Then, I called the billing department of the doctor's office. No one was available; there was again an automated answering machine. I left a message asking for someone to call me back. About ten minutes later, one lady called me, "Mrs. Sato, I received your message and understood that you are trying to get all documents sent to your insurance company, so we will give you another 30 days for this bill to be taken care of." I thanked her over the phone, but I still couldn't feel relieved.

From this incident, I have learned that even though we have medical insurance, it still doesn't guarantee a quick and convenient service from the doctor's office and the insurance company. Besides learning to be patient and polite while dealing with them over the phone, it also taught me to keep all records at least for a year for references and to not give up on the contact process; keep on calling until the final result. It took almost three months before $922 was paid in full by the insurance company. I really don't remember how many times I had to make phone calls.

American living is fast-paced; people are very busy and stay active. They work long hours and sometimes hardly take time off, because the more you work, the larger the paycheck you will earn. Some people actively exercise and learn how to manage stress and take care of themselves physically and emotionally, in order to prevent doctor's office visits or dealing with the insurance company. While I was a student, one of my Thai friends shared the information with me that some immigrants living here are really stressed by the issues from family members back home. Their friends and family would call and ask for help, expecting that someone working in America could afford to assist them financially most of the time. Love, caring, and the willingness to help, but limited financial capability have a strong impact emotionally. When those people refuse the request, many times they are blamed for being selfish and unwilling to share. Those family members might not really know what they are going through. Most of them don't want to talk about their problems, because they don't feel like anyone is listening to them. It is quite sad to learn that many of them don't have any type of medical insurance from their employers, and a stress test costs them a large amount out of their pocket. For most working people, medical insurance is the most important benefit they seek. I learned this fact when I personally experienced it in the years that followed. Knowledge of little things that benefit me during my studies is considered an important part of my education, and the importance of medical insurance is one of the major lessons I learned.

Education is an endless treasure that provides one who has it with benefits up to the last day of his/her life. I personally found it useful, because the benefit I have been receiving from education is not helping only me and my own family, but it also extends to my parents and some of the family members back home. Knowledge that I obtained on my initial educational path did not only come directly from the academic arena, but also from the educational environment and people around me. My future here wouldn't have happened without a strong bridge for my initial years in the American educational system.

Chapter 10: Life in Graduate School

"The point of graduate school is to learn things by going through the experience" - Dr. Ronald Azuma

For some people, graduate school in America is another educational path through which they have to pass. For many, graduate school might really be a great way to further their education, some attend graduate school because they wish to fulfill a requirement for employment promotion, and others might just see it as a place to gain wonderful experience while living legally in this great country. Graduate school serves different purposes for each individual. But for me, a master's program in graduate school is an educational dream come true for an average person. Graduate school is a place that allows me to really find out about myself, my interests, my skills, and a career ideally suited for me. It is also a place that helps me to develop better self-confidence and gain better personal and life skills. It is a place for me to take control of my emotions in different circumstances to actively work toward my educational goal. More than anything else, it is a place that provides me the most essential and valuable educational life experiences.

My learning experience in American graduate school began in the spring semester in 1997, at Texas A&M University-Commerce. On my first day in a big university, I remember standing alone beside a big pond with a big winning smile looking at a high, beautiful water fountain in front of the university, inhaling the fresh morning air and slowly exhaling to release my excitement, anxiety, worry, and relief. It was the day for which I had waited for a long time in the hope of having a chance to walk inside the university as a graduate student. Looking back at that moment, I am thankful that I didn't give up on the word of the admission evaluator who said, "We can't honor your bachelor degree's transcript because the college you graduated from, in Thailand, is not in our references." That was it. There were no further instructions or assistance. I looked for instructions from many sources until I later received suggestions from one Thai student who was in the same situation and received the same response about his transcript. His said, "Don't worry, it can be done. I know a place that can work with you on your transcript. I got my evaluation done by them before I was accepted in the university." I contacted the translation and evaluations agency in Houston, Texas, to get my B.A. transcript evaluated. It took almost two months and cost me $450 for their work. I clearly recall the months of worry waiting for uncertain news. That was another emotional period in my life during which my heart had to work hard to get through. I finally received the evaluation, and I took it back to the office. The words of the same lady, "You can bring all of these documents to the graduate school downstairs to put in your file. Then you can start the registration process," were like holy water pouring into the hopeless heart. I walked down the stairs to the graduate school office with joy. After I finished registration, I felt so relieved, and I looked forward to seeing what the next step in the process was. I then went to the pond, looked at the ducks swimming and finding their food in the water, and it became my favorite spot on campus. The day that I learned I was accepted into graduate school was a happy day. The following two years were happy ones for me.

For many people, the first semester in grad school might go smoothly and they may be able to enjoy the university life. They might be pretty clear on the goal and direction of their field of study. Unfortunately, my first semester was somewhat different; I was totally lost. I faced many life challenges from back home. I was stressed, confused, depressed, and emotionally I felt alone, while I was physically among many international students from different countries. At that moment, I asked myself a question, "Why me? Why do I have to deal with so many problems that I didn't create and find a way to fix them?" Enrolling in three computer science classes in the first semester, with tough life situations and a part-time job, had made my school life even more demanding. I even considered dropping classes. On days that I felt so down, I was thankful and fortunate to have a few friends, especially my godmother, who spent time to listen to my problems, put up with my frequent frustrations, and even allowed me to cry on their shoulders. When she observed all of this, she would say, "Everything will work out." With emotional support, positive encouragement, and understanding, I finally could face those problems with a clear mind, and a positive attitude and approach. I was able to get myself back on track and concentrate on my educational path.

My first semester, I started the master's degree program in the college of science and technology. My initial study was in the area of computer science. My primary interest was not really in the program itself, but the employment, pay, and benefits afterwards, since those years was a boom period in technology. That was the wrong focus for pursuing a degree. In addition to that, I failed to realize that I didn't have a strong and proper background for the field. I also just wanted to follow what a friend suggested. I didn't realize the significance of my poor decision in choosing a field of study, until I reached the point that I didn't enjoy going to class. Some projects that I had no interest in had negative effects on me physically and emotionally. I observed many of my classmates finding class work challenging and interesting, while some of them were struggling with those projects. Half of the semester passed, and I made pretty good grades, but I still didn't have a good understanding about each of the subjects I studied. I realized my weakness in the field, and I could not see myself struggling through the program. I certainly didn't think of working in that field of work for the rest of my life.

Before it was too late, I started searching for another field of study. I tried to find out what I really wanted to do in this country when I graduated. I visited a few departments and inquired about information to support my decision. This time, I didn't follow any friends, but sought my own field of interest, until I found out about one of the fields in the department of education. It was **Learning Technology and Information Systems**. I asked for permission to sit in on a few classes and observe activities for almost two weeks. I enjoyed the classes and had fun with the activities presented. Even though I was not a student in the program, I was allowed to participate, and it seemed to be what I could do well. I finally decided to switch my field of study. My suggestion to those of you who are not quite sure about your field of study and want to search for the right one, please don't hesitate to ask the program advisor for a trial period; you might have a clearer understanding of yourself, your interests, and your strengths and weaknesses. Sometimes, only thinking about the pay and future employment when you choose your major doesn't guarantee that you will be happy. Changing a major might delay your graduation; mine was delayed one semester, but it was worth it. Of course, it would pay off in the long run in terms of the time and money you have wasted for that period. You especially won't have to be miserable in your career choice.

In the 1997 summer session, after I expressed my interest in the education field and was qualified to study in the program, I was informed about the degree plan. It consisted of all the core courses and elective courses of study, the required credit hours, and other requirements in order to successfully complete the program. With good assistance, I was clear on what class I could start taking first the following semester and those I could wait until later to take. Each class was taught by professors who have the prefix "Dr." in front of their name. Each of them had different teaching styles and used their preferred teaching methods to deliver their instructions. Each class required a lot of research, presentation of information, and discussions. The most interesting thing was that we were allowed to choose many of our own topics within the subject of study. After our research, we were to present to the whole class and create a portfolio for the class. I enjoyed Dr. Sue Espinoza's classes. The majority of her classes involved technology in the classroom and the empowerment educators to become more effective in teaching technology classes. The other multimedia and video editing classes were also very interesting. We didn't have any textbooks for some classes, but at the end of the semester, we got a big portfolio of projects from all our classmates' research on various topics. Enrolling in these classes and studying with American educators was the beginning of my interest in a teaching career path. I was lucky to find my own interest, giving me the opportunity to set goals and making me keener to have more experience in the field, which allowed me to consistently work to pursue success in reaching them. While in the department of education, I sought every way to gain experience. Besides having the opportunity to study, research, present, and discuss with a professional group of people that I enjoyed doing tasks with so much, I started thinking about doing more in terms of providing training to the others who wanted to learn. I certainly put full effort and concentration in searching for possible ways. When I had free time from study and work, I offered to help my professors with their workshops and training within the university. By doing that, I benefited a lot in terms of the opportunity to communicate in English, learn how to conduct training sessions, prepare training materials, and work with other people as a team to achieve a common goal. Due to the lack of real world experience in the educational field, I was quite fortunate that I was given the opportunity to explore and experience through practice and observing experienced professors.

I gained more experience in the field, after I received kind advice from Dr. Espinoza to start working as a **G.A. (Graduate Assistant)** in the department's computer lab. Working there while studying provided me an excellent opportunity to be within an academic setting, which also allowed me to use English daily in guiding lab users to accomplish their tasks, and communicate with my supervisor and my co-workers. I was lucky that all of my lab co-workers were international students with whom I had to communicate in English. Also, the majority of my classmates were Americans. A lot of them were educators who were working or teaching in public schools; I did not know then that they would become quite a positive influence on my career choice. They are a wonderful group of people who didn't mind sharing experience, useful information, and helping out by explaining things, such as class projects and assignments when I didn't understand them clearly or got stuck. They had such a good sense of humor and were really fun to be around and study with. I still remember one of my educator classmates who was then the assistant superintendent in a public school. He was smart, friendly, but so playful and always busy at work. It seems to me that he took classes as a part-time student to obtain some class credit to help him move up in his position. We were always paired up for class projects. His busy work schedule many times resulted in me doing a lot of research alone in the library and completing assignments by myself a few times. The last semester of our time in grad school, he jokingly said to me, "Pat, I appreciated that you always put my name on the projects when you submitted them. Your work helped me to graduate." "Don't mention it. Actually, your delivering pizza and Chinese food helped our class projects to be completed. Without eating the food you ordered and having it delivered, I wouldn't have had the energy to do the work." He brought another good luncheon for a few of us in class. He always brought fun, friendly discussion and laughter to the group.

There were only four Asian students in our program at that time, including myself. There was one female student from China, one male student from Japan, one male Thai student and I. The only time I spoke Thai was when I spoke with my Thai friend, but most of the time I asked him to speak with me in English, so both of us could improve our language usage. Graduate school allowed me to learn from some international students that they spent a large amount of money to attend language school for quite some time, and they took different levels of English classes before passing the TOEFL exam to be accepted into grad school. While in graduate school, many of them enrolled in the same classes and stayed in their own groups, and of course, spoke their native language.

The graduate school was also a place that gave me the opportunity to realize that working while learning is definitely possible through good time management. I learned that from seeing the routine of many fellow students. While I was studying at Texas A&M University-Commerce, there were about seventy six Thai students, but I did not have much of a chance to get to know and associate with the majority of them. Most of them were working on their M.B.A., in the college of Business and Technology, while I was working on my M.S. in the college of Education. The only time I met many of them was at the Thai Students Association. There were a few times when I was asked for advice and assistance from two of my juniors in applying for a G.A. position in my department. Many International students would love to work in that position, because they could receive the benefit of paying only one-third of the tuition for each semester. From almost eighty Thai students, there were a few of us fortunate enough to gain this benefit by working in different department laboratories. At that time the majority of G.A. students were from China, India, and Pakistan. They were a large group of students who always participated in our International Students Association's activities. I also learned that these groups of students really strived to help each other and take initiative for the opportunity to work in a Graduate Assistantship position. They were the group that we always saw walking in and out of each lab most of the time to look for the opening position. At that time, in the education lab, we had four students from the other departments.

While I was working in the lab, there were two Thai male students who came to the lab asking if there were any open positions. I learned from them that they wished to have a job while studying in America, so that they could have some income and their parents didn't have to worry as much about sending them money. By talking to them, I had learned that some of our native students have a strong interest in learning and earning extra money at the same time, and they don't want to be a burden to their family back home while they are trying to accomplish their educational goal. Some were allowed, under some circumstances, to work off campus. Being among them, I learned there were some international students who had to travel from Commerce to the Dallas area to work as waiters and waitresses in the different restaurants on the weekend. They sometimes got paid lower than minimum wage and had to work quite long hours. Tips are the biggest motivation for their job. Many of the students didn't have to worry about working at all, because they had good financial support from back home. Once I learned from a group of my Thai friends that some students didn't take their studying time seriously. They had a lot of money and time to party and travel. Probably, coming to America to study was not a big thing for them; unlike many students from China, India, and Pakistan, who worked so hard in restaurants and devoted all of their time to study, these other students participated in activities sponsored by the university. Their main goal was to gain as much experience as possible while being a student. Then, after graduation the main focus was to seek employment and make a living here.

These days, some of my International student friends are successfully working for American companies in different fields and using English in their daily communication at work. I met a few of my Thai friends at the Thai temple and learned that they are successfully making a living by working for a Thai owned company or managing their own business here in America. Some are still working in a Thai restaurant. I learned that the majority of International students during my time went back to their native country after graduation. I think that it is just a different path for living life. People have different goals and they pursue them differently. I asked a friend if he plans to visit home. He told me that he could not go back, because he did not have the proper paperwork to return. Some are saving, sending money back home to invest, and expecting to retire in their homeland.

Another thing I experienced in my graduate school life was that some American professors were really willing to help and followed through knowing that we were trying hard, striving to better ourselves, and English was not our first language. In contrast, the other professors might tell you straight that their class is a technical class, not an academic class; there might be some who even go so far as to say, "My class is not an ESL class where you will learn your English." I was fortunate that I had never received that type of response, but one of my friends faced that problem while he was working in the doctoral program. One friend, who was not able to move his legs, after knocking on the professor's door, was greeted by "What do you want?" Well, if you encounter these situations, don't let it hurt your feelings or make you give up the whole idea of reaching graduation day in an American university. Don't let them intimidate you. The suggestion is to keep a positive attitude and keep your politeness. Remember one thing: you are in control of your own attitude, while dealing with your professors. Understand that they are human beings who have good and bad days just like we do. They might not mean to hurt your feelings, but that might just be his or her personality, or you might happen to be with the right person at the right place, but not the right time. Or you might encounter the situation of what many people call "culture shock," when seeing how some professors do their business in the educational setting. There might be a time that you are shocked by the straightforward talk of Americans, since attitude has to do with many things, learning being no exception. Your positive view and courtesy will help you successfully deal with even a negative professor. You can even schedule to speak with her privately. The stern and rude professor might become your favorite one during your grad school learning experience. When you schedule the meeting, for any reasons, make sure that you exercise your punctuality and gratitude.

I appreciated the article written by Dr. Tara Kuther, "Tips for new grad school students." It provided such interesting information on how to approach a professor. She described that many students are able to work through grad school without having to seek assistance from their professors. For some students facing obstacles while pursuing degrees, they will need to seek one-on-one help at some point. Unforeseen obstacles, such as falling behind in classes because of poor health or lack understanding of class material could also require meetings with professors. Other reasons to seek help can be failing a test, asking for a make-up assignment, or if you need clarification on policies or schedules. For one reason or another, some students feel comfortable asking for help, but some students avoid requesting a meeting or asking for help. According to Dr. Kuther, they might feel that they won't be able to catch up after missing several classes, but other factors include a fear of asking silly questions, fear of meeting face-to-face, shyness, embarrassment, fear of interaction with those in higher authority, or discomfort in approaching a professor of diversity. "**If you're going to progress as a student and especially if you wish to attend graduate school, you must set your intimidation aside and ask for the help that you need,**" said Dr. Kuther. I recall asking for help from my professors from time to time in a variety of ways: scheduling an appointment in their office when they are available, stopping by their office during office hours, e-mailing them, or calling them. All professors are quite busy; if you want a face-to-face meeting, scheduling a meeting in advance is the most appropriate way.

Life in grad school is busy; there is a lot of work and study, and it requires a lot of good time management. Once you are able to manage your time, everything can move forward smoothly. I was able to enjoy many activities and gain other personal skills, outside of my study time. As a member of the Thai Students Association, I participated in many scheduled activities. That gave me the opportunity to meet the other Thai students who mostly studied in the M.B.A. program in another department. The Thai students' luncheon, cook-out party in the summer, and their Christmas party, hosted by the association's advisor, who is a professor in the business department, were awesome events.

Once I was asked to be the representative of Thai students and perform a Thai traditional dance in the university's International Students Festival. Many international students performed, participated, and introduced their own heritage. It was also a fun event. I enjoyed many performances and a variety of international foods. All participants were encouraged to wear native outfits and to be involved. I was trained to dance by one of my fellow Thai students, who loved to dance and is now teaching a Thai dancing class to Thai children in our Thai school at the Thai temple.

One American family, a retired husband and wife living near the university, serves as the international students' sponsor. They always scheduled interesting activities for international students who have an interest in appreciating and learning about American culture. They offered American cooking classes in their house and sometimes provided dinner for us. We were taught to cook spaghetti, cheesecake, and roast beef. A few times, they hosted a potluck party that we were required to bring at least one dish of our native food to participate. I still remember the evening tea meeting for just female students. It was really fun and educational, when the host taught us about what we should do if we are asked on a date by an American guy. "Be yourself and take pride in your own culture. When he likes you, let him learn something about you and your culture, too" she said. One female student asked," Do we have to kiss or sleep with a guy on the first date?" With a big smile, our sponsored lady replied, "No, you don't have to, unless you want to, but take good care of yourself." It was nice to have someone openly talk to us about her culture and have some fellow female students from different countries engaging in the discussion with an open mind. One night a week, we were also offered the opportunity to participate in an evening Bible study at the church.

The other activity that I was involved in was working closely with the international student advisor, as the international student president, in the last semester of my study. Participating in the association helped me to actively work with volunteer staff and organizations from outside the university to schedule off-campus activities. The recreational staff of a campground provided us, many international students, with a wonderful campfire on a cold Texas winter night. It was a wonderful experience. Training from one lady staff member in a fun and friendly Texas two-step dance was an awesome activity. A cook-out on the lake was also a great way to have fun, to engage in available activities, and to help clean up afterward. The night of Halloween, hosted by the International Student Association, gave us the funniest time with the costume contest. The organization had also provided an ESL class, taught by a volunteer retired English teacher. Many international students and their family members received good benefits from this offer.

The most important event in grad school came during my last semester of study. The **comprehensive examination**. What many of us call **"the exit exam,"** was required before applying for graduation. Each of us was allowed to make an appointment with our program advisor for that exam. After we knew our designated date, it was our responsibility to prepare ourselves for the date. It was the exciting waiting period that all of us in the program experienced. Seeing each one come back from the conference room after the exam and talk about their experience made me even more nervous. I recall going through each class's study materials, researching information on the major subjects, practicing the presentation alone and with friends, and looking through all the teaching and learning portfolios to review and prepare myself.

When my appointment arrived, I walked from the lab to the conference room feeling happy to reach this moment and also afraid of failing the exam. My heart was beating fast and my palms were sweating. I was nervous, even though I was prepared. There were three professors in the room. I was allowed to sit down in front of them after being introduced by the professor who was my master's program advisor. My exit exam was a one-hour oral presentation on all questions asked by those three professors. It was more like an hour-long interview on how to apply learning subjects to professional situations or how each subject will be used effectively in daily situations. My presentation was recorded. I remember how my program advisor helped me greatly on a question that I had difficulty answering. She stopped her recording and simply explained some examples to guide me through it. When I continued to present my ideas and opinions, she started the recorder again. When I had a chance to see her alone after the examination, I told her that I appreciated her help. "**I didn't help anything, you did it yourself. I just tried to remind you about what you forgot,**" she kindly replied. This is, as I mentioned earlier, how some professors have their own way of helping their students by understanding their limitations.

Graduation day was, of course, the happiest day in my graduate school life. I recall waking up very early in the morning, getting myself ready, even though the graduation ceremony wouldn't begin until 1:00 p.m. on that day. My neatly pressed dress, gown, and cap were ready a few weeks before that day. I received a few phone calls from my close Thai friends to congratulate me, and they let me know that they and their family would meet me at the university to attend the ceremony with me on my special day. It was a refreshing feeling, and I appreciated knowing that they cared. Two senior citizen students from my private training session let me know that they would love to join us for the dinner after the ceremony. One of them said, "I am proud of my little instructor." The graduation gift she presented at the dinner was adorable, and it is in my jewelry box until this day. A few of my good friends who graduated one semester ahead of me joined us at the ceremony, took a lot of pictures, and recorded the whole event with joy. Mr. Marchbanks gave me a big hug and a big smile, feeling great pride in his sponsorship. His happiness during our wonderful dinner among friends made me so happy and relaxed. When I gave my little speech after the meal, I thanked him for allowing me to focus on my studies without having to worry about any financial problems associated with education and providing me with the opportunity to gain educational experience as much as possible. Mr. Marchbanks smiled and said, "I'm proud of you, and you worked hard for it, too." One thing I greatly missed was my own parents' presence at the ceremony. They must have been happy to see me reach that day.

During our dinner time, a few friends asked about my next step to further my education in graduate school. I didn't have any plan at that time. However, celebrating a master's degree that day has led me to believe that pursuing the higher degree in graduate school can still be a dream and possible plan. These days, with work and effort, I hope that I am fortunate and have the ability to accomplish that plan before I reach forty-five years of age. Attempting this plan at this time might be somewhat more difficult, because I am getting older, have more life priorities, and the length of study will be longer. My professor, Dr. Espinoza, still kindly encourages me to pursue my long term educational goal, every time I meet or talk to her.

One day while visiting her at the university in Commerce, I was invited to go out for lunch with her and a few professors. With her kind smile, while walking toward the restaurant, she mentioned to me, "I still remember the day you told me that you don't think you could teach. Now, you have been doing it for how many years?" I told her that, "Maybe I learned how to teach students (not the subject) in grad school." Eight years since my graduation, I still enjoy what I do and plan to learn more. Some friends and family members mentioned that they don't know why I still want to go back to school, because I will have to be there for many more years. I jokingly replied to them with a big smile that "I have a dream, and I want to chase my dream before it will go far away, or before it will be gone forever." Visiting Mr. Marchbanks at his house these days, we occasionally discuss the possibility of giving myself another life experience in graduate school. This time it might be much longer than the first time, and it might put a lot more gray hairs on my head. But having the opportunity to set that educational goal once again is just an amazing feeling.

These days, looking back into other benefits that I have earned in addition to the Master's Degree that I obtained, it is an interesting and fulfilling learning experience. While life skills are presently as important as work skills and technical skills, I realize that graduate school has also allowed me the opportunity to learn many significant skills to accomplish my educational tasks: **Initiative, People Skills, Communication and Presentation Skills, Organizational skills, and Determination**. A lot of work, projects, research, study, and preparation for the tests, wouldn't have been completed successfully without **initiative**. All of the tasks associated with graduate work were the results of self-motivated, focused, consistent, and attentive effort; you will have to motivate yourself to get the job done; nobody is going to push you or keep reminding you of what you should do and when you should do it. All you would get from your professor is brief advice, a course syllabus of tasks, assignments, and their due dates. Most of the time, to satisfy those assignments, you have to choose your own topic related to the curriculum, do research, and present the information on the due date. If you want to gain the experience outside of the classroom, you have to take your own time seeking ways to do it, such as approaching your professor and asking for more work to do. Some of them really appreciate seeing the student take the initiative on new projects and present the projects to them for suggestions and advices. I recall my professor was pleased, when she learned that I established a private computer training session in addition to accomplishing all of my class work. Initiative helps me to set goals, work toward my goals, and look forward to seeing the completed projects. Basically, you have to get up and go all the time.

Even though I took initiative to study the tasks and topics, I was often unable to accomplish those tasks without the ability to work with other people. I found, through a grad school, that **people skills**, are essential. Establishing your own topic, working on your own projects, and trying your best to stick with it, you sometimes might find yourself getting stuck on some thoughts and strategies; you might have to ask for other people's ideas and opinions. Since some of them have more experience in the field that I was researching, my classmates or my fellow students sometimes helped me out by making good recommendations of books, articles, and websites that provide good additional information to better help me on my projects. The ability to openly listen to constructive feedback and suggestions is also very helpful. Sometimes, you might have to ask for your close friends' time to listen to your presentation, before you actually present it to the whole class on the due date. Many times, in addition to spending a lot of hours in the library, working very hard on your research, and typing up your report before finally submitting the paperwork, you might also have to work closely with the staff in the writing lab in the English department to help check your work. Instead of spending all your time searching for many books while researching on your topic, learning a good way of using a library from its staff is quicker and more effective. Here again, your good people skills come in handy. Good people skills will help you excel in working with others who are not even in your own department. One thing I realized was that studying in the Education Department, I was always involved with learning, teaching, and associating with people; without good people skills, studying would have been quite difficult to excel at. Good people skills are also based on how you treat others and how you want to be treated. It is based on recognition, respect, and showing appreciation for the time given, assistance, and suggestions. One group of people that you shouldn't overlook is the clerical staff in your own department. They can be very helpful with all types of office work and those times that you are hardly able to reach your professor. They are the insiders with whom you need to remain on friendly terms. Strong people skills will allow you to effectively interact with people in different situations, while you have to be among them trying to reach your academic destination.

The good people skills – respect, friendliness and politeness – are very helpful when you are among many fellow students and faculties. These skills help you easily get along with others, especially when you have to work closely with diverse groups of people on assigned projects. You sometimes have to meet with those members outside of class time, in new environments and different places. Seeing something different from your own way, you shouldn't judge or criticize it without a real understanding. Most of the time, you have to take the time to learn about your teammates and their personalities, along with learning the assigned projects. Nobody really likes a stranger in their group, specifically a stranger who always strongly believes in his/her own ideas and opinions and refuses to listen to the group, or a stranger who always aggressively speaks his mind. However, if you are nice and friendly, they appreciate you more. Being the international student in the group, most of the time, you have to express your ideas in a friendly way. Some of your group members might overlook your ability, if you are too shy to speak while working on the team. You surely don't only want your name be put on a sheet, without having a chance to really work with your team. One important thing is that being polite, respectful, and friendly doesn't mean that you have to be intimidated by your group members who don't have stronger qualities or significant skills. Also, you might have to learn to manage the culture shock from hearing some conversations that are open and direct, or seeing independent behavior. My daily awareness of being friendly is that you always have a smile on your face. Nobody can deny a sincere and smiling face. We certainly don't have to buy it. I don't know exactly where I read this, but it says, "Smiling uses fewer muscles on your face than frowning." So, it was quite common that while we were working, Pat, most of the time, had a little joke or small Asian craziness. Of course, my lovely Thai-English accent made it even more fun for reducing tension while completing our group projects. Good people skills also means to not looking down on others. When I was back home, I heard a few people who looked down on students who received a degree from America, saying that "They just bought it," or "All degrees are being sold in many colleges." I then had no idea how it was really like and how realistic it was, until I had to work so hard to get my degree. I could now straighten my shoulders and be proud that I earned my degree with a lot of effort and determination. I am definitely sure that my university didn't grant its graduate students a degree simply because of "money can buy a degree." I sometimes wonder if people who like to look down on other people have earned a M.S., M.Ed., or M.A. for their educational achievement.

Being an international student who has strong people skills, it is very significant meeting a new group of people while being away from home, especially meeting people in the local area. Some of them are very understanding and helpful. Some really care and don't mind providing whatever assistance they can offer. They acknowledge that you don't have any family members around. You are fortunate, if you find you own country people who are willing to help and eventually allow you to be around in their families. You will be able to learn a lot of thing that you can't find in a book. You might be able to excel academically in your own studies, but these people will help you excel in living the American way; they will guide you in ways that you can apply for your own good.

Besides my own experience under the American family's care, I recently have learned that one Thai student has been accepted into a well-known private university in the Dallas area. He was so lucky to find a generous Thai restaurant owner who is my friend's good friend to help him in different areas while adjusting to the new environment and to his studies. This student had been in America for a month and has neither met any Thais nor made any friends. One day, he looked in the yellow pages and found out about this Thai restaurant and the directions to get there. The restaurant is about four miles from the university. He walked to the restaurant in the evening and knocked on the back door. When the owner opened the door, he introduced himself. He was a very polite and soft spoken young man who has a strong desire to finish his law degree. These days he is being well taken care of, provided good suggestions and advice, including receiving assistance in obtaining a driver's license, requesting a Social Security card, and buying a good used car. We always joke with him that he would also enjoy Thai food at every meal. Another example of good people skills is a Thai student by the name of "Chatchai" who was reaching for help and friendship He is being provided with such good care from an American family, who don't have any children. They even helped him to find a loan for his study. He is now pursuing his B.S. degree in nursing, and he has a strong desire to become a medical doctor in America. One day when we met he told me that, "Aunt Pat, my family back home would never be able to send me to school here. It cost a lot of money, and we don't have that money. Since my American family is helping me, I will study hard and do my best. I will make them proud of me." He is the most ambitious 21-year-old young man I have ever met, since I have been living here. He works hard to achieve his dreams, personally and academically.

Communication and presentation skills are definitely important. In one way, I was lucky in that my group always assigned me to present our projects. I appreciated that they gave me the opportunity to do public speaking. Presentation time is our show time. It is the showcase for our research and study. It is time to show off all the good things we know about our project. It is the time that we can use the ability to use technology and multimedia equipment in presenting our work and ideas, and make sure we know what we are talking about. In class, many of my classmates told me that my presentation was not only informative, but also entertaining. Completing each individual project in different classes provided me the opportunity to utilize my communication skills, both written and oral. After a project presentation, I was required to submit a report or a portfolio. I spent time writing a report and took my work to the writing center to get my work checked and corrected. I also spent time rehearsing my presentation. I practiced saying things right, especially some difficult terminologies that I had a hard time pronouncing. Sometimes, my close friend laughed and thought that I was too crazy about presenting my project. One lesson I presented related to cultural teaching; I presented a lesson on Japanese culture. I did show and tell time, providing some Japanese tea and snacks, and I put on a native dress, a kimono, while presenting my information to the class, and it drew the full attention of my classmates. It was a fun project that I spent a few months preparing. Everybody seemed to enjoy the presentation very much. I remember what my professor said in my initial class: "when you present your information, present it with confidence. To be confident, you must be fluent in the topic you choose to present. To have knowledge of the topic, you have to do a lot of research, study, and reading."

Organizational skills are a must to obtain. Imagine this: you are enrolled in four graduate courses, so your class runs from 7:00 p.m. to 10:00 p.m. Each class requires your study time and effort to complete the projects and pass the exams. All of the assignments must be submitted on time. You work in the lab all day at least 20 hours per week, before you go to class. You provide a private lesson all day on Friday, and work part time at the retail store that sometimes requires you to work 30 hours. You also have to take care of the rent house business and take care of the household for the host family during their absence. Your attendance in different areas has never been discussed. You still have a little bit of your time to socialize with close friends and take some trips to New York and Las Vegas. In the end, you never fail in all the tasks. I admit that I wouldn't have accomplished all of these without organizational skills. Some of my friends say my life during that time had always been on the clock. I accepted that it was really true. I managed everything by keeping a To-Do list to prioritize all tasks, and I reduced stress by walking a few miles every chance I got. I have learned that when you are able to organize, you will also be able to learn how to be flexible.

I personally believe that the secret of reaching any goal and becoming successful in any area is **determination.** It also allows you to determine where you want to be and which direction you want to take to reach the destination in your graduate school life. Even though you might not be the smartest student among your fellow grad students, with determination you will still be able to set goals and not allow anything to interfere with the goals you have set. Of course, there might be many obstacles, but with determination you will be able to stay focused and not allow yourself to be distracted. For me, I was determined to finish my Master's Degree before the age of thirty and look for a job. My practice through those two years was like the old saying, "when you start it, don't let go until you accomplish what you want." You can determine how long you want to take classes, and what classes you want to take this semester or later on. The difficulty of each class is unique, and it also could bring a lot of tension, frustration, and even depression. In addition to that, you might face many life obstacles, but stick with your studies. Don't give up. The basic foundation of determination is that when you want to accomplish something so badly in the timeframe that you have set, you will have to put your full effort into it and do whatever it takes to reach that goal; sitting around or just working on your projects whenever you are in the mood will delay your completion.

In graduate school, I was not the smartest student, but I was one of the hardest working ones who was determined to complete all of my graduate work in a timely manner. I also wanted to seek employment here after my graduation. When I found myself heading in the right direction, based upon the goals I had set for myself, I was able to take control of my studies. Besides actively focusing on all of the academic courses to pursue my graduate degree, I learned many significant things along my educational path. I still remember my godmother's encouraging words on my graduation day: "**Don't feel bad about the ups and downs in your life, while you were studying; recognize each challenge as an outside classroom teacher that is teaching you a valuable life lesson. Be proud that you have a chance to learn both academic classes and life lessons at the same time. A diploma in the life experiences that you learned, besides the academic diploma that you have also earned, will support you to do better in life. Your ability to combine them together will help you maximize their available benefits.**" Eight years has passed, but her teaching on that day is still around. These days, every time I look at the result of my own educational accomplishment in a nicely-crafted wooden frame displayed on the wall both at home and at work, I realize what I had put in to earn my diploma. Even though some might just refer to it as "**a piece of paper**," for me, **it is a paper of pride**, a paper that allows me to claim the excellence achieved in the academic arena that I had never dreamed of.. It is pride that provides me the opportunity to develop, manage, and utilize different skills to live and to work in this country. I still remember one guest's compliment when she came to visit me at home. After she took a look at all of the pictures in the frames around the house, she said, "I found the nicest frame on your wall. That is the frame for your diploma. I wish I could accomplish that for a frame." I smiled and replied without hesitation, "Yes, it has always been beautiful to me. It is a frame of pride." That was not my showing of the moment, but it was the moment that I recognized my own success. I normally don't talk about it a lot, but inside I am always proud and determined that I will carefully utilize what I have learned to pursue my dreams every day. Graduate school was my best start for a career and in achieving my dreams.

M.S. Graduate

Chapter 11: Dream Catcher

Many people are fortunate to have been granted a working visa prior to coming to work in America. There are many who were sponsored by American contracted companies, to work in different areas. Some people have come to America on different types of visas, but primarily they desire to seek employment. Many international students have the opportunity to work on campus while attending school. After graduation, many students gain experience working in America through curricular practice for one year. If they are lucky enough, they might be continuously sponsored by their employer, so that they may obtain an H1-B type visa to legally work here for another three to six years. Many skilled international professionals from all over the world are beneficiaries of the introduction of the H1-B visa by the American government, which enables immigrants the opportunity to legally live and work in America.

I consider myself one of many fortunate people who have had the opportunity to gain work experience while studying and to eventually obtain a full-time professional employment after graduation. I appreciate the privilege to legally work in the United States after obtaining permanent residency status through my blood ties as an immediate relative of a US citizen. In twelve years of living, studying, and working here, I definitely have gained valuable working life experience.

Initially, I was given a chance to work at House's Good House Keeping, Inc. It is an appliance store owned by my American family's best friend in Paris, Texas. I worked there while attending classes full time at Paris Junior College. I worked as an account receivable clerk earning $5 per hour. My work there required only a few hours a day after school to enter the customer's data on a computer, including the date when an item was bought, personal information data, and the payments customers made on the outstanding balance on the appliance bought from the store. There I gained many important work skills, such as the ability to use a computer, customer service skills, and organizational and detail-orientated skills. By entering the data, I learned that accuracy is really important; if I was careless, I could mess up the store's customer record, including his/her balance. I first made many mistakes spelling the customer's name, which left the business unable to identify many existing store customers. I am thankful for a salesperson in the store that patiently answered my questions about American names. I later learned to correct those mistakes by carefully paying attention to details instead of trying to get a job done quickly.

My second job started in March 1996. I got a part-time job as a cashier at Wal-Mart in Paris, Texas. Wal-Mart is considered the biggest and the most popular retail store in America. By working there, I am proud to say that this job was my first job for which I started paying the federal income tax on every little paycheck that I received bi-weekly. It was a job for which I started making a contribution into a Social Security fund, hoping that one day when I reach retirement age, I will securely receive that pension. My hope is not much different from that of many American workers. They all expect to gain the benefit from their last drop of sweat. I worked about 20 to 32 hours per week. I was a minimum-wage worker who then received about $5.15 an hour. There were not any full benefits provided for part-time employees; there was no paid vacation or medical insurance, but I did receive a 10% employee discount at any Wal-Mart store. This was my first official job in America while attending school full-time. My work hours were mostly from 6:00 p.m. to 11:00 p.m. on Friday evenings and 6:00 a.m. to 3:00 p.m. both on Saturday and Sunday. I used most of my one-hour lunch break to finish my homework or prepare for a test. As a cashier, I learned the responsibility of handling cash, working with other people, and most importantly, customer service skills.

When working with money, of course, accuracy is the primary goal. I paid attention to my starting amount on each shift. I counted back change every time customers paid by cash. I also learned how to carefully handle the customer that paid by credit card or check. The most important thing I tried to avoid was having an overage or a shortage of cash in my drawer. The last thing I wanted to receive from the cash office was a "Pink Slip."

I was neither hard to work with nor difficult to get along with. I treated people like I wanted to be treated. I helped other cashiers, when I was not busy on my line; I helped to zone merchandise when it looked unorganized; I filled in when other cashiers called in sick; I assisted in cleaning up when it was needed. Many times I had to stay late after the end of my shift due to the business being busy and because service help was needed. I volunteered to help at the other branch during the holiday season. Learning to do these things helped me to become a person who does not hesitate to take initiative in life.

The company's goal was to have the best customer service and satisfaction, and it was my goal as well. I learned the basic principle that if there are no customers, there won't be any business. Without the business, I would not have a part-time job. Without a job, I could not earn money and gain work experience. I recognized the customers by politely greeting them when they came into the store. I would say their last names when I received a check for their payment and also when I returned their credit cards. I concentrated on checking them out, instead of talking and visiting with the other cashiers at nearby cash registers. I tried to memorize the products' code, so that I could quickly check their items instead of having to call other staff to check for me and keep my customers waiting for a long time. I did not want to spend a lot of time looking up on the sheet provided in the back of the register. I offered to assist my customers carry out their bags, when I saw they had many items and obviously needed help. Through servicing my customers, I even made a friend. I observed one family that always came through my line and sometimes had to wait a while, due to my line being occupied. They always had a little girl with them. I later learned that she was their grandchild. The little girl initially shook my hand, and after a few weeks gave me a little hug, showed me her dolls or toys, asked me to look at her new dress, and just wanted to have a little chat with me. I guess I was her favorite cashier. One day while checking them out, I was invited to attend the little girl's birthday party. I could not go due to my school responsibility and a tight schedule. However, I gave her a cute doll I bought at Wal-Mart with my employee discount. While I was checking out my customers, I had a chance to meet a friendly Thai lady, who has been in America for almost 40 years. Her name is Mrs. Ubon Thurman. She later became a very good and close friend of my family. Even now she still visits and spends some weekends with us. I was allowed to call her "mom," and my children also call her "grandmother".

While working at Wal-Mart, I also learned punctuality and time management. It has been said that time itself cannot be managed, but we can learn to manage ourselves to utilize the time we have. If we choose carefully, we can manage the way we spend our time, in order to pay attention to the things that are most important to us. Time management requires self-discipline and the ability to make decisions and set priorities in our life. I usually reported to work at least 5 to 10 minutes before my shift began. I had to clock in on a time clock at work for actual work time and break time. For every two work hours, I got a 15 minute break. Fifteen minutes was not much; I tried to get my personal business done and clocked back in when break time was over. During lunch time I had a one-hour break. After my meal, I spent time reading my textbook or finishing my homework. Even though I was working, my priority was studying. I worked at three different part-time jobs and studied full-time, but I tried my best to keep my priorities straight and to stay focused. While on a job, I did my best on the duties I was assigned. I was never corrected by my supervisor for being tardy or absent.

I was twice chosen as cashier of the month and cashier of the quarter. My work skills, performance, and check out speed were considered for the award. When I went shopping while visiting my parents back home, I saw some cashiers working slowly on duty; some were talking excessively and sitting on a chair while servicing customers; I was annoyed. Working at Wal-Mart was not only a job from which I could learn the importance of good work skills, but also one that provided me the opportunity to communicate in English with people from diverse backgrounds. I always think that if I can speak English, at least a few sentences a day, it will help me improve my English skills.

In January 1998, I was employed by the Department of Education at Texas A &M University-Commerce as a department lab assistant, while in my second year of graduate school. Being service-minded helped me to successfully provide services to both staff and students who used the lab. This opportunity would never have happened without the help and encouragement of my professor, Dr. Sue Espinoza. She suggested to me that I should make an appointment with Dr. Abbey, who at that time was a lab director, to express my interest in applying for the open position. Fortunately, I was given the opportunity to earn more work experience in the educational setting environment. This opportunity impacted my career a great deal.

My primary responsibility was to assist with the duties in the instructional laboratories by preparing educational labs as needed, ensuring that faculty and students were able to perform assignments properly and safety; I also received directions from appropriate faculty members and the department administrator.

In the computer lab, I was required to work three days each week from 7:00 a.m. to 4:00 p.m. While working there, I attended all my graduate classes from 7:00 p.m. to 10:00 p.m. In the lab, I worked with a few international students from China, Pakistan and India. There were two lab assistants on one shift to provide help. All of us were working on our degree. I enjoyed working with them and learned the importance of diversity, since our cultures were different. We all had to work as a team for the same common goal, which was to provide the best service in the department computer lab. Since our working environment was diverse, I learned to respect others, be tolerant, and appreciate others who are different from me. It was a great challenge. Sharing is another thing I learned while working there. Basically, as lab assistants we had to share office and work space. I kept the office and lab clean and organized, so the others wouldn't have to worry about cleaning up the mess when they took over the shift. We also shared useful information and time. We shared the equipment and material to best serve our lab users. My good co-worker and I even shared lunch, when we were too busy and did not have time to go get one. I had fun working.

While working in the lab, I got a chance to work closely with one of my classmates from China. She was a great classmate and a wonderful co-worker who was hard working, kind, polite, and unselfish. We mostly had the same shift and helped each other in the lab and with personal matters. We covered the work shift for each other, when we had important personal business to take care of. When we were not busy, we took time to learn something new to improve our skill and knowledge. We spent time helping each other finish our class assignments. Sometimes, after work, I was invited to have supper at her apartment before we started our evening classes. She later became my closest friend, and she is the only friend I still keep in contact with after graduating from graduate school.

Gaining more work experience, learning more technical skills, finishing up all class work, and always making good grades, I became more confident in myself that I could help others to learn, and I was pretty clear on my career goal. I learned that I love to interact with people. I enjoyed helping people to learn and to get things done. I was delighted thinking about the positive outcome while preparing the lesson plans and handouts for class and for the lab. I began to think about providing private training in computer classes to different groups of people. Fortunately, I was provided three brand-new computers and work stations in one room at home for this challenge, after talking to my American family. I contacted the classified department of Paris News to inquire about what a weekly advertising fee would be on a small ad in their newspaper. In the mean time, I started creating the promotional materials for my training: flyers, brochures, business cards, and even a simple website. If my professor had known at that time, she would have been so delighted that I actually put the skills learned in her "Desktop Publishing" class to work. I planned to give training only on Thursday evening and all day on Friday due to the fact that I did not have to work at Wal-Mart or in the lab. During my private training, I learned the importance of many things. Through continued learning and practice, I obtained these skills: self-awareness, self-motivation, self-confidence, patience, courage, and knowledge.

Self-Awareness

Self-awareness involves discovering your strengths and weaknesses. I learned to be aware of who I really am and what I can do, what I am good at, and what I like and enjoy doing. I was happy in creating all of my materials to market my training. I was delighted when I got phone calls asking for information on my training. I was so proud of being able to use my specific skills I leaned in class and to be able to apply it to my work experience. Overall, I learned that I love to interact with people.

Self-Motivation

I did not wait on others to motivate me. I knew what I wanted to learn and was so determined to see a positive result from what I got started. At that time, my motivation was not money that I would get from the training, but the challenge of establishing my own small training sessions to gain professional work experience, the satisfaction from my ability to create something that I enjoyed doing, and an acceptance of my American family. Keeping those goals in mind got me going and moved me forward.

I updated my technical skills by reading books, learning from college friends and professors, and spending more time searching information on the internet. I also developed relationships with people around me that would be beneficial in learning. By being self-motivated, I had no fear of picking up a phone and calling prospective clients and explaining what I had to offer. It helped me to overcome a fear of communication in English. Self-motivation not only helped me to develop my dream that one day in the future I would become a professional trainer or educator, but it also gave me a dream of having the ability to establish my own small informative, friendly, and enjoyable learning and training center. Actually, when I started private training, I did not expect much of an outcome. I expected to gain more experience and knowledge than I had before, which was working to increase the sense of motivation to handle new challenges in life.

Self-Confidence

Only you can take initiative in developing self-confidence. I have a positive outlook as a good foundation within me. I believe that I have the ability to teach my students and offer something good for their learning. I can confidently answer their questions and behave positively to let my prospective student/client know that they will at least get the best training for their money. I once heard that, as a teacher, "Believing in yourself and believing in your students" is half of teaching success.

Patience

Never…never give up. No matter how many obstacles I faced, I patiently reached out for help when I needed it. I politely asked my American family's friends for their referral. A few weeks after I placed my advertisement in the newspaper, I received many phone calls inquiring about the training, but no one actually enrolled. I did not give up or become discouraged. I kept thinking that there would be someone who wanted to learn something new. There would be someone who would think that the training would be beneficial. I continued networking with people I knew; I told my classmates and professors what I was doing, and I asked them if they knew anybody who wanted a private lesson or training sessions for a reasonable cost. Soon, I received phone calls from clients wanting to enroll; they signed a simple contract for the sessions. The following is the advertisement I placed in the newspaper weekly:

> Texas A&M University-Commerce Graduate Student, majoring in Computer Learning Technology, would like to teach Introduction to Windows 95, MS Word for Windows, MS Publisher, MS PowerPoint, MS Excel, Creating web pages, and Introduction to the Internet in my home; Computers available for hands on experience. Call Pat at 785-1946 or cellular 737-7188.

I patiently trained my clients, who did not know anything about a computer. My clients' ranged in age from 8 years old to 76 years old; one client was an elementary school student whose mother also asked me to pick her up at the daycare to train and bring her home after the lesson. She was the youngest student I had. It was fun having her, because I had a chance to teach, baby-sit, and learn basic English from her at the same time. I could learn good things in English from American children, in terms of greeting and some useful vocabulary for daily situations. That year, she did not have to buy a birthday card, a Mother's or Father's Day card for anyone in her family, because she created cards especially for them by herself.

Another client was a seventy-six-year-old retired nurse who just had a love of learning new things in her free time; she also said, "I don't want to attend continuing education classes because I can not catch up with the rest of the class."; she wanted to learn to use the internet for her personal leisure. She wanted to scan pictures to send to her children, friends and grandkids; she was willing to spend extra time learning to create her very first basic web pages; she enthusiastically wanted to learn to create Christmas cards for her family and close friends with personalized labels and envelopes. She was the one who made me learn a sense of success as a teacher by her simple sweet words, "Hey, my little teacher what will you teach me today?", when I walked into her apartment or sometimes before her schedule. I sometimes got a call asking, "Can't you come a little bit early today, so we can eat sandwiches before starting the lesson." What a kind offer, "Of course, I will be there!" I replied.

She was a client who jotted down almost everything I taught her and reviewed it after I left her apartment, because she always had questions to ask me. I loved to see her try to learn something new on the sites she visited online. When I was teaching her, the Internet was new to her. She really spent time trying to understand its useful tools. She spent her time creating something nice to show me when we met the following week. She phoned or sent me e-mails when she had problems or questions. She also referred me to a few of her family members and friends. That meant I had new clients because of her. This self-motivation allowed me to take pride in my work and to build a good reputation of the work I did. I did not know that I would be able to use this quality a lot more in my current position; it is important to me not only to take pride in my own work, but also to motivate others to take pride in the things they do. I did not know that eight years later, I would have a number of students say to me, "Mrs. Sato, one interesting thing about you is that you have a lot of patience to deal with us. We thank you for patiently dealing with our foolishness."

Courage

I learned courage, or the willingness to take risks while striving for success, through the process of starting a private training. I certainly hoped for a positive response when I asked for help from my American family for the office space in their house and three brand new computers in the office. I knew it was a lot to ask. There was a possibility to get **"NO"** for an answer. I took a risk to ask, anyway. I took a chance on having to pay a weekly advertising fee for the advertisement I placed in the newspaper, and that no one would give me a call. However, I am a person who never thinks that I will get things exactly the way I want, so I was taking a risk, too. The worst thing that can happen is somebody saying "NO" to my request. It would not hurt to ask and accept the outcome.

Knowledge

I never think the knowledge and technical skills in class are enough to become successful in private training, without the knowledge of the clients. The more I know about them, the better services I can provide. Knowledge of what they want to learn is essential in providing the appropriate level of training or helping in creating a lesson plan and teaching material. One of my prospective clients called asking if I could help her set up a basic database record of her customers, using Microsoft Access. This database was a convenience for her position at work. She did not have the time needed to attend a continuing education class at a local college. She wanted to schedule a time that fit my schedule. She requested Friday evening for two hours every week. A few months later, I helped her to establish something that effectively helped her at work.

Another example was a lady working on her graduate school work, which required Microsoft Excel and PowerPoint in order to finish her class projects. Because she was working full time, she did not have much time to complete her work or to attend a formal class to learn the software program. She asked me to train her on a software program for a few hours at night, so she could use the skill gained to finish up her class work. Some projects really needed to meet a deadline; I had to do them for her. One time she had to use a statistics software program to complete her project, and she did not know the program. I did not know the program either. She bought the program for me to learn and teach her to do her class work. What could beat that deal? I could learn the program for my knowledge without having to pay for it, earn money from a training session, and gain experience while training my client. I did private training until I graduated from graduate school.

After my graduation from graduate school, I quit working at Wal-Mart, stopped assisting in the department computer lab, and canceled the private training. It was not because I did not enjoy doing those jobs any more; I wanted to devote my time to seeking a full-time professional employment or career. I believe that all new grads have this dream, a dream of getting out of the academic world and getting ready to go into the work world. My dream might be more challenging than others -- I am going to be one of the working women in America. I thought I was ready to apply the skills, knowledge and training that I had obtained. I graduated from Texas A&M University-Commerce with a Master's Degree in Learning Technology and Information Systems, in December 1998. It was an academic success for the average person that I am.

Chapter 12: Job Hunter

As part of my graduation present, my American family kindly gave me a round trip ticket to visit my family in Thailand. I was there for two months, and I came back to America in the middle of March 1999. I was quite fortunate that I did not have to worry about acquiring a working visa as many of my international student friends did, because I already held residency status. After coming back from visiting my home country, my employment journey began. I was actively seeking full-time employment in America. Getting a job in America sounds really good, but it was not as easy a task as it may sound.

For those of you who think about seeking a professional job here, please keep in mind that you need to initially obtain a proper working visa; this is the biggest problem for many people wishing to work in America. However, after graduating, international students are allowed to work on a curricular practice for one year. If you are lucky, there might be companies who will sponsor you to work for them for three years. After that, your visa can be renewed for another three years. Some companies sponsor you, but you pay your own expenses. Many companies take care of the process for you, which might include all of the fees associated with immigration. It depends on how bad they want your skills. I had a friend that had an American company sponsor him for permanent residency after working with the company with an H1-B visa for three years, and he continued working with the same company.

He has been there seven years. Some lucky international students were able to obtain residency status through their employment and were able to work and live in American legally. If you want to complete all of the paperwork by yourself, it is a long process, but it is a wonderful learning experience. You could gather information from a good source site http://www.uscis.gov/graphics/index.htm, and follow the step-by-step instructions. You can save thousands of dollars in immigration lawyers and legal fees.

For me, applying for a full-time job demanded a lot of time and effort. I think looking for a job is a full-time job in itself. After two years of educational and technical classes, I was now learning how to get a job and to keep a job. After two months, I learned that the following job seeking skills are important:

- Performing a self-assessment, by writing a résumé and the cover letter
- Searching for a job, by filling out and sending application forms
- Interviewing for jobs and accepting offer letters and considering employment benefits
- Performing the job

Self Assessment

For most people self-analysis might not be a difficult task. For me, it was not only difficult, but it was also hard to know where to start. I was encouraged by one of my good friends who told me that no one knows you better than yourself, in terms of your abilities, skills, interests, experiences and background. So, I started thinking about all the little things that I am good at and jotted them all down.

While doing a self-assessment, many questions can be asked, such as: What are your strengths and weaknesses? What have you gained from education, training, or previous employment? How much do you know about the companies with which you are seeking employment? What qualifications do you have that make you think that you will be a good asset for their firm? If you can not answer all of these questions by yourself, a good close friend or classmates can help. I even asked my professor what type of career I would be good at in her opinion. A few years working with and teaching me, my professors had learned a lot about my personality and ability. These people might observe skills that I did not think I had. I am currently in a career which she told me I would be good at. Ask them for their feedback and add to your list of good qualifications. Don't be shy to ask; sometimes a stupid question in our mind helps us learn a lot. You also have to do some research on the company or the organization through the websites, brochures, newsletters or any other type of literature available. The more you learn about yourself and the prospective company, the better you are prepared and the more confident you become with the next step of job seeking.

Writing a Résumé

After you know yourself, your skills, and your abilities, now it is time to put in a professional format to market yourself. Keep in mind, though, from the management standpoint, there are so many applicants seeking the same job you are trying to get. Marketing yourselves well is the way to win. This starts with filling out a job application and submitting a cover letter and a résumé. Preparing an impressive résumé helps the applicant to get in the door for the job interview. It has been said that a résumé is the greatest marketing tool; the first paragraph of a résumé should be able to close the sale and get a job in a few seconds after the employers read it, and the interview that follows only serves to support the employer's decision. Besides being a tool to market oneself, a résumé is also a short account of one's career and qualifications, a personal advertisement that shows job skills and their value, a showcase of one's professional goals.

Initially, I did not know much about how to create a professional résumé. I did not learn while in school and did not pay much attention until it was time to be serious. I had the time I needed to find good resources and information. I went to the public library to check out books and search the internet for informative sites. Following the provided formats, guidelines, and suggestions, I started to write..... rewrite....rewrite...and rewrite my résumé until I thought it was good enough to send out to apply for a job. I let my friends who had gotten a job check it for me. They helped me make some changes where they were needed. Many companies requested a cover letter to accompany the résumé; I learned to create one, too. A cover letter allowed me to briefly state a detail of the specific job for which I was applying. It also gave me the opportunity to let my prospective employer know about me, including my personality, interests, qualifications, skills, and specific interest in the company to which I was applying. About the company information, I spent time doing enough research to know the mission, interests, services, and goals of that company. I made sure to write the letter to reflect that knowledge.

I sent out many résumés each day via post mail, fax, and e-mail all over the Dallas/Forth Worth area in Texas. I received many phone interviews in response to my résumé, but there was not yet a chance for the first in-person interview. Was I giving up? I sometimes wanted to, but I just could not afford to do so. I was hoping that there would be a company that would give me a chance to present what I had to offer. I remember many times being frustrated while I was conferring with my godmother about having no positive result on getting a job interview for almost two months. All of her kind and encouraging words are still not forgotten and they added to my personal experience.

There are so many helpful books and informative websites about job hunting. A book on creating an impressive résumé for a computer and technology field that I found helpful is *Winning Résumés for Computer Personnel*, by Anne Hart, M.A. She has more than fifty effective sample résumés presented in her book. It is also a book I am currently using as a guide in helping my students to create one. Creating a résumé can easily happen by writing everything on paper and then typing it, using any word processing software programs. I personally prefer Microsoft Word. It even has some templates available to help create a quick résumé. When starting to create one, I paid attention to the following important basic elements.

- Identification Information
- Career Objective
- Summary Of Qualifications
- Education
- Work Experience
- Special Skills, Computer Skills and Training
- Reference

Identification Information

This is the first part of my résumé; it consists of my name, address, telephone number or cell phone number, fax number, and e-mail address. I ensure that the e-mail address is appropriate and professional by not using a nickname or a funny phrase. If you have your own website, you can also include the URL under the e-mail address.

Career Objective

It is the focus point of my résumé. It describes the position I want and then is supported by the body of the résumé. It is also a reference point for choosing the most important thing to say about oneself for the goal of seeking that position. Actually, it can be as short as the name of the position.

Summary of Qualifications

This section immediately follows my career objective. It is used for people that have a lot of experience and long résumés, but I tried to summarize all my experience. I just want the reader to get the essential points I am presenting. It is also a brief overview of the qualifications related to a career field in which I am seeking employment. This section can be a paragraph summary, summary statement, or a list of outstanding points. The words used should be good action words.

Education

I list all schools attended and training I received. It consists of name of schools, location, degree earned, years of attendance, major, and possibly G.P.A.

Work Experience

It can include part time, full time, or field experience that starts with the most recent and works backwards; list the names of employers, their locations, and your job titles. I also briefly list duties and responsibilities that I did while performing a job. I make sure to use action words.

Special Skills, Computer Skills and Training

This section includes seminars, certifications and licenses, professional training, and any software programs or equipment that I can operate.

Reference

I did not include references directly on my résumé; instead, I created a separate reference sheet with at least three professional people that know me. I certainly call them to ask permission to use them as my reference. One of the references I used was my educational program advisor. I am now asked if I can be used as a reference. It is a nice feeling to be asked this question in America by my own students, and it is quite a learning experience to know what type of questions are being asked by prospective employers when my students seek employment.

Job Searching

During my job search, I learned that I need to contact as many prospective employers as possible; the more job applications I completed the better chance I will have to find the right job. For the part-time job I had previously, I got help from my American family by referring me to the employer, and a friend helped to refer me to another person at Wal-Mart. While looking for a full-time job after graduation, I used many methods, including asking friends or previous classmates to tell me about open positions in their organizations, applying in person, calling on the phone, sending out an e-mail, and writing a letter. The method depends upon the type of job, situation, qualifications, and experience required. I was advised that whatever job I seek, I need to market myself properly and appropriately. I sought employment using the following methods:

- Networking – I asked my friends, classmates, instructors, and professors if they knew individuals or companies that were hiring or looking for someone with my teaching and training experience and qualifications.
- Apply in person – When I learned the company had open positions, I went to apply for the position that

I thought I was qualified to do. Sometimes, I just drive around to look for "**Now Hiring**" signs, or I go into organizations like schools, churches, or other professional organizations to see if they are hiring.

- Visit a local Texas Workforce agency to see available job listings.
- Visit a state employment or job services center.
- Apply for a job through recruiting agencies.
- Newspaper – I looked in a local newspaper, which included a "Job Opportunities" or "Help Wanted" section, especially in the Sunday issue. There are more jobs listed on Sunday than on a regular day. Luckily, my American family subscribed to a daily newspaper; I did not have to buy one. Everybody in the house knew the classified section was my favorite section in the paper. When I found positions that I thought I was qualified to do, I used a marker to circle the advertisement and got ready to send my résumé.
- Web sites – This method was one to which I really devoted my time. I created a personal employment account on different sites to post my résumé. I kept checking my account daily to see if there were any possibilities. If there was someone keeping track of my hits, he would have been annoyed by my logging in the account. The sites I frequently visited are Monster.com, American Job Bank.com, Texas Job.com, Computer Job.com, Career Builder.com, and any sites that provided job opportunity links.

Sending and Filling Application Forms

I don't think this process is much different between America and my home country. In America, I have learned that if people start looking for employment, the first contact they have with the prospective employers is when they file a job application with the firms. Filling out a job application can be very time-consuming. The application will be the first document the employer will see about the applicant. If you happen to look for employment here, keep in mind that a good overall impression can be created by a clean looking appearance. It is a means of presenting a positive and interesting image. If your application has a lot of errors, mistakes and corrections, that is another image of you for them to judge as well, so take time to fill out a job application. The impression you create here might lead you to a job interview.

While I was seeking a job, I had to fill out many applications, both on paper and online, sometimes taking as long as 45 minutes to complete. Some companies want job seekers to only submit the résumé and application online. It seems to me that these days, it is the first thing many companies want to be completed. If you fill out an online application like I did, you should spare the time to complete a form in one stroke if you can, because all information can be deleted if you delay for a long period of time. I made sure all sections were completed before I clicked the **"Submit"** button. Some companies allowed me to go back and correct or edit, but for many I had only one chance to be considered. Keep in mind, there are so many applicants for one job, the company has many choices to select from and they can't interview all applicants. Most of the applicants get eliminated in the initial screening. The companies generally keep applicants who most meet their criteria. Every time I filled out an application, I made sure I had a résumé with me, a driver's license, a Social Security card, and a green card – in case I would be asked for my alien number. Normally, in America, a driver's license is used as an identification card. Presenting an application form effectively is crucial, and you need to prepare for it well. I never feel that it is easy to sit down in the Human Resources office to do justice to myself at any given time. I have sometimes made a copy of the original one and filled it out, then rewrote in the actual one to prevent mistakes. I learned to treat the process of job seeking with great care. They will see my application, before they will allow me to see them. There are many questions asked about me and I have to complete many of them just to get one interview. The questions generally are divided into sections: personal data, education, work experience, job choices, position statement, and additional information. This is why I think having a résumé with me is essential.

Job Interview

The phone call for a job interview was the most wonderful call ever. I did not take my job interview period lightly. They were the most anxious and exciting days during the job seeking period. It is a day I had the opportunity to present and market myself in person with prospective employers, a day that I had a chance to create the first impression that leads to the next step in the employment process. I am not ashamed about the valuable job interview experience gained during my first full-time employment search. I failed completely. Did I do my homework? Yes, I absolutely did. Obviously, it was not good enough.

It was a job interview for a computer software training position for a Credit Union. It was a newly established position for this organization. They had just opened a new in-house training center that specialized in filling the needs of the organization. The job description sounded really interesting. I was so confident that I was qualified for the position. I thought I would nail it. After I got a phone call confirming the date, time and location for the interview, I went to survey that area one day before the actual interview date. The main purpose was not to be late trying to find the location.

I practiced my interview questions and answers in front of a mirror a few times. My American family laughed when they saw me talking to myself. I did some research about the Credit Union. I selected my appropriate job interview outfit. I even remember neither wearing a lot of accessories nor strong perfume. All was set, I thought.

I arrived at a lobby and found that it was so beautiful, clean, and organized inside the building. The atmosphere was so professional. The workers dressed nicely and looked so professional. I showed up with a lot of anxiety, but I tried to calm myself down inside. I was asked by a well-dressed lady to fill out a job application in the lobby. It was multiple pages in a folder with many promotional materials and information about the position benefits. There was a lot of information I had to fill out. I got my résumé and my I.D. out while I began to fill out the application. I made a mistake on the form. I asked the lady if I could have white out. She was kind enough to hand me one. I continued filling out the application more carefully. Well, I didn't ask for a new package.

After I submitted the completed application, I was escorted to the second floor of the building. It was the Vice President's office. It looked neat and beautiful. There was a Human Resources Manager in there, too. The interview started right after they introduced themselves. It continued in a friendly and professional manner. I answered all questions to the best of my knowledge and also thought that I kept my professionalism. It lasted almost 40 minutes. I walked downstairs and got out of the building with the hope for a positive result.

I got to my car, where my friend was waiting to hear the result of my first job interview. I was asked, while removing my beautiful jacket, "Pat, look up! Let me see your face." I smiled and said enthusiastically, "I'm definitely fine. Don't worry, the interview was nice. I have a good feeling about it. If you think my face is red, I might be just too excited about it."

"Let me see, do you have one noodle on your face?" We had gone to eat before the interview.

"What?" I could not smile anymore.

"Look at your face in the mirror." My friend offered.

I looked, and guess what I found in the mirror. I saw my well–made-up face with a long thin white line on my lower chin. It was obvious that it was not a birthmark. I then realized that it was a line caused by the correction fluid I used to correct a mistake while hurriedly filling out my job application. That meant I had this white line on my face through the professional interview. I wanted to scream out loud at the top of my lungs. I thought those interviewers might want to laugh so hard seeing me confidently answering their questions throughout a 40 minute interview with a white line on my face.

The day after my interview, I sent a short Thank You letter to the interviewer, even though I knew that the memory about it might not be too good. Sending out this letter was an opportunity to mention any experience or skills that were not discussed in my interview, in addition to thanking the interviewers for taking their time to interview me and for letting me learn about their organization.

The following week, I got a letter from the Credit Union saying that they thanked me for interest in working for their firm, but my qualifications did not fit their needs at this time. Was I sad for losing a chance? I would say not really, but I kept blaming myself for that carelessness. However, I learned from that job interview failure. I planned to be more careful on everything and to take care of my personal grooming beforehand.

My Useful Note: The mistake should not happen. There should not be correction fluid on a job application. It should look neat and clean.

I actively continued sending out résumés to apply for jobs and received some phone interviews. In late April, I found a job opportunity advertised in the Dallas Morning News, ***"Vinnell Corporation is looking for a Desktop Publishing Instructor."*** I faxed my cover letter and résumé right away. A few days later, I got a phone call from the Human Resources Specialist asking if I wanted to come in for an in-person interview. Of course, I accepted the appointment without hesitation. I found out about the location and directions. Then, I got myself ready again for my second full-time employment interview.

I got to the office a little bit early and was asked to fill out a job application right on the spot. It took me almost thirty minutes to complete the form, but this time there was no mistake to be corrected. I was told to wait for the interview after I submitted it. For this job interview, I carried with me a portfolio of my desktop publishing work that I created in college and created during my private training. It was an exciting waiting for the interview.

I was interviewed by the vocational manager. It was a really nice and friendly interview. I was calm and comfortable while being interviewed. I also had the opportunity to present my portfolio during the interview. He informed me about the company and the services they provide. He offered to allow me to visit the classroom and meet the students. I followed him to the classroom and found students who were physically bigger than I am. The interview lasted about 40 minutes and left me with a positive feeling. A few days later, I got a phone call from the Human Resources Manager of Vinnell Corporation, who offered me a full-time teaching/training position in the vocations department at The North Texas Job Corps Center in McKinney, Texas. She told me about the position's compensation and benefits as well as informed me of the required background check and medical examination. I was so excited about the phone call; I accepted the job without hesitation and planned to start soon after the acceptable result of a medical examination. It was like a dream-come-true to find a job after many hard tries.

Medical Examination: It was the first requirement by the company for me to have the pre-medical examination. My employment would be based on the result of the exam. I kept in mind that an offer of employment is subject to a clean health result. Good health shows the importance of safety on a job. The examination was performed by a doctor nominated by the company. I got a phone call asking to report to work a few days after my medical examination. I assumed that the result was acceptable.

Throughout my job-seeking experience, I have learned many things through researching, reading, and practicing. The interesting thing is that, in my current position, I am able to use what I learned to teach and help students. I am currently discussing the following tips daily with the students in my training area. Some useful tips were gained from my reading from different resources. They can be summarized as follows:

Useful Interview Tips

- Bring only essential items to the interview: extra résumé, references, portfolio, licenses/certifications, and date book.

- Arrive 15 minutes early so you can relax and review what you would like to say. Don't just be on time, be early.

- Be pleasant and friendly and businesslike to everyone you meet.

- Shake hands firmly. Be yourself and use natural gestures and movements, stress qualifications without exaggeration. Emphasize experience and training related to the job opening.

- If you know about the company's products and services, you should refer to them as you answer the questions. It is impressive if you have positive knowledge about the company.

- After being asked a question, it is okay to pause and think about your answer. Answer questions with more than a "yes" or "no." On the other hand, do not ramble. A successful interview occurs if the interviewer talks 50% of the time.

- Speak positively about past employment and avoid discussing personal, domestic, or financial problems.

- Know your salary range from research. When asked, "What are your ideas on salary?" answer with a question of the interviewer. "What do you pay people with my skills and experience?"

- Ask probing questions about the company plans and the nature of the job. These questions will indicate interest and motivation.
- Be prepared for "When can you start" questions. Or if they ask, "Can you start tomorrow?" Be sure to make a wise decision; most interviewers will allow you sufficient time to make this decision. Remember, many of you will already be employed and will want to respectfully give the current employer two weeks notice.
- Thank the interviewer even if they indicate that you are not right for the job. Ask about any additional positions they feel you might be right for.
- Send a brief Thank You letter after the interview process.

Sell Yourself in Print - Portfolio is important: It is a Show & Tell Time

For my job interview, I prepared my portfolio, which is in a good size binder that contains a collection of my work, design projects, and lesson plans. I present my portfolio during the interview. A point I like to stress to the interviewer is that I know that I can do it; here is the evidence of my experience. However, I keep in mind that there's a right time and a wrong time to present my portfolio or its contents to an interviewer.

I don't hand over my portfolio at the beginning of the interview, because I have learned that the employer may be tempted to look through it while talking to me and may not give me his or her full attention. The interviewer may also listen to me while I am talking, but not see the great examples of work I have included. On the other hand, I don't save my portfolio until the end of the interview. The interviewer may have a very limited amount of time to spend with me as a candidate, so he or she may not have time to skim through my portfolio. Also, I do not put the original document into the portfolio; I make sure I have my files saved on my computer or other storage devices. Sometimes, the interviewer may ask to take the portfolio with them. I am prepared to make copies of everything that I include and be willing to leave this copy of my portfolio upon request.

The way I present my portfolio

When the interviewer asks me a question, I take a moment to think about my answer and to pinpoint it to what I think is specially related. I show something that I include in my portfolio. Also, after answering the question, I then say, "I have an example of this in my portfolio." While presenting the portfolio, I ensure that I open it and find the document as quickly and as smoothly as possible.

For instance, when I introduce the document to the interviewer on the question related to the lesson plan preparation for class, I say something like, "During my student internship at Texas A&M University -Commerce and when I conducted private training, I designed a user-friendly and easy step-by-step PowerPoint, as well as a "How to Create your first Business Card" handout for my students. I have the process of my lesson plan that I believe demonstrates the skills we have been talking about." I show my lesson plan and stay quiet. Wait for the interviewer to look up (this is a signal that the interviewer has finished examining the document) or until the interviewer asks a question about my work or asks me another question.

At the end of the interview, when the employer asks "Is there anything else you want to share with us?" I joyfully show a project that I feel especially proud of from the portfolio. Or, sometimes I ask the interviewer, "Can I share with you any other items from my portfolio?" I ensure that I prepare the most impressive portfolio possible.

I learned qualities that American Employers seek in their employees

- Communication skills (verbal and written)
- Honesty/integrity
- Teamwork skills (works well with others)
- Interpersonal skills (relates well to others)
- Motivation/initiative
- Strong work ethic
- Analytical skills
- Flexibility/adaptability
- Computer skills
- Organizational skills

I learned about applicants whom American employers do not want to hire

- Poor personal appearance and/or hygiene
- Overbearing, "know it all," or high pressure types
- Inability to express one's self clearly
- Lack of planning for career: no purpose or goals
- Lack of interest and enthusiasm: just shopping around
- Lack of confidence and poise
- Overemphasis on money: interested only in salary
- Poor grades :just got by
- Makes excuses
- Speaks badly of past employers
- Fails to look interviewer in the eye
- Limp handshake
- No interest in company
- Late to interview without good reason
- Failure to express appreciation for interviewer's time
- Asks no questions about the job

- Unwilling to begin at the bottom
- No definite response to questions
- Wants job only for short time
- Lack of courtesy; ill-mannered

During the job searching period, I was not easy on myself. I set a schedule as if I was on an actual job. I got up early to finish my personal business, sat in front of a computer, looked through the newspaper, and searched websites. When I saw the open positions, I sent my résumé to apply. I took a lunch break and started searching again. I took a long walk in the evening to exercise and release tension. That was my routine for two months. I finally got a job. Thank Goodness!!!!! It is a job in a field I would like to do, **teaching and training**. It did not come easily. It is the result of hard work and a great deal of determination. My American family once said, "If you want to make good money, you should not get into this line of work." I took the job opportunity as a challenge with pride in mind, "*What would it be like teaching in America, having Americans students, using language that is not even mine?*" Then, I did not know that after seven years, it would still be a fun, challenging, and rewarding professional working experience.

Finishing the interview and accepting a job offer, I am proud of my achievement in searching for employment. It might not be a big deal for many people, but it is a fantastic and unforgettable life experience for an average person from Thailand like me. I tried to the best of my ability throughout the whole process. These days, in my current position, I have a chance to tell my students that, "If I can become successful in America, you can do much better. You can speak your language well, and you know your country better than I do." After a job hunting period, the next thing I do after getting a job is to learn how to keep the job. I plan to perform my job to the best of my ability. I am teaching a vocational trade for the Job Corps program, a company contracted by the U.S. Department of Labor. I teach Desktop Publishing. It is one of many available technical education classes on campus. Career technical education is the field in which I am certified to teach by the state of Texas.

Recently, I have decided to take on another challenge in the whole job searching process. Updating my résumé is not quite as difficult as writing the first one. This time, I have more than eight years of teaching experience to offer, and I am ready to take the opportunity to learn something new. In the initial process on this challenge, I have to write a written response to some questions along with my application. This process also gives me the opportunity to learn that looking for employment has always been a big and challenging task. It is quite an experience to learn that some companies asked for five references along with the application; I have to ask my references before I have any idea whether or not I will get the interview. In terms of the written response, I never know if my answer will fit in with what they are looking for. I just want to share it with you, in case you can get something from my learning. The questions and my answers are as follows:

1. *Our teachers may be asked to assist with compensation with curriculum development during the spring semester either in the evenings or on Saturdays, and during the summer. What level of commitment can you make to participate?*

   I am committed to assist on the level of "whatever it takes" to get the job done. My experience in graduate course work, instructional design, and current suggestions and participation in revising training record in the desktop publishing field, should be beneficial to the students.

2. *The Academy's summer camp is tentatively scheduled for June 5-30. What level of commitment can you make to participate?*

259

I will be happy to give 100% to engage in the activities and assist in the program. My experience as a president of the Business Major Student Association, while studying in Business School in Thailand, and the International Student Association, while studying at Texas A&M University - Commerce, have provided me the opportunity to gain a knowledge of organizing and participating in activities in both an academic setting and outside of the classroom.

3. How do you define academic rigor?

The academic setting that consists of:

- A well developed curriculum on offering subjects
- A group of professional and knowledgeable educators and staff.
- A positive campus culture and healthy relationship between teachers and students.
- Challenging, advanced, and creative projects or assignments to enhance and motivate learning.
- Incentive and positive reinforcement to support students to maximize their potential.
- Life skill and employability skills program to prepare students to excel in their interested learning field or careers of their choices.
- Belief in the foundation of "Personal skill + Technical skill + Academic skill = Success."

4. Explain the phrase, "all students can learn."

Every student has the ability to learn, but each of them has different learning styles; each student will have an interest in at least one thing. It is a teacher's responsibility to find out what it is and use that knowledge as a foundation in assisting the student to relate to learning the subject area. Looking for that interest by establishing a healthy professional relationship between teacher and student will be the best way to help that student learn. It is also a teacher's job to develop the plan to fit and support her student's learning style.

I remember one female student who progressed very slowly in class. When she was assigned class projects, after a few times of instructions, she hardly completed them. When I asked if she needed help, her response would be, "This class is too difficult. I can't understand the program, and I can't work on the computer to finish the work." One thing I observed everyday when she came to my class was that her hair was always well done and looked so pretty. After I asked her about her hair one day, it was quite surprising when she told me that she worked on it by herself. I started complimenting different hair styles that I saw, and she started working on a PageMaker program, based on the way she got her hair done each day. She was so happy and became more cooperative in class. She completed my training using the principles from her own interest in hair styling.

1. *What have you done for your own professional growth? Why did you choose what you did?*

Attend conferences and seminars that relate to my teaching field. This way provides me the opportunity to gain and obtain knowledge that can benefit both my students and me. It gives me a chance to meet a new group of professionals in the industry, to listen to their experiences, ideas, and suggestions on new tricks and tips as well as new versions of software programs that I use in teaching. It also gives me a chance to participate in the discussion on similar problems in the field and get help to seek solutions. For instance, I attended the seminar "Hats Off to Teachers", hosted by TEA, in 2001. I frequently attend the Conference of Desktop Publisher, conducted by CompuMaster, a Division of the Graceland College Center for Professional Development and Lifelong Learning. I participated in "Effective Publication Design," conducted by SkillPath Seminar. Annually I received approval from my supervisor to attend the Adobe PhotoShop Conference, conducted by the Rockhurst University Continuing Education Center. I once got the opportunity to attend the Motivational Seminar in March 2005, to listen to many great national and motivational speakers, such as Zig Ziglar, Rudolph Giuliani, George Foreman, and Pete Lowe.

Regularly attend available "in-service" training provided by the Human Resource Department.

This allows me to gain the specific knowledge that is needed to effectively perform a job in my current position. I also found it beneficial for personal and professional growth. For example, I attended the training on *"Effective Classroom Behavior Management Training,"* facilitated by Dr. David Hurr, who is an experienced classroom teacher and administrator; *Adolescent Growth & Development,* facilitated by Dr. Kevin Steed. Some department managers also provide their training on different topics, such as diversity, communication, team building, and setting appropriate boundaries. This training also gives me ways to work with my students more effectively.

Read books/articles and search for useful resources online.

This allows me to learn from others' experience and ideas, to obtain knowledge for personal growth. However, I like the way the author Les Giblin, stated in his book, *Effective People Skill* that "knowledge itself is no value, unless or until we learn to put it to work." I like the information that I learned from Mr. Henry K. Wong, in his book *The First Days of School: How to Be an Effective Teacher.* He talked about many useful methods for classroom management and effective teaching styles, the three characteristics of an effective teacher, the four stages of teaching, etc. I have experienced fantasy, survival, mastery, and impact stages, in my teaching career. In my current position, I have passed each stage with pride. Reading many interesting articles on the Teacher-to-Teacher website gives me a chance to know about other teachers' experiences, and to get tips and techniques on classroom activities and discipline.

Accept challenging projects.

This allows me to not only put different skills to work, but also learn from my "on the job" mistakes, take the heat, learn to leave the mistakes behind, and move on. I use my knowledge and skill not only to educate my students, but also to provide technical training to the center staff on different business software programs, such as Microsoft PowerPoint, Publisher, and Excel. I was assigned to design all art work, forms, and publications used on campus. I established the center newsletter. I certainly make a lot of people happy by using my design and computer skills, to create artwork or desktop publishing projects, to enhance the performance in their positions.

Write Journals.

This helps me to use my free time to concentrate on improving my English competency, and to take time to review the experience in different area; doing so has allowed me the opportunity to set goals, work toward goals, improve weaknesses, and celebrate accomplishments. I spend time writing a personal experience book in three different areas: living, studying, and working in America. I intend to publish my writing for others to learn from it. I certainly believe that every day is a great day to learn new things, and my desire to learning is never-ending.

6. Describe any industry experiences you may have:

- Career Technical Education Instructor - Desktop Publishing and Graphic Design.
- National Job Corps's curriculum implementation team member to develop visual communication training
- Job development/placement, advance training, military, and college enrollment.
- Extended Learning Experience Trip Organizer.
- Desktop Publishing Freelancing – designed presentations, newsletter, and promotional materials.
- Graduate Assistant in Education Department – Texas A&M University-Commerce.
- Student Teaching with professor in graduate school.
- Private training in basic computer class.

7. *Describe ways you could bring your experiences into a teaching environment.*

- Develop lesson plans and training achievement records.
- Create positive learning environment to enhance and motivate learning.
- Network with industries to establish the internship programs to assist students to gain real world working experience.
- Establish a healthy working relationship with the other staff and departments in assisting students with job placement, including military recruiters.
- Introduce "Get to Know You" program in business cluster.
- Establish the "Creative Contest" to motivate students to take pride in their work.

- Introduce "Recognition" program to give out incentives for students who do and behave well in training.
- Utilize skills learned to effectively perform job.

8. *Describe techniques for problem solving that you have used in your work experience.*

For Example: Discipline negative problems in class: sleeping, talking excessively, profanity, tardiness, fighting, disrespect, failing to follow a dress code, or instructions, etc. The fairest thing I do is to let them know the expectations up front. I believe in a fair and firm approach when approaching students on these kinds of behavior. I stay calm and guide them with a firm tone of voice. I initially give a verbal warning and one-on-one counseling. If the behavior continues, I would discuss with the student's counselor or set up a meeting with the student to address the issues.

One recent incident occurred when one female student became very angry with her classmate, screaming, yelling and acting very disrespectfully toward me when I tried to stop her. She responded to my instructions negatively, with a high angry tone of voice. I kept calm and let her finish without responding. The next day with her counselor, she mentioned that she expected me to argue back with her or yell back at her. She remarked that my calmness and positive poise surprised her. "You didn't even seem angry at me," she said in our meeting. My response to her was, "I am here to work with you, not to be angry with you."

9. *Describe any experiences you have had as a mentor either at a school or in the workplace.*

I was a few times assigned as a mentor for new students enrolled in the program. As a new member in a new environment, I acknowledged that new students have difficulty. I welcomed my students by scheduling to meet with them after school in the campus cafeteria; I introduced myself, asked about their initial experience, offered any additional help that they needed to make their stay and learning experience on campus more pleasant. Then, I showed them around the different training areas, so that they could receive more information on their training choices. Once they choose their field of training, I keep close contact with them and monitor their progress. I meet with them on a regular basis to see if there is any area they need extra help with or if they have any problems. This mentor program allows me to utilize different skills, such as communication, interpersonal skills, team work, and problem solving skills.

I also provided help to new teachers when the help was asked for. When asked, I shared with them some classroom techniques that I have found effective. I worked with them on scheduling field trips, and I initially help them with reports. While working with them, I always keep in mind that I wouldn't suggest anything that is not being asked for. They have full control over their on-the-job learning, as I too learned in my first year. Working and having good relationships with them helps me to learn and grow in my teaching career. **The teaching field is definitely still my career of choice.**

Chapter 13: Bread and Butter

"See it and be it" seems to be an important thing you can do when you seek employment. It is good to know what you are worth — your preferred salary as well as the benefits that are offered, for the job that you will perform. Many people may think that they will never be paid what they are worth. That might be why some Americans do not like to be asked about their salary. Asking how much you make seems to be a rude question in America, while in my country this question is not a big deal. Currently, in my position, I jokingly respond to my students when they ask about my salary that it is "not enough to deal with you guys." Most of the time, it brings the laughter to the whole class.

I started working for Vinnell Corporation at the North Texas Job Corps Center in McKinney, Texas, on May 10, 1999. This corporation was contracted by the Department of Labor to operate this center. It takes me about 45 minutes to get from home to the center. I never felt happier and more excited than when I got up early, got dressed, and prepared myself for my first day of a full-time job in America. Everything I have tried, learned, and accomplished in my search for a job had paid off. I was ready to go to work. "Today, I am a vocational instructor. I am going to teach American students and will be in charge of a vocational area of Desktop Publishing," I told myself while driving to work. At this point, I am satisfied with my third step toward an average person's success: good education, good home, and good job. I am thankful for what I have, especially since none of these things came easily.

I reported to the Human Resources office after I got there. The Human Resources specialist presented me with a folder containing a big stack of paperwork. She also clearly explained everything, including the position as per the job offer, the position salary and benefits, work hours, company pension plan, health insurance, annual vacation, paid expenses, personal & special leave, and education and training. She also made sure I was eligible to work, by making a copy of my alien resident card. She also had me sign to acknowledge the job description and took me to get my identification card made. The morning time of my first day in my full time job was devoted to paper work. I learned many things on my first day.

Job Offer Letter: It is a letter printed on company letterhead stating that the company is pleased to offer me employment as a Desktop Publishing Instructor at the North Texas Job Corps Center. The letter also confirmed the details of my employment, particularly that the offer of employment is contingent upon my ability to successfully pass a pre-employment drug screen and background check. The instructor position is a full-time exempt position for which I will be compensated annually and to be paid bi-weekly. The company provides medical, dental, and vision benefit insurance; life, accidental death and dismemberment, and short-term disability coverage to all eligible employees. Insurance for my dependents is also available, but does require an employee contribution. Insurance benefits will become effective the first day of my employment. A 401(k) retirement savings plan is available to all employees with immediate eligibility. The company is now matching twenty percent of the employee's 401(k) contribution up to 5%.

Salary & Benefits: I learned that "exempt employee" means the one paid by salary. My salary was stated in my offer letter. It will be directly deposited in my bank account, the information for which I provide to the finance department. I will be paid on 26 pay periods per year. Each pay period, I will receive an itemized pay statement detailing all deductions.

Work Hours: I am required to work 40 hours per week. I work from 7:30 a.m. to 4:30 p.m. I have read that working hours in America depend on employers, positions, or type of industry. Most Americans work many hours per week. Some also work 12 to 14 hours per day. Employees in most businesses work around 40 hours a week, which is considered a standard working week in America. American companies are often strict about permitting time off during working hours; some do not even allow paid time off to visit a doctor or dentist. Employees must deduct that time from their sick leave entitlement and vacation time.

Company pension plan: The Company I work for provides a 401(k) company pension plan, to which I must contribute. I will become eligible after 90 days of employment. The contribution will be deducted from my gross salary every paid period. Within seven years of my employment, I will contribute 10% of my salary to the plan. I am hoping that by my retirement age, I will have a good pension on which to live.

Health Insurance: Health insurance is one of the benefits included in the offer. I was given a package from which to choose a group insurance in which to enroll. Each group lists the premium I have to pay. Health insurance is important in America, and it is not free.

Vacation and Sick Leave: It is another benefit on my job offer letter. As a new employee in an American company, I received only 12 paid days a year. My annual vacation will accumulate each month. When I want to take a vacation, it must be approved by my supervisor. It should be about two weeks ahead of time. I must keep in mind that not every request will be approved. It depends on department coverage. Sick leave must be approved by my supervisor two hours before a work hour. The doctor appointment should be a week before the appointment date.

Personal & Special Leave: Company provides paid personal time off for military leave, leave to attend the funeral of a family member, or for jury duty. However, it depends on the status and position on paid time off.

Paid Expenses: This company provides travel expenses, especially when traveling for a company's business. All costs will be paid from home to the place of work. The company also provides a mileage allowance, if I am authorized to use my car for company business. I also can get a lunch allowance.

Education & Training: This company provides a tuition reimbursement benefit. If I am interested in attending classes or training that is related to my job and it will benefit the company and the students, the company will pay for the costs. I must submit all necessary documents for approval prior to registering for classes.

I was really lucky that when I first started teaching, I was able to attend so many seminars and conferences. All my expenses were paid for, and I learned a lot of new skills that I did not have when I was in school. Later, when I was working on my teaching certification, all my tuition and conferences were also paid for by the company.

Throughout my job search, I also learned that the benefit package is as important as the position salary. I have acknowledged that it is imperative to study and do some research about the benefits related to the position for which one is applying, at least get a general idea. There are many available resources: the internet, good friends, books, or the states agency's handbook. It is essential to think about all benefits while making the decision whether or not to accept a job offer.

After I reported to work, during the first week of my employment, I learned more about my work place and the service it provided. North Texas Job Corps Center is one of many Job Corps Centers in America. My supervisor informed me that "Job Corps is a no-cost education and vocational training program administered by the U.S. Department of Labor that helps young people aged 16 through 24 to get a better job, make more money, and take control of their lives." Later on, I was also told by my colleagues that," It is a government program funded by all American taxpayers."

Each student who enrolls in a Job Corps program will have the opportunity to learn a vocational trade, learn marketable skills, earn a high school diploma or GED, and get help finding a good job. Most jobs will focus mainly on selected training areas. When students join the program, they will be paid a monthly allowance; the longer they stay with the program, the more their allowance will be. Job Corps also provides career counseling and transition support to its students for up to 12 months after they graduate from the program. Since the Job Corps program is funded by the United States Congress, some requirements were established. To enroll in Job Corps, students must meet the following requirements:

- Be between 16 and 24 years of age
- Be a U.S. citizen or legal resident

- Meet income requirements
- Be ready, willing, and able to participate fully in an educational environment

I also learned that the Job Corps program was established in 1964 to provide meaningful career training for American youth. The program's main purpose is still a commitment to offer all enrollees a safe, drug-free living and learning environment where they can take advantage of the provided resources to better themselves and become productive members of society. Its training is a combination of classroom, practical and work-based learning experiences to prepare youth for stable, long-term, high-paying jobs. Trainers or instructors are skillful and specialized or certified in their training fields.

When I was first told by my co-workers that I would be teaching **"At Risk"** youth, I had no idea what that meant. Later, I learned that **"At Risk"** students are a group of students who come from either broken or low-income families, who have dropped out of school or college, and who are unsuccessful in employment. Some are from middle-to working-class homes that generate reasonable incomes, but their intolerable negative behavior at home, makes their parents enroll them in the program. So, my main teaching responsibility is not only to teach them the technical aspects, but also to teach marketable skills and life skills to help them get and keep a job. They could eventually have a life long career. I have also learned that after teaching them, I would be assisting in their placement, helping them to find a job, helping them to create a resume, and preparing them for a job interview. At first I was worried about how I was going to do all of this. It seems to be interesting, and I later on found that the task is quite challenging: a Thai instructor teaching American students and preparing them for the American job market.

Can you imagine me on my first day and first week of a teaching career in America? I believe I am not much different from many teachers who just got into a teaching profession, and found that the first day and first week of teaching are an incredible experience. I was overwhelmed with information and responsibilities. I was uncertain how to start off my teaching and what to teach them. I had so many questions that needed clarification. I spent a lot of my time thinking back on how I was taught by my teachers and professors. I tried to remember what they started teaching me in their first class meetings that helped me to learn their subjects. What did they do to make me memorize things in class? What effective ways did they have to get all of the students involved? I recalled one of my professors saying that whatever we started in our first day of class will set the tone for the rest of the teaching year. So, what I did was at least set the tone for "Desktop Publishing," which is that it is fun and creative.

I also learned from educational experts and applied their advice to my own classroom. I found useful information presented on the website by L. Dee Fink at (http://honolulu.hawaii.edu/intranet/committees/FacDevCom/guidebk/teachtip/firstday.htm). The article was about nine effective ways to get class started on the first day, and I still follow this process in my teaching with every group of students:

- Acquire students' involvement
- Recognize the importance of the subject
- Set class expectations
- Create rapport with students
- Disclose something about teacher
- Institute the credibility
- Set up a classroom's climate
- Present useful administrative information

- Begin the subject matter

Acquire students' involvement: The way I get my students involved is that I simply provided donuts and juice for the first class meeting. I got my students involved quickly in my first class meeting by telling them briefly about myself and my background. I told them three interesting things about me that make me so unique; one of the three definitely is that I am Thai. Then, I let them introduce themselves and tell the class what three things we need to know about them. When they all finished, I asked if anybody remembered each of their classmates' good qualities. They participated quite well. I got them!!!!

Recognize the importance of the subject: None of my students clearly answered "what is desktop publishing?" when I asked it in our first class meeting. Some of them could answer that it involved computers. They did not really know why desktop publishing was important, why they needed to learn it, and what they would be taught in class. After learning what kind of job they can seek, they learned where they could find a job. I helped them to understand what I meant, by briefly explaining it to them and promising them that I would have an informative handout for them about my class within a week.

Set class expectations: First, I had the opportunity to find out what the students wanted from their selected class. I asked what they expected to learn and how they think a class in desktop publishing would help them. I gave them enough time to think and speak. Then, I jotted down what they said. After all of them finished, I took time to inform them of my expectations from them as a class. I created posters for my classroom. A few students asked if I really created them myself and if I was going to teach them to create things like it. I grabbed their attention with the design part of the desktop publishing class, at least.

Create rapport with students: After I shared a little information about myself, and the class told me a bit about them, it became a more relaxing in class. I also told them that after a class meeting, I would have them spend time on the computer creating a one-page flyer about them. Whoever created the most beautiful flyer would get a little prize. Oh....they loved it!!! They did not know that was my way to establish a rapport with them.

Disclose something about teacher: I remember many times in my own student life, I wanted to know about my new teacher; especially my favorite one. I briefly shared information with my students. For instance, I told them about some mistakes I made when I was their age and was a student; I told them that I used to fall asleep in class, skipped class, and turned in my homework late. I am a human being, just like they are. I shared with them about how I learned from my mistakes and how I improved. It was fun to share my stories with my students and to be able to laugh at it. Some students even asked if I used to do stupid things. "Like climb up a tall mango tree to steal mangos?" I replied, and I did that too. Telling a personal story helps students to effectively relate to the teacher, instead of seeing them only an authority figure.

Institute credibility: Many students really want to know about their teacher's prior work experience, educational background, and accomplishments. It automatically helps students to feel confident with their teacher. They just want to know if a teacher is really an expert in their field and knowledgeable in what he/she is teaching. One of the methods I used to present myself credibly in class, by having a graduation picture, diploma, certificates of accomplishment, and a family picture displayed in my office. An image means more than a thousand words. My students can see that I am accomplished in different things.

Set up a classroom's climate: Each teacher is unique, and each prefers a different climate in the classroom; intense, relaxed, formal, personal, humorous, or serious. I learned that the climate established in the first week would most likely be the tone for the rest of the teaching year. I would say my classroom's climate was combined. It was quite relaxed but structured. I did not make personal jokes. I set a boundary between me and my students. However, I am a serious teacher. Some of my students said to me, "Mrs. Sato, you are cool.", but a few students that I did not let behave inappropriately in my class would say, "Mrs. Sato, you are mean, strict, and too difficult." Many students said that "Mrs. Sato is strict, but fair." I think the fairest thing I can give to my students is to tell them about my expectations of them while they are with me as trainees.

Present useful administrative information: I provided all necessary information about my class and my teaching to my students. They would know about the location of my office and my work hours, what projects they would be working on, how each project would be graded, how much time was given for each project, class attendance, and students' evaluation. I would not only verbally tell them, but they also got a useful handout containing all the information related to my class.

Begin the subject matter: In the first class meeting, I took the opportunity to tell my students about the training. Since my training is "Desktop Publishing," I would let them know what it is, what they will learn in class, what kind of hardware and software involved, what kind of job they will be able to get after the training, and how much they will possibly be able to make. I tried to be as clear and straightforward as I could about my training. I just wanted to give accurate information to help them make a decision on what kind of training they really need. I always encourage them to pursue the degree after the training to further their education.

These days my current students tell the many newcomers to my training about my classroom's climate on the first day, particularly my expectations, class projects, what will be taught, and most importantly the phrase, "Mrs. Sato does not play." "She will surely write you up if you act foolishly in class." Sometimes, the class does a lot of its own discipline in terms of inappropriate behavior or class activities. I just play the role of a teacher some call a "ring master."

There are a few major parts of my teaching as a vocational instructor. The parts I am required to give the students as an introduction to Computer Desktop Publishing, are what I call "Technical Skills," and Marketable Skills, and I evaluate students in both areas during my teaching. Each student enrolled in my class will receive a package during the first week that consists of useful important information about the class. The following information is the basic thing my students need to know during their first week.

Desktop Publishing Class

Welcome to Class

"Welcome to Mrs. Sato's Desktop Publishing class. I hope that you will enjoy your stay and your time learning in my class. You will help to make this class a successful learning experience, if you have the desire to come to class on time, have a positive attitude, are able to follow instructions, and are willing to work and do your best during the time you are in the classroom.

Setting goals each week will help you start achieving success. When you begin this class, you will be an exploration student for one week. You will have to complete a folder of assignments by the end of the week. Initially, you will be working with Microsoft Word, Microsoft PowerPoint, and Microsoft Excel, or AppleWorks on the Mac. Mrs. Sato will check the completed work, and the student will be graded on the projects at the end of the week. At the end of your training, check to see if you reached your goal and continue doing this weekly. If you start now, it will always help you later in college or in your job.

Your work and projects should be a challenge to you-not an easy one-but a challenge that helps you to learn the software programs available in class. You will have enough time for each assigned project. If you need help on class projects, always let me know, but try first. You are in competition with yourself- not with anyone else in class. On a job, however, you will have to compete with a lot of people, so try to do your best now. Enjoy your learning."

Instructor's Information

Instructor: <u>Mrs. Patcharin Sato, M.S.</u>   Day: Monday - Friday

Office: Building 222 Room 125B   Phone: 972-547-7788

Time: 7:30 a.m. - 4:30 p.m.

E-mail: <u>Sato.Patcharin@jcdc.jobcorps.org</u>

Class Information

Desktop Publishing is a process of combining text and graphics to produce professional looking documents. This course is designed to provide hands-on training for students to utilize computer and design skills in creating a variety of publications. The training includes a historical overview of desktop publishing and a review of microcomputer software and hardware available for desktop publishing. The student will also be introduced to desktop presentation and basic web publishing techniques.

Class Objectives

The students enrolled in Desktop Publishing class will:

1. Learn a brief history of Desktop Publishing.

2. Describe the desktop publishing process, the components and hardware used, and available software programs.

3. Demonstrate preparation, presentation, and evaluation of desktop publishing projects.

4. Create slideshow to present and share concepts related to the effective use of desktop presentation, and desktop publishing.

5. Demonstrate preparation of publication design.

6. Evaluate appropriate software in desktop publishing training.

7. Assembly of personal portfolio prior to the completion of the training.

Class Projects

Students in my class will be learning different types of desktop publishing software programs to create the following publication projects: Flyers, Posters, Banners, Letterheads, Forms, Newsletters, Business Cards, Greeting Cards, Certificates, Bulletin Pages, Coupons, Bookmarks Signs, Brochures, Calendars, Menus, Presentations, and Basic Web Pages.

Class Expectations

As Desktop Publishing students, you are to meet these expectations in class. Students are to remember that Desktop Publishing is a job training program. The instructor expects all students to have the appearance and behavior of mature young adults.

1. Students are to be on time to work each day.

2. If students have an appointment, they must show the instructor a pass. If there is no pass, it will be counted as an absence for that period.

3. Students are not allowed to sleep in class. If the students head is down, it will be assumed they are sleeping.

4. Students are not allowed to sit or lie across the desk or table in classroom.

5. No horseplay in the classroom.

6. No profanity used in class at any time.

7. No improper use of government equipment.

8. No other computer programs may be installed on the computer without the instructor's supervision.

9. Only specific Desktop Publishing programs are allowed for use in class.

10. No music during class time, other than the multimedia presentation projects.

11. Classroom and work areas are to be kept clean.

12. Students are expected to be polite and courteous at all times.

13. Students are expected to obey the dress code during training hours.

14. Students are to be back from break and lunch on time for class.

15. Students are to do the cleaning assignment as scheduled.

16. Students will be warned about the class expectation when they fail to follow the first time.

17. Students will be written up and fined if they fail to follow class expectations.

Desktop Publishing Software Programs

The following are different types of software programs used in Desktop Publishing Training:

Word Processing & Spreadsheet: Microsoft Word, Corel Word Perfect, Lotus Word Pro, Microsoft Excel, Corel Quattro Pro

Graphic: Corel Photo Paint, Corel Photo House, CorelDraw, Adobe Photo Shop

Presentation: Microsoft PowerPoint, Corel Presentation, Lotus Freelance 97

Page Layout: PageMaker, QuarkXPress, Microsoft Publisher, Print Shop Deluxe, Print Master, Corel Ventura, Adobe InDesign

Internet: Basic HTML, Internet Tools, File Formats, Finding Information, Save Text File, Save Image File

Desktop Publishing hardware

My students will be able to gain experience using the following hardware in class: PC, Macintosh, Laptop, Scanner, Inkjet, LaserJet, and DeskJet Printer, CD/RW Drive, Digital Camera, Heat Press Machine, Laminator, Copy and Fax Machines, LCD projector, Overhead projector, and Flash Drive.

Besides teaching **technical skills** to my students, I am also required to teach "**employability skills,**" which I personally called "work skills." These are skills that they must have in order to get and keep a job. There are thirteen employability skills I demonstrate daily in class and expect my students to practice. The majority of them are doing much better than when I first started working with them. Unfortunately, I still have many students that need a lot more push in training them these skills. It is quite a big challenge to modify the behavior of someone who comes from an environment that had no structure, guidance, and discipline for many years, within a few months of training. I am required to teach the employability skills class on Friday afternoon each week.

- Being on time to work
- Dressing appropriately for work
- Responding positively to supervision
- Following directions
- Providing customer services
- Explaining Procedures
- Asking for clarification
- Working as a team
- Working with diversity
- Taking initiative
- Troubleshooting and solving problems
- Accessing and using information
- Maintaining good hygiene
- Staying on task
- Using tools and equipment properly

As another part of my job, every forty-five days (45), I am required to do a student performance evaluation. I am to evaluate students who are currently on my class roll. The evaluation must rate the student on the twelve (12) evaluation factors listed below, using the 1 to 5 performance scale. Instructors must base their rating upon the student's past performance and/or displayed ability.

Evaluation Factors:

1. *On Time to Work Consistently* - The students are expected to demonstrate punctuality and consistent attendance. My class starts at 8:00 a.m. The majority of students are sitting and waiting in front of the classroom around 7:50 a.m. There are a few students in each group that I have to meet with, about their tardiness and unexcused absences. After a few times warning them about tardiness, those students are documented. There are some students who give me a call or come back to class with an excuse note from the other staff who have them during that period. This way I can hold my student accountable, while they are scheduled to be with me. I also address their ability to turn in their work on time and ability to meet a deadline when they accept the projects to work on.

2. *Dress appropriately for work everyday* - My students are expected to wear clothing in accordance with workplace requirements. The center has a uniform for students enrolled in the program, and they are expected to wear that uniform neatly and properly during training hours. The biggest problem about dressing that I see daily is sagging pants. It is not only male students, but some female wear them that way, too. In my opinion, it does not look good, but for some of the students it is a fashionable thing they like to do. It is what I can't allow in class. Each morning, I inspect my students' uniform by having them stand up and take a look from head to toe. If I see what is not appropriate, I politely correct it right on the spot. This is a routine in class every morning after the greeting and the calling of the roll. The funny thing is that a few students wear

their uniform correctly in class, but once they walk out of class on break time or lunch time, they pull their shirt tail out and wear sagging pants. Before they reenter the classroom, they tuck their shirt tail in again. It is one of many challenges I meet daily with these students.

3. *Respond positively to Supervision-* Accepts constructive feedback with a positive attitude. Some students need to take more time in practicing this skill, because they are so argumentative on everything. Their tendency to talk back is such a major issue that I have to meet with them consistently. Many really have problems with their parents concerning supervision.

4. *Follow Directions* – Each day I observe whether my students are able to actively participate and complete assignments in class. Some students can work independently with limited supervision. Many of them, I have to guide almost every step of the way. Training this group of American teenage students in their ability to follow directions each day is not an easy task for me. The majority of them have difficulty following directions, not only on class projects and class behavior, but also in their personal attitude toward their classmates during class time. That is really a big worry to me, because it could affect how they are going to do on a job. For some students who demonstrate excellent ability in this category, I have no hesitation to give my letter of recommendation when they ask for one. These students indeed make a day on my job pleasant. They are also a good example of students who make it easy for me to help those who are still behind them, stuck under the mud and still not able to recognize the importance of the ability to follow instructions in the workplace and life.

5. *Effectively Satisfies Customers-* Students are expected to produce substantial work each day and to effectively address the expectations

of their "significant others." They have to demonstrate using trained skills, in order to get work done on time, both their class work and in taking work orders from other people. The quality of work must be satisfactory.

6. *Effectively Explains Procedures*-Demonstrates a practical understanding of subject matter; follows professional standards of procedures (verbally and in writing).

7. *Ask for Clarification*- Students are expected to actively participate in discussions and to seek additional information to accomplish a task in class. A few always ask questions that are related to class or just want to disrupt the class. Some quiet students are too shy to ask for help in class. They will wait until class ends and talk to me after school.

8. *Effectively Works well in team*- They are expected to work harmoniously with diverse races, sexes, ages, cultures; accomplish tasks with others. I sometimes assign them group projects and observe how they work and interact with each other, and how they solve problems and conflicts. Some male and female students just want to fight to solve their problems in class. A few times in my seven years teaching, I have had to break up a fight in class.

9. *Listens Effectively*- Student is alert, attentive and responsive to directives and discussions. Many students don't have a problem, because they listen to instructions in class. They pay attention to what is expected, both with class behavior and with class projects. A few students still need a lot of guidance in this respect. They have "Know-It-All" attitude and have tendency to interrupt while being instructed.

10. *Consistently Takes Initiative*- Students will be evaluated on whether they are a self-starter, self-motivated, stay on task, and whether they require minimal supervision to complete tasks. Some students

always take work orders from other staff and get it done beautifully. They volunteer to help out in class, to complete extra activities, or to clean up. They also offer to help newcomers to get started in class.

11. *Troubleshoots/Solves Problems* – They are expected to demonstrate the ability to analyze situations and determine effective approaches to resolving problems.

12. *Accessing and using information from different resources* –They have to demonstrate the ability to use a variety of resources to complete projects in class: the Internet, books, magazines, and dictionary, etc.

13. *Maintaining good hygiene* – Since we all have to share a training facility, students are expected to take good care of their personal hygiene. There were a few times we have had to have a "smell check" in class on a person who does not give priority to hygiene. Putting some students on a hygiene contract was an interesting thing I experienced.

14. *Staying on task* – Students demonstrate the ability to stay on task and complete all assigned work in reference to instructor/classroom requirements.

15. *Using tools and equipment properly* – Students demonstrate the ability to use equipment available in class and assist in good maintenance of the equipment in the training area which included PC/Mac, digital camera, printer, scanner, LCD projector, and overhead projector, etc.

Below are general guidelines for applying the scale:

1. Unacceptable: Student regularly demonstrates a lack of skills, is resistant or hostile to staff supervision and intervention, and unwilling to follow instructions or try new skills.

2. Poor: Student seldom responds to supervision or demonstrates good skills; does not attempt to try new skills; does not accept intervention willingly.

3. Satisfactory: Student usually acts in an appropriate manner; responds satisfactorily to supervision and intervention, and attempt behavior change.

4. Above average: Student almost always acts appropriately: shows a willingness to practice new skills and behavior; is respectful to supervision and intervention.

5. Outstanding: Student always acts in an appropriate manner; student serves as a role model for others.

After I evaluate my students, I meet with them individually to discuss their low rating areas and find out their goal and plan for improvement, and I give them sufficient time to work on each area before their next evaluation. If I do not see much improvement, I will call a meeting between the student, the student's counselor, and myself, to discuss the student's lack of progress in class. Sometimes, the counselor places the student on a contract and watches them closely. This meeting for some students is effective, because there is more than one professional who is monitoring their progress and it helps them to stay focused on their goals in learning.

Sometimes, doing student evaluations reminds me of my own annual evaluation as a staff member. I have a chance to sit down and think of things that I have accomplished, look at what is still behind me, and take time to do a self-evaluation in a different area each year. If there are some areas that need improvement, then I can stay focused on doing better. When I first started working, my senior instructors suggested to me that I write down and keep track of projects that I have completed, extra tasks I established and finished, in addition to doing my job. It is a good record that I could look at in terms of my own accomplishments on the job during the review or evaluation time. I was also told that some supervisors do not recognize the extra things the employees do, so our record will become helpful for discussion while being reviewed.

Recently I completed a self-assessment. I am so proud to share that I have had a successful year. With my knowledge and skills, I am professionally and technically providing desktop publishing training to my learners. I am enhancing students' practice and understanding, by working with the MIS department to implement new settings for the hardware in the classroom to better prepare students for the office environment, and by working with the other departments in the center on tasks that involve designing and printing publications and artwork. I took the responsibility for designing forms and creative print work used in the center by different departments, working with printers outside of the center to print and perform a color separation of the material used at the center, including newspapers, newsletters, and quarterly graduation programs. I took an assignment to provide business applications training to clerical staff at the center when requested, assisting in students' discipline on campus by conducting a weekly peer council, and establishing and designing the center and student government association's newspaper. I am consistently assisting center staff with software applications troubleshooting.

There are some areas in which I am planning to improve, such as volunteering extra time for students' advancement and success after class. I want to be more accessible to students during training day, to try to adjust my training methods to better fit the special needs of students, and to have an open-door policy for students who need immediate professional attention. I would also like to keep learning and seeking new sources of knowledge for self-improvement and to better serve students, to seek more resources on the Internet and professional training on subject matter, to become more proactive with students in training, trying to better understand each individual's needs in class, to teach more one-on-one with a hands-on approach, and to continue to update DTP programs in training to better prepare students for the advanced American job market.

Patcharin Sato
Career Technical Training Instructor

Chapter 14: I am a Teacher—a Nation's Molder

"To the world, you might be one person, but to one person you might just be the world." Author- Unknown

A teaching career had never been a clear choice in my mind, until I reached the age of thirty. When I have time to think back, I recall what my mother used to tell me about the times that I spent occupying my sibling. She told me that I spent a lot of time playing a teacher role, having all my elementary school playmates sitting around playing my students. At that age, I might not have had any idea what I wanted to be or do for a living. It might have been just a fun activity to do. I was only a girl without a really clear idea as to which direction I should take. When I was studying in business school, I dreamed that one day I might become a businesswoman who worked in a firm. Unfortunately, it was only a dream, because I later found that I had no interest in it and did not really want a chance to pursue it.

I definitely decided that I wanted to be a teacher when I was working in a computer lab while working on my graduate degree at Texas A&M University-Commerce. I enjoyed helping and working with people, staff and students, on the computer. I was delighted to see that they accomplished their tasks. I was happy that I could help them learn something new. I was also having fun spending time preparing lesson plans and interacting with my learners.

At the beginning, my lack of confidence in my ability to use English was a major concern for pursuing a teaching career in America. My professor, Dr. Sue Espinoza, was my inspiration. She encouraged and motivated me. She was very supportive of my work in the department's computer lab, in student teaching, in an internship, and in class. She made me feel like I was someone special that could become a good teacher. My summer graduate class's instructor, Mrs. Moffitt, placed a big post-it on my folder saying that my work and lesson plans looked good. She thanked me for being a good asset in the Texas educational system. Their inspirational words energized me to keep improving myself and pushed me to move forward in the teaching field. That helped me gain confidence in becoming a good teacher.

Since I decided to be in this profession, I have yet to regret it. I always keep in mind, like many people in this profession that "teaching is my job and making a difference is my goal." I love my profession. I believe in myself, my knowledge and skills, and I also believe in my students and am willing to help them to pursue what is best for them in their education. It has always been an enjoyable experience seeing their development and growth. Their successes serve as evidence of the mature fruit of my labor.

Education to me is a lifetime learning experience. It is a continuous process. I believe that there is no age, background, culture, or race barrier in education. Everybody can learn, but each person might have different ways of learning the same subject. As an instructor, it is my responsibility to find out which way my students learned best.

I always try to find the ways that I can best deliver the instructions that fit their learning styles. It takes time to reach each of them, but in the end I can ensure that they learn something from me. It can be identified by observing their improvement in projects, some behavior, and achievement.

Besides teaching my students the subject matter, I spend my time talking to them about the significance of education. Education is an important gateway to many opportunities. It is a passport to a bright future. It is a tool that one can use to make a living to support themselves and their family for a lifetime. However, that tool needs to be sharp at all times. I keep telling my students that having knowledge is important, but knowing how to apply it in life is even more important. Knowledge is an endless treasure.

I encourage my students to always seek the opportunity to further their education. Skills and knowledge they have should be updated at all times due to the rapid changes in the competitive job market, so that they can be the best candidate during a job interview. Educating students to me is more than teaching; seeing them develop what they learn is much more valuable. I also told them that knowledge from me is free, but they have to build their own container to hold it. Yes, some students build a big and secure container for themselves to become successful, but many might need more time to learn the consequences of not retaining the information. However, I am honored and pleased to be a part of my students' learning experience.

In my seven years in the teaching profession, I have developed and learned several valuable things, such as to **have a high expectation of the learner, to listen to them, to be patient and creative, to value the power of teaching, and to keep learning from experienced teachers.** Firstly, I have learned to become a person with high expectations for my students, especially the expectation of acceptable behavior in class. When students understand what types of behavior I expect in class, then teaching can happen quite easily. My senior instructor once said,

"Don't lower the bar; your student will try to jump as high as the bar has been set, but keep it up with consistency." Each day, with each student, and with each group, I consistently keep to these expectations. I also hold them accountable for their choice of behavior. Secondly, I have learned that I should talk less than my students do in class. That way it will help me to watch what they do and listen to what they discuss while they are working. Also, I can hear what they think about my class and the subject when they are sharing information with their classmates or with new students. It is quite interesting when I listen to my student class leader every week giving a trade tour to a group of new students or prospective students. She shares with them about the class expectations, the class content, and the class teacher. It is nice to listen to the advanced students in class helping the beginners on some class projects. It is amazing to hear some of them explain to their classmates the procedure they followed to accomplish the assigned tasks.

It has become clear to me that they understand my expectations of them, even though many times they act as if they do not care about what they are expected to do. Most of the time, I allow them to help each other on projects. I believe that without an encouraging atmosphere -- listening to each other and learning from each other -- learning would not occur as much as it does.

One thing I encountered as quite a problem in class is that my teenage students love to talk to their peers in class. Many have problems talking excessively, arguing loudly, and using profanity. When they talk, they do not know how and when to listen. They have a strong tendency to easily get off of the subject. Some can not stay focused when talking. Sometimes when I correct them about using profanity, they would tell me, "Mrs. Sato, this is what I hear all the time at home. My parents even cursed at me. I cannot just stop. I am working on it." I heard what he told me, and I told him that he has a choice not to use profanity in his conversation. Then, a few minutes later, I heard profanity again. I expect this inappropriate language daily in my class, though I keep fighting against it. Listening to their conversation allows me to guide them back on track. It also gives me a chance to discuss with them the benefit of having good listening skills.

I told my students that being a good listener is not easy. It takes a lot of effort on their part during a conversation. However, when they are on the job, having their supervisor compliment them for not having to tell them twice about an assigned task, is the finest compliment they should want to hear. I am fortunate to have had the opportunity to hear such compliments from my American supervisors many times. I think that credit should go to all my teachers. I have always kept my assignments and due dates on a work book or calendar, jotting down the details that needed to be completed. So I will not have to come with the excuse that I forgot. Most of my assigned projects are never delayed.

There are several listening tips I have learned and I love to share with my students during our class discussion. The first important tip is to *always look at the speaker* while listening to what is being said. By looking at that person, you can concentrate on the message he/she is sending. Your eye contact will also send a message to the speaker that you are listening.

When I talk to my students, if it is unclear due to my pronunciation, I encourage them to *take the extra effort to listen* carefully. I will always keep in mind that it is my responsibility to get my point across to all of the students as a class and to be a good message sender, but they should take advantage of receiving the message as clearly as possible.

When I teach my students new terms or new tricks on class projects, I encourage them to *jot it down* in a notebook or repeat it a few times in their mind to *remember the message* I send to them. If they are still unclear, they can always repeat what they understand to me, to make sure they got it right. It is surprising to me that not a lot of my American students like to take notes. They are not prepared when they come to class. I had one female student employed in a doctor's office. She was a nice student, but she could not articulate many of the messages she gets. Unfortunately, her employment was terminated because of her lack of listening skills. She missed filing many times after a few instructions were given to her for the same task. She refused to jot them down for her own memory. Her employer informed me that she asked the same question many times and still did not get the task done correctly. I believe that if she took an extra effort to improve her listening skills and to write down the instructions, she might have been able to keep the job.

I also tell my students, *"don't come up with an excuse"* when they receive criticism from anybody. They will improve more if they listen to what they are doing wrong, instead of being defensive. I told my students that they refuse to learn, when they find excuses for everything that they do wrong or do not want to admit. Of course, I see it is not easy for this age group to be open-minded about accepting criticism. They think that whatever they do is right. Observing a few students reacting inappropriately to a staff member's feedback on their design, allows me to see that my students have a lot more to learn. I just hope that with more maturity, they will learn that nothing in life will always be done in the way we think it should be.

Another tip on listening skills that I encourage my students to practice is to *think* after they receive the message. They can reply briefly if it is needed to make sure what they are thinking is the correct message. They then should continue to listen so that they receive the complete message.

I also give them the opportunity to *always ask questions* and do it right away if they don't understand what I am teaching in class. Some of my students never hesitate to ask, but a few are still shy to ask questions in front of their classmates. Sometimes, those students stay after class to ask questions. I emphasize that if they do not ask for clarification at that specific point, they may not fully get the message that follows.

The other important tip that I share with my students is that when they find themselves having a conversation with a person who is overly talkative, they should *politely interrupt* after a period of time. If they do not interrupt, they may become irritated and will not want to listen anymore. In class, some students quietly work by themselves on assigned projects while many are very talkative and distract others with their excessive talking. I often have to tell my talkative students to be considerate of their classmates' feelings and respect their efforts to learn. These important listening tips are the main things that we always have to discuss. Of course, listening requires concentration.

As a teacher, I have learned that it is important for students to know they are part of the classroom. Everything in the classroom is not mine, but it is ours as a class. I always emphasize that they come to study in their classroom everyday. Their job is to keep the classroom running smoothly and to keep their work area clean and organized. They are in class as a team, and they are treated as a team. I let them use a digital camera to take pictures, including a class picture, and we place it on the classroom door or put it in the frame set on the table in our class. Some students use a PhotoShop program to touch up or manipulate pictures before using them on a big poster design. I also display their work or class projects on the bulletin board in front of the classroom or on the windows around the classroom. When people walk by, they stop and take a look. Many have received compliments on their work. That encourages them to do better and gives them a pride in their own classroom. They enjoy seeing their products being displayed, which motivates them to put more effort in their work.

They receive awards or incentives from me for good behavior and perfect class attendance that they demonstrate monthly. I treated those who perform especially well with a Chinese lunch. I sometimes reward students who try really hard to produce an outstanding class project with a flash drive for them to save all their class projects. The award is something for them to look forward to as a member of a team. It is a way of my recognizing their good work and their effort.

When I listen to my students, I don't mean only class-related issues and concerns, but I listen to their personal problems, when they need someone to talk to. I keep in mind that the problems they encounter can affect their performance and behavior in class. I provide help in any way I can. One of my male students who used to actively progress in class isolated himself and stayed very quiet after he got back from summer break. He repeatedly asked my permission to see his counselor. I asked if I could talk to him in the office one morning before class started. I found out that his mother was hospitalized due to HIV. I understood his great concern about her condition. I worked with his counselor on this matter to arrange time for him to be with her. One of many issues in this age group of students is relationships; girlfriend and boyfriend issues. It has such a big effect on their behavior in class. Dealing with my students during this condition is not an easy task. It takes a lot of understanding, even though I see it as a small, manageable problem. To them, it is really a big and meaningful problem that needs to be fixed right away. My question to you is how would you react if two of your female students openly told you about their personal experience of being sexually molested? One girl's story happened between the ages of seven and twelve; it was her mother's boyfriend, and her mother could not do anything about it. The other female student has to go to court to testify that the man is actually her own uncle. These two stories certainly didn't bring me in a good mood.

Another thing I developed is the ability to be more patient with disruptive behavior and to find creative ways to deal with my students more effectively. Disruptive behavior and inappropriate language were the most intolerable problems in class when I first started teaching. It bothered me so much that these young students couldn't conduct themselves appropriately, but after I learned about their background and the environment they were from, I found out that a majority of them were from a negative environment and areas of poverty. Some were sexually abused at a very young age. One of the sad parts is that some got abused by their own family members. I trained myself to be more assertive and firm, by attending many seminars on dealing with negative behavior, instead of responding to their negative behavior aggressively. I also participated in misbehavior training among teachers, taking classes in classroom management and effective teaching. Experience in the classroom teaches me to look for things behind that "acting out" behavior. One thing I saw in my American students is that they are so outspoken. Most of them always speak their mind without caring whether it is appropriate or not. Many of them display very disrespectful behavior toward their classmates in class, sometimes even toward me. I tried to be patient and calm while dealing with them. I wanted to be honest, but I wasn't successful every time. A few times, I reacted negatively to my students' negativities. It did not help the situation, nor did it make them change their behavior; I just realized that I expected these American students to be like students in my generation from my country who were very obedient and respectful. This will never happen as I expected in many of my American students, who survived on their own on the mean streets of America. The most effective way I use to deal with my negative students is to learn to treat them as an individual, who should be respected and who is important. I guide them in the right direction to the best of my ability. Whether they take it or not depends on the choice they make. I tried to change my way of teaching, instead of changing their way of learning.

As a teacher, I always appreciate an awesome power: the power to teach, a power to guide, and a power to impact another's life. I certainly plan to use this power well and wisely to help my students learn and grow.

> As a teacher, I possess a tremendous power to make a child's life miserable or joyous. I can be a tool of torture or an instrument of inspiration. I can humiliate or humor hurt or heals. In all situations, it is my response that decides whether a crisis will be escalated and a child humanized or dehumanized. — Hiam Ginott

In my role, it is important for me to make an effort to help my students to become productive and successful. I attempt to create and maintain the best possible positive learning environment for my students in class — to operate a *firm, fair, friendly,* and *fun,* classroom is my goal. I don't believe that a negative and hostile environment can help students learn and produce a positive outcome. Creating the positive environment means I am developing the class where my students can be themselves, while being respectful and considerate of others. They should feel comfortable working and communicating with me, and with their classmates. To me, the positive learning environment should be happy, stress-free, and energized. It should feel safe and sound respectful, supportive, and friendly. I am exhibiting myself as an example and I lay the foundation by establishing the ground rules. This is the first step I take. When they start the day with me, I talk to them about the class rules and my expectations of them. The ground rules serve as the class norms by which everyone in the class agrees to abide. I ask students to develop these norms by thinking about what classroom conditions would have to exist in order for them to feel that they can share their ideas and feelings openly. I keep these rules and expectations posted in the classroom at all times, and I remind students that every person, not just the teacher, is responsible for seeing that the ground rules are adhered to. I also print out the expectations sheet and place it in each student's folder, when they come to explore my class for one week, before they actually enroll as full time desktop publishing students. I professionally demonstrate a good example of a desirable office employee at all times. I do not use profanity and inappropriate language in class. I make sure I get out of my house in the morning with the proper and appropriate outfit for work. It has not been once that I got sent home because I did not abide by the workplace dress code. When I first started my teaching career, one of my senior instructors taught me that, "the students are watching you, be aware of everything you do in class. They might pretend that they do not pay attention when you teach, but they will point out when you say something that you are not supposed to say in class." I treat each of them fairly and with respect. If I can not do something for all, I will not do it, even small things like giving out candies. When I bring donuts to class, I will be sure to save some for the afternoon group instead of giving all of them to the morning group. There have been a few times that a student questioned my fairness. I called that person into the office, and sat down to talk with him/her until he/she understood and accepted what I did. The type of fairness that my students observe in my judgment is punishment for inappropriate behavior in class. When they do well, I reward them and when they misbehave, I punish them. The fairness thing that I do is to let them know class rules and consequences for misbehavior at the beginning of class. I hold them responsible for their own actions. When I correct inappropriate behavior, I try to do it firmly rather than aggressively. I am aware of my tone of voice and my reaction to hostility from some students. Sometimes, it is very difficult and I get frustrated. I try to forgive their bad behavior and I think that they don't know any better. It is my job to train them, and everyday I am pushing them to improve.

To make for a friendly class, I interrupt name-calling, slurs, jokes, teasing, or other prejudicial behavior, whenever it occurs. Failure to address an incident of prejudice can signal to students that such behavior is acceptable in class. My class is diversified. I tell students to respect the others' cultures and practices and encourage them to be proud of their ethnic background. I share my personal experiences with my class. Sharing life experiences in class can help students develop empathy. It can make the classroom a place where students' experiences are not marginalized, trivialized, or invalidated, at the same time acknowledging that experiences in which prejudice and/or discrimination have occurred are unique and cannot be equated with each other.

It seems that my students have fun in class. I often hear friendly joking among them while they work on class projects. Some simply have fun by mocking my accent, and teasing me, "Mrs. Sato, please go sit down at your desk, you walk around the classroom too much, making it so we us can not go to sleep." Sometimes, I have been asked if they are special, and I simply reply that they are and it takes a special teacher to teach special students. They just laugh, understanding that

I mean special education rather than special…special…. person. I think a little appropriate joke can make the class more relaxed and friendly. However, working with this age group, I have to clearly set the boundary. That means I have to let them know when to play and when I really mean business. When I know the birthday of my students, I acknowledge it by having one of the classmates create a birthday card for them and getting it signed by the members of the class. I also have the whole class sing a birthday song to that student. Sometimes, I bring the birthday cake to class for them to enjoy a little birthday party.

To make a fun class, I create activities to enhance their learning: creative contests, presentation of the most sought after class projects, or educational field trips to different organizations such as *The Dallas Morning News*, *The Star Telegram*, The Western Currency Facility, as known as Money Printing Facility, and EDS, a big computer network corporation. Sometimes, I take them to the Fry's Electronics – a big electronic and computer store, where they can explore the new technology, listen to music, watch movies, read books and magazines, buy things they want for class, play computer games, or even apply for a job. A few times I assigned them a project on the most fascinating piece of technology they found in a store on that day. They then had to verbally report to the whole class and send their report to me in the form of a memo. This activity helps to prepare them for public speaking and writing communication within the workplace.

Every time I schedule a field trip, I have to work with people both off and on campus; I contact the person in that organization to request the tour. I communicate in the form of a business letter, an e-mail, fax, telephone and sometimes in person. I ask the campus safety-transportation department to transport us back and forth, and I contact the cafeteria manager and staff to request a sack lunch. The final thing is to notify my supervisor when writing on the activity's objective and outcome. I plan an extended learning experience trip almost every month. My students love it and successfully co-operate with me during the trip. Through scheduling a field trip, I not only provide my students an informative and fun learning experience, but it also enhances my personal growth by establishing a good working relationship with others and an effective use of my communication skills. Many times, I planned the field trip for three classes combined. They are for desktop publishing, office technology, and accounting. I call the field trip the business cluster trip. I organized the trip with the great support of the two class's instructors. This task helps me to learn the importance of team work and information sharing.

One day out of the week, I let my students do a presentation on their best assignment. They have to set up the equipment such as a laptop or LCD projector to present their work to the whole class. In this way, I can ensure that they not only know how to work on their projects, but also know how to present themselves to people. Some students present their projects created in Adobe PhotoShop and CorelDraw and the others present their PowerPoint projects about themselves. It seems to me that they put effort into their work, because they want to show their classmates the best they can do. It also gives the students the opportunity to learn from each other. They ask questions about how some tasks get completed when the projects are presented. Then, they keep trying to use the tips they learned on their own projects.

The other way I make my class fun, while focusing on the learning objectives and helping them to be motivated, to take pride in their work as well as to enhance their creativity in class projects, is by establishing **"The Creative Contest"** for our daily bulletin, for book covers, and for coupons, which are the files sent out electronically through our center network for the center staff to view daily information. I planned this activity, before discussing it with my supervisor. He was very supportive of the idea when I presented it to him. He even asked if I needed anything from the budgets for the prizes I planned to give out to the students who would participate. Actually, I was planning to give out only the big bag of Asian coffee candy or peppermints to the contest winners. After his support for this activity, I had enough from the budget to buy many flash drives to give to my students, so that they can save their files in class. I assigned four students to design the Monday-Thursday bulletin, the completed file for which I send out in the morning each day. On Thursday morning, I send out four files for the staff to review, and I request their votes by 3:00 p.m. for the file or the design that they like the best. Before the contest, I assigned one female student to work on a one-page flyer about this activity. She did an excellent job. Her work got a few votes from the staff, even though she was not even in the contest. I personally do not know whether the staff did not pay attention to our voting information and rules, or my student's flyer looked too good to be overlooked for the vote. It was a huge success. My students had fun and stayed motivated. The staff also had fun viewing the good work. Some even sent in their constructive criticism about my students' work. I certainly shared the criticism I received from the staff with my students. Some samples of critique are as follows:

"This is a very good design by Ms. Barrett. Clean, clear and good use of page, but not over stuffed. Ms. Sato, we know that we are to vote, but just thought that she should know her work looked good." Critique from student services staff who always participates on our activity.

"SUPERB!!"

"Clarity with negative space!" (Comment from scheduling clerk).

"Colorful and creative, but too busy." (Comment from finance staff).

"'Hi! I am Eva Tibeus, will vote for Daisy Montano, she did a really great job."

"Today's bulletin is very difficult to read. The color choices are not only unattractive (pea green) but also do not contrast with the background which is very busy and distracting."

"'I like the one dated 3-20-06 because it is not cluttered up and is easy to read without my glasses. Background is very good and so are the designs in the way they are placed on the paper."

"My vote is in strong favor of the Winnie the Pooh Design. I absolutely love the way the background and characters blend to create a "complete" presentation."

"This is the one I am voting for. It was designed very well, print was clear, display of the menu was good, the color was fantastic, and the print was readable, not too fancy."

"'All of the designs were great, and this was a hard decision to make. Most liked over all is by Heather M. Crawford, design, layout and use of color, with simple bold letters are eye catching."

"NICE and DIFFERENT!!" "Very interesting, I liked it. This student has good concept"

We as a class enjoyed reading those comments and learned to accept them. For the few students who did not like the given criticism, I took time to talk to them about the important way that we all can improve our own skills. After the contest was over, I made sure to send out an e-mail to the staff. The staff certainly wanted to know who won. They have been very supportive of my class's activities and help to encourage my students to put more effort in their work. They praise my students for their work. Many of them appreciate my students help on designing, typing, scanning, copying, and laminating different things. Many people called asking if I could send my student to help them type or create the form in their office. A few staff members keep coming to my class using the same student over and over. I received a lot of nice replied e-mail after I sent out my e-mail on different creative activities.

From: Patcharin Sato
Sent: Friday, April 07, 2006 9:26 AM
To: All North Texas Users
Subject: Contest Result

Good Morning Staff,

This week, the DTP class has finished its **"Creative Contest"** for our center bulletin from Monday through Thursday. I do appreciate your encouragement regarding my students' work by sending in your votes. Your votes and constructive comments really made those students happy and made them want to put more effort in their work. Next week, I will have another four students participating in the contest. The following week, I am planning to have each week's winner competing with each other. Each week's winner receives the "Jump Drive" to store his/her work. **Please stay tuned!!!!**

This Week's Winners are:

Jeremy Parker
Whitney Davis
Alyssia Gonzalez
Delisha Benson

Thank you,
Mrs. Sato.

I have learned a great deal from many experienced teachers and educators about the qualifications of an effective teacher. I especially learned from my own teachers who always give me good advice on my teaching problems. I called them or sent them e-mails asking for effective way in some situations, after many tries of my own. I read information from good and useful resources, such as books and online sites. I particularly like the effective ways of teaching presented by Mr. Henry K. Wong in his book ***The First Days of School: How to Be an Effective Teacher.*** He talked about many useful methods for classroom management and effective teaching styles, three characteristics of an effective teacher, four stages of teaching, etc. I have experienced the fantasy, survival, mastery, and impact stages in my teaching career. I have passed each stage with pride. Yes, I agree with an experienced teacher that it is a big difference between the ideal of teaching and the reality of the classroom. The manager of a classroom must really be a multitasking person.

As a teacher, I absolutely wear many hats and play many parts. Some of the hats are not even mine, but the duties I perform are certainly one of the hats the other professions should wear. I am a communicator, a presenter of information, a disciplinarian, a classroom manager, a counselor, a member of many teams and groups, a decision-maker, a role-model, a foster parent, an performer, an evaluator, a janitor, and even sometimes a reluctant baby sitter. These are just some of the roles assumed by me. Each of these roles definitely requires practice and skills that I did not learn in school.

I gained the skills mostly while on the job; I also learned from my senior instructors and attended educator training to learn from other teachers. Many of them share their valuable teaching experiences. I strive to build a solid foundation for learning how to teach, using their advice, by hoping to excel and become a better teacher. I listened and learned tricks and tips. I am open for suggestions from other teachers. I am willing to adjust my teaching style and methods. So far, one thing I have learned is that teaching is not just about loving children, but is able to work with them effectively with love and care.

Even though I dismiss students when the bell rings at 3:45 p.m., it does not mean that my day ends. I am involved in department meetings, center meetings, student evaluation panels, career meetings, career transition panels, center event committees, as well as assisting students, grading papers, evaluating projects, typing reports, assisting some staff on computer matters, preparing class rolls and plans for the following day, and sometimes cleaning up after having two students sweep and mop the classroom. All these responsibilities demand a great deal of personal time. I am committed to excellence as a teacher, and I acknowledge that it is a sacrifice with which I am able to live. I feel quite comfortable with it so far. Sometimes when I feel very frustrated and exhausted, I remember reading one handout. Then, I accept that I chose to get into this profession.

Seven years on a job as a vocational instructor and by learning from other teachers and educators, I have gained priceless experience. I certainly appreciate the value of being a good teacher. I enjoy reading the article *Tips on Becoming a Teacher* written by Dr. Bob Kizlik. He stated that there are many qualifications for being a good teacher. Following are some of them that I found beneficial:

- Good at explaining things

- Keep their cool- Be patient
- Have a sense of humor
- Like People
- Be fair minded
- Have common sense
- Have a command of the content they teach
- Set high expectations for their students
- Hold the students to those expectations
- Be detail oriented
- Good at time management
- Can lead and follow
- Don't take things for granted

First of all, good teachers are **good at explaining things**. It is an essential skill for teachers. Teachers have to explain how something works, or how something happened. Initially, I learned from my professors, watched how the other instructors did. I found some interesting topics to talk about, and I practiced teaching them in front of the mirror. It took a while for me to become comfortable. I always try to keep my explanation short and easy, before I lose my students' attention on a topic.

There will be times when teachers will be tempted to scream or yell at some students, other teachers, administrators, or other workers. Teachers must **keep their cool**, stay calm, and successfully resist aggressive behavior. I took a walk out of class many times in seven years to release the annoyed and irritated feeling when my students pushed me to the point that I wanted to scream out loud in class. I confided with the other instructors. It helped me to calm down and to handle my students' behavior more effectively. These days, one of a few challenging students misbehaved in class, angrily yelling and being very disrespectful, but I was able to keep my cool. She later told her counselor that she was surprised that I didn't scream back at her for that type of behavior. She has no idea that it is pretty hard not to do so.

I am considered a person that takes things too seriously. My teaching profession has helped me to develop a good **sense of humor** and learn to use humor as part of my teaching method. I also use humor with groups of people I work with on campus. I always keep in mind that if humor is used properly, it can be a powerful tool that can help me to do my job easily and more effectively. It also can help me have fun doing my job each day.

Good teachers **like people**, especially students in the age range in which they are teaching. "Most teachers choose an area of specialization such as elementary education, special education, secondary education, or higher education, because they have a temperament for students in those age ranges. If you are not comfortable working with young children, don't major in elementary education," said Dr. Kizlik.

I like to interact with people, and I like to be part of their learning. I love creating beautiful publications on the computer. I enjoy seeing the others learn to do the same. I feel a sense of accomplishment after guiding my students step-by-step and seeing that they have completed the assigned tasks. That might be why I chose to teach in a computer and design field.

Good teachers **are naturally fair-minded**. When assessing students, as a teacher, we should be able to assess them on the basis of performance, not on the students' personal qualities.

Having **common sense** is one of the many good qualities of good teachers. Many situations can occur inside and outside of the classroom.

Using common sense, a teacher can size up the incident quickly and can help to make an appropriate decision in each case.

Common sense can help me in many areas, such as managing my classroom, leading students on field trips, confronting inappropriate behavior, documenting incidents in class, moving from one instructional procedure to another, supervising my students, submitting reports to my supervisor, and dealing with many people that I encounter on a daily basis. There is nothing that can replace common sense in my daily routine.

Good teachers should be **knowledgeable.** Teachers should be an expert in their field of teaching. They should have knowledge of a broad range of content — enough to pass on the information in a meaningful way to their students. I am fortunate to work with many vocational instructors who are certified in the area of teaching. I also have to be certified in the Office Education area to teach the class that I am teaching right now.

Teachers should **set high expectations** for their students and **hold the students to those expectations**. I have always said that I believe in myself and I believe in my students. I set high expectations for myself, and demand excellence not only from myself, but from my students as well. I remember that one of my senior instructors once told me to never lower my own bar. Students look at teachers as good role models. Working with them a little bit at a time will help them to approach the bar that each teacher has placed for them.

Good teachers should be **detail oriented**. The way you manage your classroom will reflect how you are in your personal life. If you are disorganized in your private life, you might find that teaching will be quite uncomfortable for you. Each day you have to work with a pound of paper work and submit many reports, which are usually demanded in a timely manner. Grading students' work must also be completed. Students' evaluations must be finished. There are meetings at which you must be present and many activities in which you must be involved. Teachers must be organized in their professional and teaching duties.

Good teachers should be **good managers of time**. Time is one of the most precious resources teachers have. The ability to manage time will help teachers to be more effective and efficient in their classroom. In seven years, I have done and have seen many instructors spend more extra time at work than at home. There are so many things to complete each day, besides teaching students during class time. Teachers have to learn to manage their time for lesson plan preparation, grading papers, guiding and motivating students, evaluating students, and working with counselors, etc.

The ability to both **lead and follow** is another good quality teachers should have. There are many situations at work, which require teachers to be involved. As a member of the situation and activity, teachers should be able to function well. Sometimes, teachers assume leadership roles; the ability to lead other members and to get tasks done is essential, and they must be comfortable playing that role.

Dr. Kizlik. Also emphasized that "**Don't take things for granted**." This refers to everything involved in teaching; it starts from selecting a college for education to become a certified teacher. I am like many teachers in all different areas of teaching; we don't learn to teach by going through college, participating in teacher preparation programs, getting a degree, getting certified in a subject area, and becoming a teacher who knows how to teach. We all learn to teach by teaching. When we make mistakes, we learn from them and improve. We also learn from other experienced experts in the field of teaching and apply what we learn to our own teaching style. We all should keep in mind that good personal habits can benefit our teaching profession in all aspects. The degree and training we earn are an essential foundation to help us get started.

Everyday is a day of learning. Being in the teaching profession makes me strive for the opportunity to improve, update, and advance. I have opportunities to attend professional seminars, training, and taking classes. I am fortunate that all learning activities are paid for by the company. I always encourage my students to ask questions. When I really do not know the answer, I spend time searching different resources, books, and internet sites, and sometimes I call on my previous instructors. I sometimes learn by observing the other instructors' way of teaching.

One afternoon, my supervisor also allowed a few instructors, including myself, to discuss the importance of professional development in technical careers in a conference call with many job corps centers around the nation. The conference was facilitated by a national office. It was an informative conference. I was encountering many vocational instructors' views and thoughts in their areas. Some instructors have been teaching in their area of expertise for almost thirty years, but have yet to be certified. They have done such a great job of helping, guiding, training, and placing students on different jobs. Their view was that whether or not a teacher is certified is not as important as the ability to do the job. Thirty years experience has proven that they are also able to create an environment that is safe and calm, so that the teacher can teach and students can learn. Some certified teachers, however, might not be able to manage their classrooms and deal with students. Yes, they have a good knowledge of their subject area, though many instructors discussed the importance of professional development. They all agreed that it is important, but a lack of time and a supportive budget prevents many from paying much attention to it.

I personally think that professional development is important, especially when teaching in a technological field. New inventions are developed every day. Updating skills and keeping up with new knowledge are not only beneficial to personal growth, but also to helping students to learn. Yes, every student's learning is every teacher's business.

Pat & the training curriculum implementation team

Chapter 15: Working and Bonding

My profession as teacher in America allows me the opportunity to work with and learn from different groups of people. I am gaining significant life experience and acquiring useful skills to improve myself from every group with which I associate. On a daily basis, I interact with my direct supervisor, department co-workers, other department staff, and most importantly, the group of students under my supervision.

A working relationship with my supervisor is significant. It certainly can speed up my progress or slow down my production at work. I believe that a good and positive working relationship with a supervisor can make going to work everyday a productive and enjoyable experience.

As a vocational instructor, I report directly to a vocational training manager. I was fortunate to initially have the opportunity to work for a good, knowledgeable, and professional manager. My first supervisor interviewed for my position back in May 1999. He was the one that helped me learn strategies for a successful interview. A few years of working experience under his supervision was a wonderful opportunity to develop my life long learning skills. He was a supervisor who assumed three different roles for me. Firstly, he was my teacher. He not only taught me a routine for my new job, but he also had a great influence on my attitude toward my job. My first day on the job, my supervisor spent all afternoon training me on the forms and reports that need to be completed in my position. He took me around the campus to see different training areas and see all of the vocational instructors and the other staff. He gave me the information about the company and its services. He informed me about my students, and guided me about becoming a classroom manager.

Secondly, he was my counselor. He gave me assignments and he told me that he expected the best out of me. He encouraged me to do my best on the job. He listened to me when I had job-related problems, and I struggled to find ways to solve those problems. He helped me to develop better ways to find solutions. When I was out on sick leave after an operation, he personally called to see how I was doing, sent me a "Get Well" card, and offered his help. I recall the experience after I turned in the assignments that he gave me. If it was correct and satisfactory, I always saw a yellow post-it in my mail box stating, "Thank you, Pat," "Job well done!," "Great Job, Pat," "Looks Good!," and "Wonderful." It was a small thing, but it sure did make me feel good and helped me to have energy to work on my following projects. The little things he did showed me that he recognized my work.

On the other hand, when my completed assignments needed some improvement, I would receive a note or a phone call saying something like, "Pat, let's discuss the project at 4:30 p.m." or "Pat, can you please come to my office to take a look at this project to see what can be changed." While he had to correct my errors, he never put me down or made me feel small. Instead, he gave me tips to improve myself as an employee. All his encouraging words and advice made me strive to do the best I could do on every project I was assigned.

Finally, he was my leader. His important task was to provide the leadership my department required. He certainly provided motivation and support to all employees.

"What can I do to help you to do your job?"
"What tools do you need to do your job?"
"How can I support you?"
"My minimum expectation is……."

I remember hearing my leader lead our departmental meeting every Monday after school. My first supervisor was a professional who earned my full respect. He was not soft and easy; he was a strong leader who helped me build good work skills for my teaching. He helped make my working days a pleasant experience. He made himself approachable when I needed help on both personal and professional matters. He was a leader that managed his employees with a heart and recognized his employees as important individuals who had unique skills and personalities. He provided help and made recommendations whenever he saw the opportunity for career growth for his employees.

Since my first supervisor left the company, I have had the opportunity to work under a few more supervisors. They were absolutely different in both their personalities and in their managerial styles. They created different working climates in the department. Recently, I had the opportunity to work for one manager who really was different from the previous ones. Our working climate was somewhat dictatorial and tense. This manager was something of a micro-manager. Many employees under his supervision were very unhappy; for some, they even updated their resume to search for another opportunity. Interestingly, one of my co-workers listed many of the things that we experienced as a department under his supervision. It was wonderful for me to learn about her skill in shorthand after a year of working with her. At that point, I did not know that I would be able to learn many things from her life experience. She was a mom who sacrificed her own time to raise her children, while being a wife to a man who some Americans would categorize as a "high profile" and a "well-earned" professional. She was one of a few co-workers who were somewhat irritated by our supervisor's unprofessional treatment.

On two occasions, when I had meetings in the Vocation Manager's office about a field trip and center projects, I found a sheet of paper lying on the floor. I attempted to pick it up, thinking that my supervisor might have dropped it. Very rudely, the Vocation Manager told me to leave it on the floor because that is where garbage belonged. I was quite surprised at his behavior and social manner. I didn't say anything about it when he said, "I'm sorry Mrs. Sato, and it's not you. It is someone in our department." I just continued my meeting with him. Personally, I was thinking that we were a training facility that sought to produce employees that would behave in a mature manner in the work place; throwing paper on the floor and telling employees that garbage belongs on the floor doesn't sound like something I would want an employee of mine to do. As members of the staff, we are also supposed to demonstrate appropriate behavior in order to be good models to our students. I thought what he did was not proper; it is just my personal opinion. Later, I was told by one of my co-workers that someone submitted work that he was not pleased with.

I remember questioning whether it was the right thing to do for a person in a supervisory role. In Desktop Publishing class, we have an Apple laptop computer that is used in class for training, purposely for the students. The Vocation Manager "borrowed" it for his presentation one afternoon. A week later, he still had not returned it, and I asked for it back, so I could give it to one student to use in class. I was told that he wanted to borrow it for a few months. He also said he was going to reconfigure it during the time he had it. I was quite surprised and did not understand why he needed to make changes on equipment that didn't even belong to him. Since I needed it for class, because many saved work projects of my students were still on the hard drive, I finally asked him to bring it to me only one day before Thanksgiving, because I was going to save the information on the CD, so that my students could use it on another computer. He said, "Yes, sure, tomorrow I will bring it."

A week after Thanksgiving, he told me that he had left it at home. Three weeks later, I still had not been able to recover the information on the laptop computer he "borrowed" from my class. When I mentioned this matter to some senior instructors and the property warehouse supervisor, I was told that all equipment assigned to my class should always be in the class. No equipment should be transferred without proper paper work, and according to the warehouse department's record, my supervisor was assigned one laptop. He shouldn't have needed to borrow another one from the classroom for his personal use.

I didn't receive the laptop back from my supervisor until two weeks before his resignation from his position as Vocational Manager. He didn't return it to me directly; one of my students needed her file, so she went to ask his secretary. The secretary went to his office and got it for us while he was out on a leave. I told him about this matter when he came back a few weeks later. He apologized for not returning things that I needed to teach my class.

There were a few more occurrences that happened between my supervisor and some of my co-workers that taught me his management style created an unpleasant work environment for many employees. For instance, another instructor had not had any experience with

Microsoft Excel, which is the program on which our reports have to be filed, and she asked if she could take a class, so she could understand it better. Instead of allowing her to attend class, he sent a student from the Business Technology class to help her for 45 minutes. When she still didn't understand some tasks of the procedures, he was extremely rude to her in front of the entire staff.

Another instructor was trying to explain her problem because of the way the report was set up, and again he was rude to her and told her he couldn't believe that she still couldn't get it. I am sure that she felt humiliated. He also said that she frustrated him.

We received a gift card from the Corporation and one instructor thanked the Vocation Manager for the gift card. His extremely rude reply was that he did not have anything to do with it; he wouldn't give any rewards until his requirements were met.

He was not really rude toward me, nor did he try to intimidate me, but I saw that he was not good to some of my co-workers. One very good instructor had been in her position for almost 20 years and had earned awards for excellent teaching. She was about to turn in her resignation, because of the way he treated her. Since he knows that she arrives on campus early every morning, he told her that if she can't complete students in her class during the day, she could go to the dorms in the morning, find one of her students, and bring them back to her class to individually tutor them before class started.

I learned that in her twenty years, she had worked under many operation contractors and managers; 36 of them had come and gone. This supervisor was just one of those 36. I remember during a usual Monday afternoon meeting for the vocation staff in which several points from the student satisfaction survey were listed on the board.

He told us that we were to make sure that we answered every one of the questions on these topics on the student satisfaction survey during the next week, because he was not going to get a bad rating on this survey. One female instructor was sitting at the table shaking her head. When he asked her why, she said she did these things every day, but it sometimes doesn't sink into the students.

When one of the instructors tried to explain that some students have problems in class, his comment was that there are no bad students, just bad instructors. That really hurt the feelings of many wonderful, long-time instructors in our department.

In seven years working in a vocational department, I have experienced working under six vocational managers. I have never had any problem with any of them, personally or professionally. I choose to learn from each one's strong character and skills. I accept the fact that they might have a strong personality, which gives them the confidence to become a supervisor. They might also have their own supervisor who might put a lot of weight on their shoulders, too. They absolutely have authority over me. I certainly want to learn new things from them, but it doesn't happen every time. To me, liking or disliking a supervisor is not really important; the most important thing for me is how well I can deal with each supervisor and how productive I can be under their supervision.

The second group of people with whom I work closely is my department co-workers. They have been a wonderful group of colleagues. In seven years, I have seen co-workers come and go. I was the only Asian instructor among them. It was quite special, because I got a chance to sit on the front row during training or meetings, being that I am the smallest and the shortest one. A few jokingly refer to me as "A little Asian lady", or "A desktop lady." However, like many new instructors teaching in a new environment with a new group of experienced instructors, I felt small and was not very confident. It remained that way for a little while, because they helped guide me and worked well with me as a newcomer. None of them intimidated me, despite my lack of teaching experience and limitation of language. I am fortunate to have a wonderful group of departmental colleagues who are willing to teach me on a daily basis. I still have an especially good and healthy working relationship with a few experienced instructors. I definitely appreciate my own personality and positive attitude that helped me to overcome panicking, anxiety, and tension throughout my first year of teaching experience.

Being a positive, soft-spoken, and polite person helps me to get along well with all of my co-workers and to have a healthy working relationship with them. I have no choice but to work with them, in order to excel as a team. I have to work with them on an hour-to-hour, and day-to-day basis. I also value the individual personalities and skills which make our department so diversified and interesting. I acknowledge that this group of people has a strong influence on my personality and productivity as one of its team members. It is my responsibility to build and maintain a healthy relationship with them. It simply starts with sincerely giving them respect, being friendly and courteous, listening to them, helping them out when they need it, and being open-minded to concerns, advice, and suggestions.

There are three senior instructors in my department to whom I could give my full respect for their practice and value of teaching. They have many years of teaching experience from which I can learn and follow. They are instructors who actually helped and guided me, when I first started teaching. Mr. Polk, Mr. Murray, and Mrs. Irving are my on-the-job role models and mentors. Seven years of their consistent assistance at work makes going to work every day a blessing. Their comfort and encouragement when I encountered times of frustration and discouragement on the job was most appreciated. They take the time to listen and seek ways to find solutions on many problems on the job. They sometimes even guide me through my personal problems, so that they will not interfere with my performance at work. All three of them are very good examples of employees who are always punctual. In seven years, I don't remember a time that I was able to be more punctual than them; their cars are always in the parking lot before mine. I think the only time they report to work late is when they have a doctor's appointment. Other than that, they would be who a few of us have to call, in case of tardiness or illness. I know that they will be in their office before 6:00 a.m.

Mrs. Irving teaches a business technology class, and she carries herself like an outstanding officer worker. She sets herself up as a wonderful example for her students. I love the way Mrs. Irving dresses for work everyday. She loves colorful outfits; they are professional and appropriate at all times, and they look fabulous on her. Her classroom is so tidy, organized, clean, and smells so good with a plug-in room fragrance that she purchased at her own expense. Her class expectations are clear, and her consistent reinforcement of them is very strict. She always strives to create a wonderful learning environment for her students.

Mrs. Irving is not only a co-worker in the same department, teaching in the same building, but she is also a good friend. She takes time to listen to both professional and personal problems and provides help when it is needed. We work together and have collaborated on different assignments: staff training, student peer court, technology training, organizing a field trip for students, and field day monitoring.

I remember times that I had to run to her office to ask for help on different things, such as borrowing a mop and bucket, printer ink cartridges, drinking water, pieces of advice, and help in discipline for some students. She helped me a lot with proofreading work I designed. Her reminder to always save e-mails helps me stay out of trouble, because I sometimes carelessly delete it. Her compliment on my appearance makes me take time to dress myself appropriately. She allows me to see her as a mother figure, in that when I do something that I am not supposed to do, she will correct me. At lunch time on Tuesdays, we always have a wonderful chat while enjoying our lunch together.

In a similar way, Mr. Polk always helps to correct the most challenging students, when I am hardly able to handle them. I took the time to learn to discipline my students before I really asked for help. He used to teach me that, "you have to be able to control your own class. When you modify your students' behavior, do it assertively and consistently. Don't get others to help you when you can do it. The students are watching you. You don't need to discredit yourself." His compliment that I am a good classroom manager motivated me to do better, even though it is sometimes so difficult with a really tough student. After an exhausting day ends, he will always hear that, "They have worn me out today. Tomorrow, I will come back with a full charged battery." He laughed, when he saw me dragging myself to my car in the parking lot in front of his classroom.

He teaches a warehousing class. He makes sure all necessary supplies I have ordered are completed and ready to be used in class. His discipline of his students is strict and consistent. When his students get out of line, if I mention it to Mr. Polk, they will be brought back in line. They know that Mr. Polk does not play around. They surely don't want to mow a big area around our building as a punishment from Mr. Polk. His long-term dedication on the job is well-known around the center. His decades of teaching experience can be beneficial for new teachers.

Mr. Murray was my next door neighbor, and he would always go out of his way to help me. He taught a basic computer class. My first week of teaching would have been difficult without his friendliness and the welcoming atmosphere he created for me. He came over to my class to see if he could help me get things started. He showed me some weekly reports that I needed to submit. His suggestions for the tasks that needed to be done in my area to support the department were really helpful. His working relationship in my teaching career is appreciated. We would always schedule field trips together, and we would combine two classes for some activities, including fishing trips and cookouts. His fun and friendly conversations during lunch would provide one hour of relaxing time at work each day. Since we both love to eat, we would always seek good places to have lunch, and we would recruit a good group of lunch peers. Sometimes, we would have a luncheon for our students who performed well in class. We also hosted a one-hour pot luck luncheon for the staff to enjoy associating with each other during lunch. I still remember times that we would get up early on Saturday morning to take our students to the job fair. While I attended class during a summer session, when I was working on my teaching certification, he always helped me out by covering my class. His help in moving all of the equipment and furniture to my new classroom in a new building during the first three months of my pregnancy, has still not been forgotten, and his friendly care during my pregnancy was awesome. One morning after I came back from the restroom due to morning sickness, I saw that he had placed a bowl of fresh fruit and salted crackers on the desk in my office. His care, assistance, and friendship will always be remembered. He resigned from teaching and pursued a new challenge in automobile sales.

Another group of people with which I interact regularly at work is the other center staff, ranging from the groundskeepers to the administrators. I give my full cooperation to all of them. I know that there may be a time when I might I have to ask for their assistance. I still remember my godmother's teaching that "whatever you do, wherever you are, you don't burn the bridge behind you when it comes to dealing with people. We never know when we have to ask for their help." "I scratch your back, you scratch mine." I provide them my help related to software troubleshooting and computer-related problems. When they want banners, brochures, flyers, or newsletters designed, I help them or assign my students to help them. In those cases my students could utilize their skills learned in my class to complete job orders from different department staff. By providing help to others, I have no problem receiving their help in return when I need it. I have a good working relationship with people across the campus. I am sure to treat people with respect, regardless of their race, position, or background. They all have a great impact on my working experience in America. Elwood N. Chapman and Sharon Lund O'Neil, the author of *Your Attitude is Showing*, interestingly wrote about working relationship that, "You must build a relationship with all kind of people, regardless of race, religion, age, sex, or personality, characteristic. Each relationship is unique. Each will be built on a different basis. Each will have its own integrity," and "Life without continuously working at building good relationships is not living."

The last group of people I work with and interact with on a daily basis is the group of students I teach. They are the most important group of all, because they are under my supervision everyday, between

5 and 8 hours a day. They are the most significant group that needs my knowledge, attention, motivation, and guidance. This group allows me the opportunity to become a teacher who can teach simply because "I love kids." They allow me to make a difference in their lives by my teaching them. A majority of my students are called "at risk" or "high risk" youth. They are the most difficult youth group in America. Many of them have failed in public schools and have been enrolled in the federal training program for a second chance to learn and even a second chance in life. According to Dr. E. Salazar, high risk youth have the following characteristics:

- Feel they do not "belong" at school
- Are very quiet/withdrawn
- Exhibit disruptive behavior and rebellious attitudes
- Have a low level of self-esteem
- Are below expected grade level for their age
- Have low achievement test scores
- Exhibit language difficulties
- Are gifted or talented and perhaps bored with school
- Have poor home-school communications
- Are frequently absent or tardy
- Request frequent health referrals
- Are invisible dropouts (present in body but not in mind)
- Are parents
- Have difficulty relating to authority figures or structured situations.

Our center recruits these groups of students from different areas. Most of them come from a low income living area and violent environment. Some of them do not have any place to live; they live on a rough and violent street. They have developed survival skills, both appropriate and inappropriate. Recently, I had a chance to go with a recruitment team to hand out flyers and talk to people in many apartment complexes. It is an amazing thing to learn and see another part of the American living environment. The environment does not seem positive or safe. It does not look clean and friendly. There are young couples raising a few children. A couple fights and a girl cries. A group of people looks so lazy and unproductive. Children were running around and talking to each other without any manners. I told my co-worker that, after seeing that environment, it made me so thankful for what I have and value the generosity of my American family who paved the way for me to create a good, positive, and productive living environment for myself and my family. My co-worker told me that I have not really seen a bad part of it yet -- the part of America in a bad area where people are selling drugs, doing gang-related activities, and prostitution. I just realized that this group of American youth is called disadvantaged or "at risk."

Yes, I have many of them in class. I was initially told that many of my students are "professional manipulators," as they lack the responsibility to admit their mistakes. They will change their story from black to white, or turn it upside down to get out of trouble. I found that many of my students try very hard to talk themselves out of the situation, instead of accepting that they are wrong. That might be the reason that they never learn the importance of honesty. Whenever an incident occurs in class, it is not easy to get any of them to tell the truth. They always refuse to give out any information, no matter how helpful it is for the investigation. The situations that they are in might force them to lie or manipulate to survive. Many of them just keep saying that they do not want to "snitch" on anybody, so that they will not get into trouble. I have been told many times by students that, "where we are from, if we tell on someone, we can get beat up or can even get killed."

One important thing that I have learned so far is that it is not easy at all to earn the trust of this group of students. However, once you earn it, it will last forever. It makes me realize that there might be many situations or people in their lives that have broken promises or lied to them. Realizing this, I try my best to keep my word and also the appointments that I have with them. If I really forget what I told them, I will be sure to sincerely apologize and make it up to them. I will not try to find any excuses.

I admit that my first group of students was not only my students, but they were also my on-the-job teachers. They helped me learn to teach and assisted me to grow as a teacher. They also pushed me to strive to make a great impact of my students' lives. In the seven years since, it has been a lot of fun, laughs, pride, tears, sadness, sorrow, headaches, frustration, disappointment, anger, and even a fast growing number of my gray hairs, but I also have a great sense of success. It has been such an incredible experience teaching American students.

These days, I have a small area of class, but a large number of students almost every week. My class is like an elective class in high school. On our campus, the students can also choose their classes freely. On my roster, if there are around 15-20 students scheduled full-time; it is considered a small load for that week. Sometimes, I have as many as 28 to 35 students rotating morning and afternoon. I have 20 computers on which to train them. When I really have many students in class, I have to let them take turns, or I have to pair them up to work on one machine. That is really inconvenient for a hands-on teaching approach.

One time I had about 42 students scheduled on my roster, including regular and exploration rosters. After I saw my roll, I almost collapsed. Can you imagine a little Asian instructor with 42 American teenagers in a small room? It surely was not a fun learning day. The following day, my roster was smaller. The class schedule was corrected and it got smaller. I felt such relief; I could focus more on teaching than spending time on discipline in class. I personally do not believe that a ratio of one teacher for a large number of students is effective in teaching, especially in a vocational area that requires a great deal of hands-on training. Sometimes, a few students choose to act up in class with a great deal of disruptive behavior; I have to spend time talking to them in the office. That time needs to be used more for helping the majority of students, but this disciplinary time is part of my daily teaching. I sometimes acknowledge that some destructive behavior is just the way my students try to get attention. It is just a negative way of getting it.

I keep my relationship with all students on a professional level. I am there for them if they need me, but I am not their friend with whom they can joke around like they do to their peers. One time, one of my female students was waiting for me in front of the building early in the morning. When she saw me parking my car, she walked toward me and said, "Ms. Sato, I did something stupid last night and now I am in trouble. My parents are mad at me. I just want to let you know before you find out about it from the other people, and she briefed me on the situation. She had to go to the court house for her actions, which were public intoxication and displaying of affection. Nobody in her family wanted to go with her. She came to my office one morning and asked me if I could go with her. I ended up sitting in the courtroom listening to her story and the penalty she received.

She graduated from the program and got employed doing a design job for an advertising company in West Texas. She was the best one in the group of my first-year students. She had a very good eye for layout and design. Actually, she was studying in college before she came to the program, but without self-discipline and direction, she failed a few of her classes and had to owe a big amount of a student loan. When I sent her for the intern position in a printing company, she did an excellent job. Her customers loved her work.

Another female student who is very negative and argumentative was really mad at me, when I corrected her inappropriate behavior in class. She became very disrespectful, yelled and used bad language. I tried so hard to calm her down and stayed patient in dealing with her. Instinctively, I knew the whole class was watching and listening to how I would react. I did not respond to her rudeness. She told me that she was going to drop my class, because she did not like me. While she was loud, I was calm and quiet. I patiently waited until she finished, spending my time helping the other students. When she calmed down, I called her into my office, and talked with her for a long time about her inappropriate behavior, undesirable work skills, and unacceptable language. She finally apologized. Unfortunately, I learned that she was behaving this way in her house; that made her mother and her not get along, and she had to leave the house because of her inappropriate behavior.

After that day, I still had to correct her many times, but her response was not the same. She responded in a respectful manner and tone of voice. I did not change my expectations of her. I continued to do the same in modifying her behavior. She told me that she realized I corrected her because I wanted her to be good, and she has been trying. Many months later, she finished my class and was ready to move on in her life. She announced that I was her favorite teacher. Yes, I almost pulled all of my hair out while pushing her through the training. However, I felt a sense of pride hearing this, after continuing to modify that negative behavior of hers. I hope that she is doing well in her life.

While a same-sex marriage is a very controversial issue in American society, I have experienced the opportunity to work with a few American gay and lesbian youth in class as well. By interacting with them daily, it allowed me to hear their point of view as a people who chose that path of life.

One of my 19 year old female students openly shared with me about her life and her decision on homosexuality, while I counseled her on her negative behavior in class. She stated that, "I guess it all started in high school that I knew I'd be gay. I just acted upon my judgment. I would always hang around a whole lot of boys or tomboyish females. By doing so, I would listen to their comments on other females and then think the same thing." After hearing this, I started asking questions about her home life. This is what she told me.

"At home, I would find myself doing the same. I grew up with three older brothers. I would never let it show to the public, but in my heart, I knew exactly what and how I felt. I was scared of being judged or criticized. I was afraid." She paused and softly continued talking while looking at me.

"The community's reaction petrified me, because I didn't want to become an outcast or anything. I knew exactly how my mother felt about lesbians, so I had to make up my mind. I wouldn't tell anyone that I had started talking to other females in a relationship manner;

I would do it only in private or secluded areas; in public, I would pretend not to know them, especially around my family and friends. Soon, after my mother began to have her little thoughts about my decision, I became more open with it."

"Only because when boys were around, I would give them little or no attention at all. I was uninterested in them. However, when females come around, we'd play and fondle on one another, but it is only in a slick manner." I was paying attention to her story while she was telling it. I was also thinking that this student would have become a very fine young lady because of her good fortune of being a beauty. However, I did not say anything; I just kept listening as she continued her conversation, "That was so; no one would notice our behavior. Then, my expression and emotion towards men slowly changed, soon men were completely banned. They were not only banned totally from my mind, but my heart as well. My caring for boys being completely gone, I started being careless about all my actions when around my friends and select family members." "How did your family take it?" I asked. She just smiled and responded,

"I would show all my true affection towards females. I am not saying that they didn't care, but I just didn't care how they felt. This is how I am going to be, but I was determined to be myself in front of my elders. I'd show the utmost respect. I never disrespected my elders; with my peers and siblings, it was a different story."

"While going to work, I met a very special woman who taught me the facts about the world and school lifestyle. Her name is Mrs. Williams. She would always let me be my true self; I opened up to her because she wanted me to really see who I actually was deep down inside. She knew I was mature enough to make my own decision. I started to confide in her for everything until one day my sister and

I decided that we were grown enough to get up and move out. We moved out from under my mom's roof with her rules and regulations. We then moved in with Mrs. Williams for several months. She cared for us as if we were her own children. She taught us that everything in this world is not free. She taught us about how life is supposed to be lived, and how to maintain self and school at the same time." I commented that she was quite lucky to have someone to guide her in a good direction.

"While living under her household's rules and regulations, I began to spread my wings and explore my other options. I was no longer afraid to be my own person; I'm my true self now. I'm my own woman and I would like to thank Mrs. Williams for giving me that opportunity.

"On August 29, 2005 tragedy hit home; hurricane Katrina devastated me. It devastated all of us; we were separated from our families and friends. My family and I were still stuck in New Orleans, before we finally were moved to the Super Dome, a stadium in New Orleans. We were all terrified because the stadium was so overly crowded with hundreds of people. Everyone was afraid to move because there were so many things that were going on; people were crying and dying. My sister and I were scared to even make a move because women and children were being raped and killed.

"Soon after, we were transported by bus to Texas. We lived in a Wal-Mart shelter where recruiters from the Job Corps program asked us if we wanted to come to the program. My sister and I were given brochures; after looking them over, we decided to come. We arrived at Job Corps on October 18, 2005. We were so lonely and we didn't know anyone and didn't know anything about Texas. The teachers and the staff were all nice. In the dormitory, I began to meet other females. Being a new student, I kept my sexuality to myself. I didn't want to be the "The new gay girl." Some females knew I was gay by the way I acted or maybe it was my rainbow jewelry that gave me away.

"I wore my rainbow necklace and bracelet that symbolizes the rainbow colors; that's when two female lesbians approached me. Both of them wanted to become my girlfriend, but I denied them because of their reputation. People may not know it, but that's important; a reputation is your past and it determines your future. No one wants a person with a bad reputation, so I decided to just be their friends."

"Now, I have a girlfriend and I am going to concentrate on my studies. I will make the best of what is being provided here."

This student has completed her training and is currently working on her high school diploma. She is actively participating in the center's projects in the community. She volunteers her time to help out when we have an activity outside the campus. She still comes by my office to say hello and to ask for help when she needs it. Whenever she sees me around campus, she always greets me with a big smile.

One day I got a chance to talk to one male student who obviously chose his own path of living. He is a good student who has a good eye for design. I encouraged him to further his education in his area of interest, which is fashion design. He has potential; I am sure that with hard work and determination, he will become successful in that field. That day, he was quietly typing his paper about himself to share with me. It is interesting to learn about my students as individuals, while teaching them in the subject area. He enthusiastically presented his profile paper. It stated,

> "Through life we all come through many trials, tribulations and choices that we make. Those choices make a big difference in life and how things will look for the near future. My sexuality

plays a big part in my experience of society. Being gay is a battle that I must fight everyday. You know, people always ask me why I choose to be gay, but what they don't realize is that it is not a choice, nor really a preference. This is my sexuality, something that I honestly can't help.

Ever since I could remember, I have been attracted to the same sex. I have never been sexually molested, touched, talked to, nor did I grow up around homosexuals or lesbians. One thing that I keep in mind and try to let other people know is that I am who I am, but it does not make me less than anyone else. My sexuality is less than half of me; I enjoy other unrelated activities just like everyone else; I enjoy things such as movies, friends (gay or straight), traveling, and family.

Being here at Job Corps and being open is hard at times. Public displays of affection is supposed to be enforced for everyone, gay or straight, but the majority of the time, I feel that when I am told to stop holding hands that it is directed towards me because of the fact I am holding hands with another man. What I am doing is something different and sorry to say, unusual to some people. You get looks, questions, and comments (bad and good ones).

Being in Ms. Sato's Desktop Publishing class has been one of the most enjoyable experiences to me. She treats me no differently than the other students. I look forward everyday to coming to class to work, learning, and laughing at Ms. Sato's funny remarks. She is a great teacher.

In-fact, I have been here in my desktop publishing class for the past four and a half months, and I have gotten acquainted with a really cool guy. He is a heterosexual male and I am a gay male, and we have never had any problems. To be honest, I kind of look at him as the big brother that I always wanted! He just works my nerves sometime with his playful acts and comments, but he's still my brother.

Overall, I try to keep everything pretty confidential, other than being here at Job Corps trying to obtain my GED and learn more working skills. Being gay states my sexuality not my individuality. I am more than a man that is attracted to other men. I hope that this brief talk will set better standards for homosexuals and let people see that this life-style is not a bunch of drag queens or a HIV/AIDS feast. There are plenty of us that think of ourselves as role-models in the community: doctors; lawyers; and political leaders in this country."

Above are just a few examples of my working relationship with various groups of students during my teaching experience here in America. Yes, I remember a great deal about them. Some students do well after completion and graduation, moving on to better and bigger things in life, but still calling and sharing information with me. However, many of them I never have the opportunity to keep in touch with and to learn how they are doing. As their instructor, I just wish them all the best of luck in life and hope that they make wise choices and are good citizens in the community in which they live.

Career Technical Training Department

Pat & Students on the field trip

Chapter 16: Lost Product—Live Hope

One thing I never want to do is to give up on my students, no matter how challenging they may be. In seven years of teaching, I try to help them in any way I can; I meet with them one-on-one to talk about the good things they do, the inappropriate things, and the misbehavior I see in class. I also discuss with them the problems that they may have. I work closely with their counselor to find ways to solve their problems, such as when my students have excessive absences in my class, and when negative behavior repeatedly occurs. When my students went home on the weekend and a few of them did not return to the center on time, I called their home to make sure they were doing fine. They might have been having transportation problems or some incidents at home that prevented them from coming back to class on time. When I know that students think about abandoning their studies without completing anything — no vocation completion, no GED, no driver's license, I encourage them to stay and put more effort into accomplishing the most they can with the services that we provide at the center. I always mention to them that they have invested their time and effort, and if they put in a little bit more, they can see the result. Some students do listen and try harder, but some students just decide what they want to do, without seeing the consequences for themselves and family.

I don't give up. Unfortunately, one of my female students decided to give up on herself and completely shut the door on people who would be able to help her. She finished all her academic classes and got her GED (Graduate Equivalency Diploma). She completed my class and worked on the process of finding a job and transitioning out of the program.

Paige Gowens officially enrolled in my class in May 2005. She was exploring my class for two weeks before being placed full time with me. She was one of several African- American students who enthusiastically wanted to come to my class. She actually worked on her assigned class projects. A majority of them just wanted to lay back, put their heads down on the desk, talk to their classmates, and not take any initiative to learn. They just want to be told every step to complete each task, instead of taking time to learn them in class. She worked quietly at her workstation most of the time and got her work done in a timely manner. I did not have to confront her about many incidents of inappropriate behavior in class, like I had to do to some students. I only had to talk to her a few times about her inappropriate public displays of affection to her boyfriend in the hallway, or sometimes in the corner near the classroom. Another thing I observed outside of my class during break time and lunch time was that she used profanity with her peers excessively. I did not hear much in class. When I corrected her behavior, she responded positively. She was a trainable student. Actually, she was the first student in the many groups that I had trained who had spent time planning her design. She sketched the storyboard on all of her presentation projects. She wrote down the information in her notebook. I thought she would be a good and successful worker. I kept encouraging the positive things she did in class.

When I had new students come into class, she took initiative to help them on the easy projects. She was volunteering to train several exploration students, while she was the advanced student in class. When staff asked our class to work on different projects, she offered to work on those projects. However, one thing I observed about her was that she was always sucking her thumb when her hands were not on a keyboard or working on a computer. From looking at her student's profile, I got the information that Paige was almost eighteen years old. She was eighteen years old and she still sucked her thumb; I really think that there is something behind this behavior. Several times, I physically and politely pulled her thumb out of her mouth without making any joke or comment about it. She just smiled at me and continued working. When I continued seeing her behavior not changing and I got a few reports on her from different members of the staff, I talked to her privately in my office. She just smiled and did not respond much. One time I asked her if she thought a keyboard that many people typed on in class was dirty. She replied, "Yes, Miss." Then, I mentioned to her about her sucking all of the germs on her thumb after typing on that keyboard.

She looked at me and said, "Ms. Sato, that's disgusting." I smiled and asked, "Why are you still doing it?" "I don't know, I will try to stop," she told me. That gave me the opportunity to talk to her about a job. "It is not employable. I am sure you can work on it. I don't think you want to sit in the office sucking your thumb while you are working. It will not look pretty." I said. "No, I don't want to do that," she responded. I offered to help her to discontinue this behavior by asking her to allow me to pull her thumb out every time I saw her doing it. Yes, she gave me permission to pull her thumb out of her mouth. We even tried putting a band-aid on her thumb. When I shared the information with my co-workers, they thought I was crazy to make that offer. She was eighteen years old; she should be responsible enough for pulling her own thumb out of her mouth. I thought so too, but obviously she could not do it. Otherwise, I would not have observed that behavior repeatedly in my class.

In the classes after our meeting, I did not see much change in this behavior. I discussed this with her counselor, and I was told that he knew about this behavior and had discussed it with her already. He was aware of it, and we decided to help each other by confronting her whenever we saw it occur. Paige did not like to go outside of class much during break time. She liked to announce to class when it was break time. Then, she put her thumb in her mouth and put her head down on the desk at her workstation to take a 10-minute nap. I corrected her on this behavior, too. It didn't seem to improve. After a few conferences with her counselors, I found that Paige was from a broken family that had no mother when she was growing up. Her father just got out of jail, and he is currently staying with his mother who no longer wants to have anything to do with Paige, due to her negative behavior. Paige did not plan to go back home. She wanted to look for a job and live on her own.

I used to tell Paige that she would be able to find an office job. With the computer skills she had obtained, she could be a desktop publisher or an office secretary. However, Paige had to work harder to stop sucking her thumb and using bad language. She quietly listened and did not respond to anything. I tried to help her look for a job, but she did not cooperate. I sent her on a job interview at a publishing company. She initially did not want to go. I encouraged her to give it a try. If not for anything else, it could have been a good experience. She completed all her class work. I gave her extra projects to practice her skills. Initially, she cooperated and did such a great job. Not too long after that, she stopped practicing and working in class.

Unfortunately, I later observed a big behavioral change in her on a daily basis. She became rude to a lot of people, especially classmates who got in her way in class. She started talking excessively in class with a few classmates. When I corrected her, she talked back and became rude and disrespectful. She slept excessively in class. She left class early for lunch and again before dismissal time in the evening. I asked her if I could talk to her privately in the office, and she came to see me; we started talking about the changes I observed. She stayed silent most of the time during the conversation. When I started documenting her inappropriate behavior, and when I did not see any changes after a few meetings with her, she became upset and really rude toward me. I found out later on that her disrespectful behavior did not happen only in class, but also occurred in different areas at the center. I met with her counselor regarding her behavior.

He met with her and informed me that the meeting was not going well. She did not respond too many of his questions, but she told him that she did not want to go back home. He finally called her family and found out that they were not ready for her to come home. They wanted her to look for a job. Her transition coordinator was working closely with her to search for a job, but Paige did not give her full cooperation. Paige also did not put her effort into seeking the opportunity. Her negative attitude and behavior still continued in class and began interfering with other students' learning. I decided to send an e-mail to my supervisor at the time, asking him to meet with her regarding her disruptive behavior in class.

I did not get any reply, but he told me that he received the e-mail. He did not meet with her. Her behavior was getting worse. Her counselor, transition coordinator, and I met to discuss her situation and to see what we could do for her. Everybody was trying to help her after training, since she did not want to go home. Our goal was to help her find a job and get settled into her own apartment, but we all expected her to do her part, which meant cooperating fully. For a reason that I did not initially understand, she told us that she did not care whether we would help her or not. She stayed silent most of the time when we talked to her; once in a while, when asked a question, she would reply, "I don't know."

Her transition coordinator called her grandmother's home to talk to her father and sometimes to her aunt. Paige's aunt informed the coordinator about her negative behavior at home. Her family asked the center to keep her a little bit longer. They emphasized that they were not ready to accept her at home. I believe they told her this when she called home, but I had no way to know for sure, because she kept silent when she was asked. Her counselor did not get much information out of her either.

One day I received a call from her father asking me to help keep her longer. I told him that I did not have any authority to keep students at the center or to send students home. However, I could help by advising Paige to stay at the center with a positive attitude and behavior, and to stay out of trouble. Basically, she needed to do what she was supposed to be doing, so that she would not get sent home quickly, especially before she had completed her training. She had skills to find an entry level job in any company. He mentioned about her often-reported negative behavior, while asking for the extension for his daughter to stay on campus. He stated that his situation at home was not ready to accept her back home. He said he needed at least 60 to 90 days to work on the situation he was in at that moment. He informed me that he was living at the student's grandmother's house, and that she had not quite agreed to have Paige at home.

During our conversation, I informed him that I was having an ongoing problem with her; her attitude had become lackadaisical, she had started showing negative behavior, and she had become very uncooperative in class, right after she learned that she had completed her TAR (Training Achievement Record). I have had to physically wake her up and pull her thumb out of her mouth, while she was telling me that she was going to put it back in. Almost everyday, she has left class early for lunch. Sometimes, she asks permission to go to the restroom and does not return to class until the class is dismissed for lunch. When I assigned her some tasks to do in class while she was present, she refused to do them and told me that she did not want to be bothered. She adamantly refused to follow my instructions. When I confronted her about her behavior, she responded negatively and stated that she did not want to be corrected or advised.

The situation was discussed with Mr. Roberts, her case manager, Ms. Lee, and Mr. Johnson, the student personnel manager. After a few conferences, there were no changes in her behavior and attitude. I documented her behavior and informed her counselor about it. Her father asked me to "Please work with her." "I am trying, sir. Actually, we all have been trying." I responded to him.

When her father called again and requested to talk to her, she had already left early for lunch without my permission. When she came back from lunch around 1:30 p.m., I allowed Paige to call him back. She certainly did not want to call. I asked her to do it. After their conversation, her father requested to speak with me again. He requested a meeting to personally confront Paige about her behavior by himself. He informed me that she did not respond much over the phone. I informed him that he could come any time. I also told him that I would notify Paige's counselor and transition coordinator. He stated that he would try to find a ride to the campus some time the following week. I had no way of knowing that it would just be a conversation over the phone. The meeting that he requested never happened. I informed Paige of her father's appointment and upcoming visit.

"What is he coming to school for, Ms. Sato?" she asked.

"He wanted to visit with you. He told me that he has not talked to you for a while, because you have not gone home." I replied.

"He should not come. I will not see him, Miss," she told me, as she turned back to talk to her friend. Her attitude seemed like she did not care about his coming to school.

"Paige, let's meet with him together. He wants to see you. He cares about you. I want to meet your father, too." I responded.

"Miss, he has never cared about me before. Why do you think he cares about me now? It was quite difficult for me to answer her question, since I knew neither of them very well at all. I did not know much of their relationship and situation at home that might be affecting her attitude and behavior. It is quite sad, because I have seen similar problems with many of my students. Some of them do not know who and where their biological parents are; some never had any good training at home from their parents.

"If he did not care about you, he would not call you and want to meet with you at the center. He might have something significant to discuss with you." I thought that was my best try.

"He just wants to ask you guys to keep me in school longer. He does not want me to go home. I don't want to go home either." She gave me her thoughts, and that was the longest conversation I had had with her in a while.

"If you don't want to go home, you can look for a job and save some money. Then you can find your own place. However, I think you should at least see your father to tell him about your plan." That was my second try. She did not respond and started to work on her computer. I just left her with her thoughts and started working with the other students. That was a Friday class.

Monday morning, Paige did not attend my class, and I did not see her in the few days that followed. I asked her classmates, but nobody could tell me much about her. Some told me that she had not been in the dormitory either. I called her counselor and her transition coordinator. None of them knew where she was. We all knew that she was not at the center. She left the center on a weekend pass and continued her absence without permission to leave. I decided to call her part time job at a fast food place. The manager told me that she asked for a few days off to take care of some personal business. I was wondering where she went, because she did not want to go home. Her counselor called her house and she was not there. We were all concerned about her absence.

Paige showed up on Tuesday afternoon one week later. I saw her standing in front of my classroom door, when I came back from my lunch break. It was her sixth day of being absent. While I let everybody back into class, I greeted her, "Good afternoon Paige, I missed having you in class. Where have you been?" She smiled and said, "Oh, I just wanted to have some time off, Miss." "Well, welcome back." I said. Since she was in class that day, her counselor called me and asked if he could talk to her in his office. She came back to class after their meeting.

All afternoon, she did not act up in class. She stayed quietly reading her book, writing on paper as she usually did, since she finished all her class projects. I asked her to laminate a few sheets of paper for staff members. She did it without any problem, like she used to do for the past few weeks. Her attitude was fine, unlike two weeks before when she was disrespectfully telling me that, "Don't tell me to do any work for anybody. I don't want to be bothered." I was wondering whether the students in my country would react this rudely toward their teachers these days. When I was growing up, I would not have talked to my teacher inappropriately. I showed respect to them at all times; even when my teachers walked by, I would stand straight and let the teacher go before me. I was not allowed to talk back for anything. It was a norm that we had practiced from elementary school, to high school, and into college. I could not expect that from the majority of my American students.

After Paige finished the work I assigned, she gave it back to me nicely. When I saw her attitude that day, I thought that she might decide to change her attitude toward my supervision and choose the right way to control her own behavior. **I was completely wrong!!**

Around 7:35 a.m. on Wednesday that week, I checked into work at the center's front gate as usual. The security guard informed me that my supervisor wanted to see me in his office. I was wondering why he was there so early. Normally, I did not see him at work before 10:00 a.m. After I sat down on the couch in his office, my supervisor told me that he went to my classroom last night searching all the computers' hard drive. I did not ask "Why?", but listened as he continued. He said, "Mrs. Sato, one of your female students, Paige Gowens, shot herself in the head, in the dormitory last night after she came back from work. It was around midnight. I have been at the center ever since" I was speechless; I could not believe what had happened. He continued, "Sorry for searching through your computers in the classroom. I was told that her suicide note was on a computer. It is a mess in your classroom now, because I did not have time to clean up."

"Did you find anything?" I asked. "No, nothing was found," he said, and I asked him about the incident. He shared with me what he knew: "She shot herself with two bullets. It was a small gun. Right now we are investigating where she got the gun. She is now on life support in a hospital in Dallas." He also asked me not to let any of my students get on any computer in my classroom when they come to class. Her family was informed and thought that she might have gotten the gun from one of her female friends' boyfriends.

That morning I did not see my students until 9:00 AM. They came to class after a mandatory assembly in the gym. The assembly was unusually quiet when our center director made the announcement to inform us about Paige's decision to take her own life. My students came to the classroom with fear and sadness. Some were crying and expressing strong interest in going home. There was a big issue concerning safety on campus. There was a big caucus in class. I spent my time talking and soothing my students. I remember offering so many hugs to many of them while I was still shocked myself with the incident. One male student who was always sitting next to Paige in class and who was Paige's closest classmate talked to me with sadness. He hugged me and started crying quietly. He asked permission to stay with me in class before starting back to work for the other department in the following hours. I was concerned about him all day long after the tragedy because he is usually a quiet student in class, and I did not really know what he would think. Paige was only one of his classmates he usually talked to. He told me that Paige did not mention anything while they were having a conversation in class the day before the incident.

All morning, I could not teach and my students could not learn. We were all in class quietly finding things to do to occupy our time and thought. Many people came to my office to check on me and the students to see if we were O.K. The following day, the center's psychologist came to make sure I was doing fine. He offered himself if I needed to talk to him. I was also informed that he talked to Paige's boyfriend, who had recently broken up with her; she was trying to get back with him. She told her ex-boyfriend that she would kill herself that night. The boyfriend did not take it seriously, but Paige did it. She killed herself around midnight, just as she told him. She did this while her three roommates were in bed sleeping. I don't really know what to call that decision: brave, ignorant, or selfish?

After I dismissed my students for lunch, one male student stayed behind and said, "Mrs. Sato, are you really O.K.?"

"I'm fine, but I need your help if you are not in a hurry to go eat lunch. I need you to help me search through every trash can in our class."

"Do you think Paige's letter might be in the trash can?" He asked me.

"I really don't know, but it doesn't hurt to look, right?" I responded, while starting my search.

He also started going through each trash can with me, and he told me that there was nothing that he could find. "Thank you very much, Bradley. Let's go eat." I said, while trying to lock my office door and get ready to accompany my co-worker who was waiting on me.

"Wait, Mrs. Sato, look! there are many small pieces of paper on the bottom of this waste bin." He told me. I hurriedly walked to him in the back of my classroom. After we got many of the pieces, we tried to put some of them together like a puzzle. I could read a little portion of it. It was Paige's suicide letter, written by her. I recognized her handwriting. I then learned that she also typed that letter and saved it on her closest classmate's flash drive. He had no idea that she had done so. I turned everything in to my supervisor, including all of the puzzle pieces. The police got the flash drive. I had no intention of knowing what was in the letter. I let my supervisor handle that matter. I focused on counseling, confronting my students in class, and listening to updated news on Paige's condition from the hospital.

A few days later, it was announced center wide that Paige Gowens passed away. It was a tragedy that brought us all sadness. Yes, she was gone as she wished to be. To many people, it seemed that Paige had planned this incident to make many people feel bad. I was informed by people who attended the meeting with her family that there was no sadness shown among her family's members. I was sad, mad, and disappointed that she chose this way to show her bravery and to prove people wrong. She would never know that; everyone grieved for a few days and they could then move forward with their lives, and she has since never been mentioned at all around campus. Later, I learned to accept that it was her life; that was the way she had chosen, I could not change anything about it. Of course, it is sad that she is no longer here for us to offer any further help.

I never thought that while America has many problems with the aggressive behavior of its young students in school (even in preschool) — teenage students abusing their freedom, which seems to me to be far too much; high school students' engaging in violent activity and even bringing weapons to school; the drop out rate increasing in public schools — that I would be experiencing those problems to the same extent. Who is to be blamed for the problem? Students? Parents? Teachers? The problem is that of raising a child in a broken home. While my students represent my professional hopes, they should also represent their parents' personal hopes. I just think that if we all do the best on our part, the number of problems might decrease. I just don't believe that education and discipline can only be the responsibility of the teacher at school. It is not a small task to teach many already misbehaving students in a very short period of time. What most teachers could hope to do is to just touch the surface, which often appears to be very calm. We never know what is really boiling under the surface. Some expect the negative behavior that has accumulated for almost seventeen years to be turned around within six to eight months, though that behavior is not removed before the teachers have the opportunity to teach and work with their students.

Dr. Shinichi Suzuki, the founder of Suzuki Method International, interestingly stated that "The responsibility for education is in the home." He said that one day he went to observe in an elementary school during the "Parent Teacher Association" meeting. He observed the principal greeting to the mothers asking for their continued cooperation in the home education of their children. The mothers were grateful and agreed to cooperate. After listening to their exchange, he thought that those people were a little crazy because of the way that they exchanged roles in their children's lives. He asserted that "The person who plants a seed in his field and cultivates it is the cultivator. Parents are cultivators. They are the ones responsible for raising their children with love. When the responsible person is asked to "cooperate" by the other person and agrees, it seems that the main and auxiliary roles are reversed. Something also seems wrong with the school teachers. If the neighbor of a farmer, who was caring for his own field, asked the farmer to "cooperate" in the care of that field, the farmer would become incensed. Nobody has the responsibility for bringing up a child to be a fine person except the parents of that child. It is the school teacher who should cooperate with the parents in educating children. It is the parents who should be asking the teacher for cooperation and the school which should agree. Remember that if a child commits a crime, it is the parents and not the teachers who are held responsible by law. This one thing shows the responsibility parents have for educating children in the home. There are parents who forget their duty to their children by leaving the education of their children entirely up to the schools. Having ignored their children, the parents feel their responsibility for the first time when their children run up against the law. This is the retribution of cause and effect."

After Paige's suicide, one of my co-workers told me that, as a teacher, we can not save them all, no matter what we do and no matter how hard we try. I have learned that all I can do is to save the rest of my students, one student and one future at a time. As I was taught to *"motivate them to be where they are supposed to be, do what they are supposed to be doing, and when they are supposed to do it,"* my primary goal each day is to do my best to train and prepare these American youths for the working world in their America. As the center's theme, *"Whatever It Takes!"* is still actively running, my hope for each of my students is to consistently help them to move forward, even though *I have lost one.*

Chapter 17: Products of Hope

In my life, I have had several great teachers who have shown me that they actually care for their students, rather than just teaching their subject areas. Due to the circumstances in my life, my graduation with a Master's Degree would have been delayed for one semester, if I had not received a long, encouraging e-mail from Dr. Espinoza in addition to the office visitations and positive discussions I had with her. In high school, Mrs. Benja Jitkrasem encouraged me to do well, and she always praised me when she saw me helping my mother sell food at the market in the morning before I went to school. When she found out I had an interest in learning English, she gave her time after school for me to practice communicating in English with her. Mrs. Sirion Kanthahat was an active role model for me, encouraging me to participate in a small business practice when I was studying for my Bachelor's Degree in a business school in Thailand. Her advice when I was in trouble helped me to graduate in time with all of my classmates. These teachers made me believe that there would not be any teachers in this world without students for them to work with. They certainly made me realize that there was hope for me as a student. On the other hand, I recall when I was in high school that there were a few teachers who were knowledgeable in their fields, but they could not teach their students. They knew their subject area, but just could not transfer their knowledge to their students, and they did not seem to care if we received the information or needed any extra help.

Since I am now a teacher, I want to be a knowledgeable teacher who can teach her students, as well as a teacher who actually cares. I once read in a book about how many students really feel toward their teachers, and it said that "They don't care how much you know, but they do know how much you care.... about them." Before I can teach, I have to learn to acknowledge who my students are by creating a good rapport with them. Many of my students learn that I will stand up for them and support them 100% on all the things they choose to do, but if they choose to do inappropriate things that are against the center's rules and regulations, I will not do anything to help them to get out of trouble. I always emphasize to them that they must learn to take responsibility for their own actions; doing the right thing in the right way makes everyone's life simpler. Is it easy for the majority of these American youth to understand this concept? No. Many of them still challenge their authority figures to prove that their views and their ways are always right, regardless of the rules and expectations. Consistency is an important key that I use when working with these products of hope. I consistently reinforce appropriate behavior, while correcting inappropriate behavior every day, in addition to teaching the class subject. Every chance I get to recognize the right things they do, I never hesitate to do so. I try to find at least one positive thing to recognize for each one of them, even though for some, it is not an easy task. I have been practicing what some people call "**Celebrating What Is Right,**" in my own little class, with the most challenging group of American students. Some students even told me that the reward they received from me was the first reward they ever had in their life. Some let me know that they had never won anything in their entire life, after they win my creative contest project. That gives me a chance to tell them that doing the right thing is the most proud experience that a winner can have before they enter into any kind of race. When you win for doing the right thing, it is always worth more than a World Cup award; it is an award in life achievement that we do not need to wait for anyone else but ourselves to recognize.

I visited the admissions office one evening for student recruitment. Looking on their bulletin board, I found an interesting one page flyer on the wall asking,

Who is a student?
A student is the most important person ever, morning, noon, and night.
A student is as dependant on us as we are dependant on them.
A student is not an interruption of our work… they are the purpose of it. We are not doing them a favor by serving them…they are doing us a favor by giving us the opportunity to do so.
A student is not an outsider to our business… they are our business.
A student is not a cold statistic. They are flesh-and-blood human beings with feelings and emotions like your own, and with biases and prejudices.
A student is not someone to argue or match wits with; nobody ever won an argument with a student.
A student is a person who brings us their wants and needs. It is our job to train them in such a fashion that will stay with them for the rest of their life.
A student is a potential graduate; it is our work to help them succeed.

The one definite thing I find as a teacher is that I can not choose my students. My job is to teach whoever enrolls in my class, regardless of their races and background; it does not matter if they are Black, Hispanic, Asian, or White. Each of them is a unique individual who needs an opportunity to learn and a chance to better their life. They allow me the opportunity to hope for them. I have decided to include this essay from a student of mine. I love to read his essay, because it helps me to understand his life and that of many of my students who are following his path. It also gives me a chance to learn about life situations they have been through and how they want to change and benefit from this federal program.

How Job Corps Changed My Life

By Jeffrey Jones, Desktop Publishing Student, 1999 (North Texas Job Corps)

Job Corps is a place where you can learn, grow, mature, and experience life. Some people find a family, learn employability skills, and fulfill a dream. Some students even have the opportunity to follow the footsteps of an admired loved one. Many people come to Job Corps seeking something and end up finding much more. This also proved to be true in my life journey.

I never took life seriously, or should I say, I never made the best of my life. Growing up I was not your typical child. I've stolen, lied, worked the street, and at times been homeless. I can remember being placed in childcare services when I was twelve years old, because of physical abuse in the home. I continued school, but because of the frequent relocating I was unable to attend school regularly. In the twelfth grade, I was on government assistance, getting food stamps, and living in a room paid for by taxpayers. Because of the frequent relocation involved when I was in childcare, in order to find suitable housing I had to drop out of school and pay my own way by working full-time at two jobs. Becoming homeless led to losing both jobs. When both jobs were gone, I started selling drugs. I never had a chance to go back to school and obtain my high school diploma.

By this time my mother had been diagnosed with an enlarged heart, diabetes, and arthritis, illnesses that turned out to be very serious. Because of these health problems, she moved to Texas. She enrolled my sister in Job Corps, where she later graduated. That's how I found out about Job Corps and the opportunities it presented. My mother has all her children's GEDs and high school diplomas on her wall. Now she can add mine.

My mother, after raising seven children and despite being ill, finally went to college and became a Certified Nursing Assistant (CNA), a job she loved. My mother's career was ended by her illness. My sister's career as a CNA that she obtained because of Job Corps was also cut short; she's 22 and has cancer. I'm proud to say that I've almost completed my vocational training and soon will also become a CNA. I've also completed a course in Desktop Publishing, and I've learned to love computers and their various functions.

I feel I didn't have a family life, because I was placed in foster care at such a young age. Being at North Texas, I met a lot of students, staff, and supporting staff (substitute instructors) that have become family. They have helped me to feel pride in what I do and to never set my goals lower than my ambition, and that attitude goes hand in hand with success. By having activities such as trips to the movie theater, basketball games, wilderness hikes (camping), and eating out, it has taught and instilled in me that good recreational and social activities are all a part of healthy living.

Everything I found at North Texas Job Corps Center can be defined as **_living_**. Now I am a twenty-four-year-old adult who can balance a check book, budget my money, and can get a good job because of the employability skills I've learned and applied on a daily basis while at Job Corps. I'm not afraid of failing, because the only way a person fails is if that person doesn't succeed at **_living_**. When I came to Job Corps, I had a hot temper, a street mentality, and a marijuana habit that kept my mind from recognizing my potential. Job Corps showed me the key to that lock. I'm a man.

I remember staying after work encouraging and helping Jeffrey to get started with this essay, after he decided to participate in the Job Corps's regional essay contest. He wrote and rewrote it a few times, before I called one of the teachers to edit his essay. He did not show enough confidence in himself that he could write well, but I asked him if living and learning at Job Corps was better than living on the street. "If it is, there are many things to write about," I suggested. He said, "You don't know because you never have to live on the street." I looked him in the eyes and responded, "Write for me to read if you want me to know." I admitted that I did not know anything about life on the street, until I started working with him. Some of my students have shared information about their lives, and it has told me a little bit about a group of Americans who live below the poverty level in this great country. The violent streets present daily challenges: killing, stealing, selling drugs, and operating gang activities. Many of my students do not want to go back to the environment from which they came. They try to study hard, do the right thing, and improve their work skills. Many of my students were using drugs prior to coming to study in this federal program. Many of them were even called "drug dealers." Several students have improved their lives, but some have not really gotten serious about meeting that challenge.

Jeffrey Jones was from my first group of students, the first group that I met on my first day of teaching at the North Texas Job Corps Center. With this group, I initially had to be more focused on discipline than on teaching the class's content itself. They gave me my initial experience as a teacher of disadvantaged youth. It was a lot of forced laughs and tears due to my lack of experience in teaching and dealing with tough American youth. Jeff is a big, bald-headed African-American young man who looked tough and rough. Looking at his student profile, I found he was twenty-three years old. He initially did not show me any respect, when I was escorted to class and introduced as their new instructor. He did not believe that he would be able to learn anything from me; otherwise he would not have asked, "What are you going to teach me?" on the first day of my full- time teaching profession. I did not answer his question right away, however. Inside, I was determined to prove to Jeff that this small teacher from Thailand can teach a difficult American youth like him. I knew it was going to be a challenging task.

When I came to the first class meeting, Jeff was the only student sitting at his work station who refused to participate in my meeting. His disrespectful behavior continued all day. He tried to get a few of his male classmates against me. At the end of the first day in class, I dismissed every student, but asked Jeff to stay, because I wanted to visit with him. He certainly did not like it, but he stayed to tell me that he did not like having a woman instructor. I told him that whether he liked it or not, he would still have me; I also told him that it was not fair for him to judge anything yet, because he still refused to try what I had to offer. He told me that he did not like to be told what to do and when to do it, because he is a grown man. I pointed out that if he claimed to be grown, he should be more mature. Refusing to participate in the first class meeting was not the appropriate way to present himself as a grown person. He went quiet after these words. He then started talking to me about what the classmates were allowed to do in class by the previous instructor: "Well, Jeff, I am not going to say anything about your previous instructor, because I don't know him and now he is no longer working here, but I am sure that as your instructor, he and I have the same goal, which is to help you learn and graduate in a timely manner." I stopped and listened to hear how he would respond. "I like the hardware part; I worked on hardware with my previous instructor. I have not yet worked on the software programs you talked about during the meeting." I felt that he did not respond to what I asked, but the one thing that caught my attention was that he mentioned what I talked about in the first class meeting in which he did not even participate. It made me think that he had gotten the information from his classmates during training hours.

I quickly replied, "Jeff, it is why I am here — to teach and train you on those software programs that you already have installed on the hardware at your work station. By knowing the hardware already, you will now be able to learn more about the software and we will start working on a project tomorrow." He was silent, so I decided to take another step, "Jeff, wouldn't it be nice if you could show your previous instructor that you have completed many projects in class, when he comes to visit our campus or calls to ask how you are doing? Do you think he will be happy, if he knows that instead of taking time to learn, you spend the time talking and acting out against your new instructor?" I asked. He kept quiet. I did not keep him long after that. After he left, I felt so tired from the first day of class. I learned later on that Jeff was only the first of many students with whom I would have to work.

I worked with Jeffrey Jones and his group for almost eight months. Finally, Jeff graduated. During the graduation ceremony, I had a chance to meet his family. They thanked me for working with him and told me that he had come a long way. Yes, I knew he had come a long way and still had a really long way to go. He gave me a big hug on his graduation day. There were also many hugs from my first group of students on that day. That reminded me of what my professor used to say in college: "as a teacher, you might not make a lot of money like the other professions, but you will receive a lot of hugs at a local grocery store like Wal-Mart."

The last time I heard from Jeff was in 2002. He let me know that he had recently gotten married and had children. He thanked me for my encouragement while he was my student, and he told me that he would keep in touch. He appreciated the fact that I did not give up on him. I have not heard from him since. I figure that he is busy living his life and making a living to support his family. I hope that he is doing well.

Recently, I went to visit my friend's mother at her nursing home. I met one of the nurse's aids who works there. From talking to her, I learned that she is Jeff's wife. What a small world! I got the opportunity to hear about Jeff again after another four years. She told me that Jeff is doing fine. He is the assistant manager of one of the popular fast food chains. I told his wife to give him my regards. It is great to know that one of my students is doing well for his life and for his family.

For the past seven years I also have had an opportunity to work with several good students from Ethiopia and Uganda. They are a hard-working group of students. They have a great determination to be successful in their education here in America. They work hard in class. They are very polite and respectful. They have a good ability to stay on task and follow directions. Most importantly, they appreciate the opportunity to better their lives in America, while many of my American students just sit back and take everything for granted, complaining about everything provided to them. They lack an appreciation for their privileges; they refuse to follow many useful instructions and directions, losing a great opportunity to modify their negative behavior. They are waiting for a miracle to turn their disadvantaged life into a success, without them having to make an effort. They dream of becoming rich and famous without working for it, while blaming their government for not providing them with enough opportunity and accusing immigrants of taking their jobs. They act crazily among themselves, using all kinds of profanity during their conversations without taking any opportunity to improve. They use drugs knowing that it will only help them escape life's problems for a short while, and they blame their parents for their broken family, while they are being given the opportunity to be better than those who gave them life. They receive welfare and still complain that it is not enough, while they sit around doing nothing; they are unwilling to get up, get dressed, and to show up for class and for work. It is really sad, pitiful, and disappointing for me to see many of my American students abusing their advantages, privileges, and opportunities. Recently, two of my American students were placed on a job. They are the "less misbehaved" students in that group. They got a good employment opportunity with a famous retail store that offers potential career growth. They went through the whole hiring process and got accepted. Unfortunately, neither of them could keep a job for two full weeks, due to their lack of self-determination and the appropriate employability skills that they failed to practice. One student chose to consume an illegal substance a few days before his employment was set to begin. That resulted in their termination from the program, without a job. The other student started working, but did not show up consistently during his first week of work. For the second week, he just chose not to show up at all. His reason for quitting was that he did not want to do it any more. Then, he was terminated from the program, because of his failure to perform a job, a job that could lead him to a future career. He just refused to do it. It is just sad that they do not realize that in a competitive job market today, finding a job is not easy, whether it is at the entry level or at a professional level.

My big challenge each day is how I will be able to train these American students who happen to be my products of hope, to do "whatever it takes" to get and keep a job, in a short amount of time, so that they can be proud of their employment check, instead of food stamps or a welfare check. Another part of my job is to motivate my students; I realize that they individually need a great deal of motivation that will help to guide them to reach their potential. Besides what I call "motivation candy," a coffee candy that I bought from an Asian store to give to students who always try to sleep in my class, I spend time talking with them individually and privately in the office when time allows, to point out their weaknesses and to encourage their strengths. It certainly requires time and great patience to motivate several groups of rough youth. Some have the willingness to put extra effort into class, but many lack the ability to be a self-starter. I do my best to offer help during class time, but some students come to talk with me after the end of school. Some never talk to me until they ask for help when they get into trouble outside of class.

I recently got a thank you card from a hard working student from Uganda. He is now studying in a community college for his Associate's Degree. He is also working as a desktop publisher in a printing company in Forth Worth, TX. He is the hardest working and the most determined of my recent groups of students. He takes his educational opportunities seriously. He was patiently getting through each of the obstacles in his life step by step, while he was in my class. It is an honor for me to help him complete the whole financial aid process for him to get into a college. I remember he was so happy coming to tell me in class about his $1,200 approval fee for his first semester in college. He is really thankful to have had the opportunity to study here. In class, he not only got assigned tasks done on time, but also took the extra time to accomplish as many tasks as possible to seize the opportunity to learn. He told me that he appreciates the chance to be in this country, and he is going to make the best of it. He created the card by himself, I could tell; the card was light pink in color, with three white roses and a lit candle. There are three different paragraphs in the card. I certainly read it with appreciation. It also made my day in the classroom wonderful.

To: Mrs. Sato, Patcharin

The little things you do each day affect many people a great deal. You inspire us with your willingness and ability to help others. You take time to create a future, one day at a time. You are continuously searching for a way to make things better, and you are seizing the opportunity to improve everyone's life.

You make a world of difference!!!

Isn't it a wonderful thing that we're all different? Each one has strengths and skills to share. And when we link our individual strengths together, we're invincible. I can't imagine us without you.

Opportunity represents itself as a door to a new level of success. One can knock and knock and never get through. You've been the key that has unlocked new opportunities and taken us to places we never thought possible. Thank you for opening the door. Thank you for being the key to our success.

By: Gilbert Habiyambere

One of my Ethiopian students is now working on the busy toll way in the city. He worked a lot of long hours on his part time job after school. He was determined to save money as much as he could, while studying in the program. When I first had him in class, he did not know how to type, but he had a good willingness to practice and to try his best. He finally graduated from the program and had a large amount of savings. He recently enrolled in a community college while working full time. He sent some money from his savings to support his family in Ethiopia. The last time he called me, he enthusiastically told me that he might be getting married, and he has filed a petition for his wife to come from Ethiopia to stay with him in America.

There are many of my students who join the service, such as US Army, Navy, and Air Force, after their training in my class. Once in a while, I receive letters or postcards from former students in Hawaii, Japan, and Germany, telling me how they are doing and how they are enjoying their endeavors in their career choices. Some shared with me their life experiences traveling into different countries and adapting to other cultures.

It was a joy having one married couple by the name "John and Samantha" as students. I really enjoyed their pleasant behavior, their ambition, and their enthusiasm, for a short period of time, because they worked so hard to complete their training. For a few months, having them in class was a wonderful experience. John and Samantha are two of my exceptional American students, who work hard for what they want and do so with a positive attitude toward things and situations. They demonstrated good and appropriate work skills in class with a "can do" attitude on every class project. After completing my class, they got jobs in Phoenix, Arizona. John is doing freelance work for an organization, while Samantha is an assistant manager for a CD duplication company. Every once in a while, I get an e-mail from them to let me know how they are doing. I certainly read all of their messages with joy:

From: John Thomas Soto
Sent: Friday, October 22, 2004 8:25 PM
To: Patcharin Sato
Subject: Your Students

Hey Mrs. Sato,

We hope everything is going well with you, class and personal. I just got an e-mail from Misty. She said you asked about us. Everything is going O.K. at our jobs. It's only part-time, so it's not the greatest. Samantha has an interview with a company on Monday for a project manager position. I have put in applications for an intern position, a newspaper, and a small business (all graphic artist position). Thanks for asking about us. We both say be safe, take care, and all that good stuff.

Love Lots,
John and Samantha

****

From: John Thomas Soto
Sent: Wednesday, December 15, 2004 2:50 PM
To: Patcharin Sato
Subject: Hello my most favorite instructor in the world.

Hello Mrs. Sato

How are you doing? I hope you and your family are doing well. Thank you for getting that information about the work and stuff. Now that I have a set rate, I have been so busy, but I like it. Thanksgiving just passed and Christmas is coming up, so I want to wish you a happy all year round. I hope that is the right way. Anyway take care and be safe.

Love
John & Samantha

****

From: John Thomas Soto
Sent: Thursday, February 03, 2005 5:43 PM
To: Patcharin Sato
Subject: Hello Teacher

How are you doing, Mrs. Sato? I hope things are going well for you and your family. We are doing well. Sam has been working for her company for over three months. I just got done doing some big projects for an event and for some doctors. If everything goes well, I will have a big job coming up for a high school. Other than that, nothing new has happened. We are just taking it one step at a time, making sure not to overwhelm ourselves. We also got lots of copies of the program that we did, and Sam wants us to send you a copy, so if you wouldn't mind giving us the address where we can send it to you, we will send it off. Hope everything is going well with your students. They don't know how lucky they are to have you as their instructor. I have to get going so take care, be safe and have fun.

Love
John & Samantha

****

From: John Thomas Soto
Sent: Wednesday, August 24, 2005 5:52 PM
To: Patcharin Sato
Subject: Hi

Hello Mrs. Sato,

How are you? We hope you are doing well with your family and your work. We both miss you. We are doing well. Sam has been at her job for almost a year and we are in the middle of getting a business started doing graphic designing. Thanks to what you have taught us, we have done things that I personally never would have been able to do. We are in the middle of designing a second book cover for an author friend of ours. I am working from home doing the graphics and stuff. We both consider you the best instructor we have ever had and hope that your future students realize how lucky they are to have you as their instructor. Please write back and tell us how you are doing. Until then, take care and be safe.

John and Samantha

****

There was a Hispanic young man in my class two years ago. His home town was on the border between Texas and Mexico. His parents were unable to communicate in English, but they invited me to visit their home for a vacation. They sent me a Christmas card and a gift from Mexico. He was a good student who did what he was supposed to do in class. He was dependable, polite, and respectful. He came to my class without any knowledge of computers. After a few months, he was able to master his computer skills. He spent a lot of time in class and after school learning. His projects always looked good. Once, when he was in trouble outside of class due to his young age, he let me know and asked for help. In a few after-school meetings, I was able to pull him back on track. He was able to graduate from my class. He still calls me every once in a while to let me know how he is doing. Because of his determination, he is one of many good products of hope that I believe will be successful.

It was a nice connectivity that my students have with me when they contact me. I am so honored to have the opportunity to hear how they are doing in their life. They are not only students who have given me a sense of accomplishment; they are proud of their success, but they are also unique products of my hopes and my dreams. I remember my first day of class in one summer session while I was working on my teaching certification. My instructor read one handout, a letter, to the whole class; it is a letter that brings many teachers to tears, including myself. I found it is a very interesting, motivating, inspiring, and energizing story for us, as teachers.

Three Letters from Teddy
(Author—Unknown)

Teddy's letter came today and now that I've read it, I will place it in my cedar chest with the other things important to my life.

"I wanted you to be the first to know." I smiled as I read the words he had written, and my heart swelled with a pride that I had no right to feel. I have not seen Teddy Stallard since he was a student in my fifth-grade class, 15 years ago.

It was early in my career, and I had only been teaching for two years. From the first day he stepped into my classroom, I disliked Teddy. Teachers (although everyone knows differently) are not supposed to have favorites in a class, but most especially they are not to show dislike for a child, any child. Nevertheless, every year there are one or two children that one cannot help but be attracted to, for teachers are human, and it is human nature to like bright, pretty, intelligent people, whether they are

10 years old or 25. And sometimes, not too often fortunately, there will be one or two students to whom the teacher just can't seem to relate.

I thought myself quite capable of handling my personal feelings along that line, until Teddy walked into my life. There wasn't a child I particularly liked that year, but Teddy was most assuredly one I disliked. He was dirty. Not just occasionally, but all the time. His hair hung low over his ears, and he actually had to hold it out of his eyes as he wrote his papers in class. (And this was before it was fashionable to do so!) Too, he had a particular odor about him that I could never identify. His physical faults were many, and his intellect left a lot to be desired also. By the end of the first week, I knew he was hopelessly behind the others. Not only was he behind, but he was just plain slow! I began to withdraw from him immediately.

Any teacher will tell you it's more of a pleasure to teach a bright child. It is definitely more rewarding for one's ego. But any teacher worth his/her credentials can channel work to the bright child, keeping him/her challenged and learning while she/he puts her major effort on the slower ones. Any teacher can do this. Most teachers do it, but I didn't. Not that year. In fact, I concentrated on my best students and let the others follow along as best they could. Ashamed as I am to admit it, I took perverse pleasure in using my red pen; and each time I came to Teddy's papers, the cross-marks (and they were many) were always a little larger and a little redder than necessary.

"Poor work!" I wrote with a flourish. While I did not actually ridicule the boy, my attitude was obviously quite apparent to the class, for he quickly became the class "goat," the outcast - the unlovable and the unloved. He knew I didn't like him, but he didn't know why. Nor did I know - then or now - why I felt such an intense dislike for him. All I know is he was a little boy no one cared about and I made no effort on his behalf. The days rolled by and we made it through the Fall Festival, the Thanksgiving holidays, and I continued marking happily with my red pen. As the Christmas holidays approached, I knew

Teddy would never catch up in time to be promoted to the sixth-grade level. He would be a repeater. To justify myself, I went to his cumulative folder from time to time. He had very low grades for the first four years, but no grade failure. How he had made it, I didn't know. I closed my mind to the personal remarks:

First grade: "Teddy shows promise by work and attitude but has a poor home situation." Second grade: "Teddy could do better. Mother terminally ill. He received little help at home." Third grade: "Teddy is a pleasant boy. Helpful, but too serious. Slow learner. Mother passed away at end of year." Fourth grade: "Very slow, but well behaved. Father shows no interest."

"Well, they passed him four times, but he will certainly repeat fifth grade! Do him good!" I said to myself.

And then the last day before the holiday arrived. Our little tree on the reading table sported paper and popcorn chains. Many gifts were heaped underneath, waiting for the big moment. Teachers always get several gifts at Christmas, but mine that year seemed bigger and more elaborate than ever. There was not a student who had not brought me one. Each unwrapping brought squeals of delight and the proud giver would receive effusive thank-you.

His gift wasn't the last one I picked up; in fact, it was in the middle of the pile. Its wrapping was a brown paper bag, and he had colored Christmas trees and red bells all over it. It was stuck together with masking tape.

"For Miss Thompson - from Teddy," it read. The group was completely silent, and for the first time I felt conspicuous, embarrassed because they all stood watching me unwrap that gift. As I removed the last bit of masking tape, two items fell to my desk. A gaudy rhinestone bracelet with several stones missing and a small bottle of dime-store cologne - half empty. I could hear the snickers and whispers, and I wasn't sure I could look at Teddy.

"Isn't this lovely?" I asked, placing the bracelet on my wrist. "Teddy, would you help me fasten it?" He smiled shyly as he fixed the clasp, and I held up my wrist for all of them to admire. There were a few oohs and ahhs, but as I dabbed the cologne behind my ears, all the little girls lined up for a dab behind their ears. I continued to open the gifts until I reached the bottom of the pile.

We ate our refreshments, and the bell rang. The children filed out with shouts of "See you next year!" and "Merry Christmas!" but Teddy waited at his desk. When they had all left, he walked toward me clutching his gift and books to his chest. "You smell just like Mom," he said softly. "Her bracelet looks real pretty on you too. I'm glad you liked it." He left quickly, and I locked the door, sat down and wept, resolving to make up to Teddy what I had deliberately deprived him of - a teacher who cared. I stayed every afternoon with Teddy from the end of the holidays until the last day of school. Sometimes we worked together. Sometimes he worked alone while I drew up lesson plans or graded papers.

Slowly but surely he caught up with the rest of the class. Gradually there was a definite upward curve in his grades. He did not have to repeat the fifth grade. In fact, his final averages were among the highest in the class, and although I knew he would be moving out of the state when school was out, I was not worried for him. Teddy had reached a level that would stand him in good stead the following year, no matter where he went. He had enjoyed a measure of success and as we were taught in our teacher training courses: "Success builds success."

I did not hear from Teddy until seven years later, when his first letter appeared in our mailbox.

"*Dear Miss Thompson,*

I just wanted you to be the first to know. I will be graduating second in my class next month.

Very truly yours,
Teddy Stallard."

I sent him a card of congratulations and a small package, a pen and pencil gift set. I wondered what he would do after graduation. Four years later, Teddy's second letter came.

"Dear Miss Thompson,
I wanted you to be the first to know. I was just informed I'll be graduating first in my class. The university has not been easy, but I liked it.

Very truly yours,
Teddy Stallard."

I sent him a good pair of sterling silver monogrammed cuff links and a card, so proud of him I could burst! And now - today - Teddy's third letter.

"Dear Miss Thompson,

I wanted you to be the first to know. As of today, I am Theodore J. Stallard, M.D. How about that!!?? I'm going to be married in July, the 27th, to be exact. I wanted to ask if you could come and sit where Mom would sit if she were here. I'll have no family there, as Dad died last year.

Very truly yours,
Ted Stallard."

I'm not sure what kind of gift one sends to a doctor on completion of medical school and state boards. Maybe I'll just wait and take a wedding gift, but my note can't wait.

"Dear Ted,

Congratulations! You made it, and you did it yourself! In spite of those like me and not because of us, this day has come for you. God bless you. I'll be at that wedding with bells on!"

I asked my instructor for a copy of this handout. For many years, I always keep it in my desk drawer in the office. I sometimes make a copy to share with my co-workers. Its main purpose is as a career learning lesson that we, as teachers, can learn from the experience of another teacher. Learning from this story makes us work even harder with every student in our classroom, who are under our supervision and expect our love and care. It is not a hope that one of my students will become a doctor, but it is my hope that they become the best they can be for themselves in any career choice they choose, and the M.D. is no exception. We all never know what will happen in the future. They might not do as well as we expect them to today, but they might turn around and do it exceptionally in the future. Each of the students is just a message that we send into a future that we might never be able to see.

I believe that I am not different from many teachers who are happy to hear about their students' achievements and successes. On the other hand, we are sad to hear about students who have made wrong choices and have not utilized their knowledge and skills to better themselves. I am quite sure that my own teachers feel the same way toward me. It has always been a dream that one day I will be able to go back home to tell my favorite English teacher, and the other teachers who care about me, about my teaching in America, and also to be able to tell them that I found myself teaching my students as I was taught. I discipline my students like I was disciplined. I want to let them know that I am their product of hope that is currently producing more hope in the American educational system.

Pat & Students on graduation day

Afterword

I started writing the last section of the book when I was on the plane, on the way to visit my parents in Thailand for two weeks. This is the seventh time traveling to Thailand within almost fourteen years. It is wonderful feeling to be on the way home. I wish I could do more often. I admire some Thais who can visit their home land every year. Some are retiring there. My hat's off to those Thais who had worked hard here and been able to enjoy the benefit in the home land. While writing, I recall encouraging words, the numerous supportive e-mails from friends, and the positive feedback from my editors at every stage. Those were great additional motivations to support my strong hope and desire to see the finished product. More than anything else, my writing this book in English is a challenging experience. I recall a few friends asking whether I want to publish this book in Thai. It is my secret hope that there will be some kind of assistance in publishing this book in my native language to provide information that benefits Thais. Of course, that will be another goal with which to challenge myself.

Each day is a learning day, and it is a great way to learn something new with a positive attitude and open mind. As a person who always welcomes all learning opportunities, after gaining professional experience, teaching insight, and a strong desire to contribute more to empower a large number of learners, I recently started updating my resume to apply for new opportunities and challenges. My job hunting experience will begin again. This reminds me of when some people say that some Americans change jobs or careers more than three times before they retire. So, it is not surprising when one of my friends say, "It is not common to see loyalty in some organizations." However, there are many people who continue working for the same organization until they retire.

My recent admission in graduate school once again and my enrollment in two graduate classes will make my Tuesday night, after work hours, even longer. Sitting in class among different professionals who strive to achieve their higher educational goals gives me a sense of fulfillment and challenges me to run a long road.

Each day of listening to my sons' conversations about their daily activities still gives me a sense of responsibility to provide unconditional love, support, and care. "Mom, this weekend we have a soccer game on Saturday evening, O.K?" or "Mom, don't forget about preparing snacks for Thai school, O.K?" or the request from my husband that "Pat, please check with the preschool teacher why Andrew didn't take a nap, because he fell to sleep while practicing piano," reminds me that whatever I do personally, my family is still my first priority. My son offering me a neck massage after my tiring day was excellent, and it gives me the energy to keep going. The little voice saying, "I love you, Mom," melts my heart and makes the exhausting day from work and study worth it. The same little voice saying, "Mom, I am going to write you a bad note because you don't let me sleep on the bed with you and daddy," makes me always spare some time for that bonding. A big hug from two little arms and a warm cuddling give me a wonderful appreciation of motherhood. My children's upcoming birthday party that will gather many of my good friends and good foods will be one of the events that give me a sense of connection with them. Our family vacation to Japan next year is quality time that we expect to enjoy with each other and family members in a Japanese culture.

My recent correction on two female students' negative and inappropriate behavior in class gave me the feeling that behavior modification is still a big task in my profession. However, one student recently enrolled in my class who has demonstrated strong learning effort and work skills makes me admire what he is working for. I was more surprised after learning that he had obtained a B.A. in Communication from a university in Mexico. He informed me that he wants to better his life in America and will try to do his best in education. The Job Corps program is his first start here. Seeing him work hard in class gives me an urge to provide him with my best assistant to support his educational growth.

My conservative daily routine continues purposefully. With each stop and step in my life here, I try to live not only for myself, but also for others to whom I can be helpful. I remember some saying that "Your life is yours, so live it to the maximum." That maximum might be different for each individual. Whether it is a suitable great life to live or not, you have a chance to choose. It is definitely up to you which one, which way, or which direction you choose. I like the way DeWayne Owens, the author of *How to Get Rich on Purpose* mentioned that "You can live no richer life than a life of purpose." Life experience is what you make and learn from your daily life. I personally learn a lot each day. ***America…A Golden Journey*** is the life I have chosen to live for the past twelve years. It has been a fantastic to live in the land that many people have described as, "great country, America." I sincerely appreciate the opportunity to share that priceless experience with you, and I welcome your constructive feedback of ***America …A Golden Journey***. If you are able to take something from my book to make an additional experience to your life, please pass it on to someone you know, so they can benefit as well. For many years, one of the many good things from America that is still in my memory is the words of the American president, "God Bless you, and God Bless the United States of America."

Bibliography

Chapman, Gary. The Five Love Languages – How to Express
    Heartfelt Communication to Your Mate. Northfield
    Publishing. Chicago. 203.
    -- Resourceful book for happy married life.

Daniel, Lois. (1991).How To Write Your Own Life Story – A Step-
    by-Step Guide for the Nonprofessional Writer. Chicago
    Review Press. Chicago. 216,
    -- Good resource for a beginning writer.

Giblin, Les. (1985). Skill With People. Les Giblin. NJ. 33. -- People
    skill guide for career success, happier family life, and better
    social life.

Hampshire, David. (1992). Living and Working in America. WSOY.
    Finland. (507).
    -- A survival handbook on how to live and work in America.

International Students, Inc. Adjustment to Living in the United
    States. [Online] Available: http://www.isionline.org/main.
    htm, November 6, 1997.

-- Good online resource for international students. This site provides information about how to adjust to live in the United State, how to make friends, how to adjust   to the educational system. It also provides student services, student resources, volunteer opportunities, and investment opportunities.

Kuther, Tara, Ph.D. Tips for New Graduate Students. [Online] Available: http://gradschool.about.com. December 30, 2006. -- Resourceful online site on variety topics for new graduate school students.

National Association for Foreign Student Affairs. (1996). A guide to University study in the U.S.A. AT&T.174. -- Excellent resource for prospective visitors, international students who plan to study in America. This handbook contains information about how to obtain a visa, how to live in campus, higher education in the United States, culture shock, and immigration regulations, etc.

Northeastern University. International Student Site. [Online] Available: http://arapaho.nsuok.edu/international/swedish.html, 1996. -- This site provides a lot of useful information about the guide to university, and international students' idea about their university and life in the United States.

Owens, Dewayne. (2002). How to Get Rich on Purpose. N-Harmony Publishing. TX. 212. -- A good self-help resource for personal and professional growth.

Rosen, Margery. (2002). Seven Secrets of a Happy Marriage. Workman Publishing. NY. (431).
    -- Seven important skills that each married partner should know to effectively work on to better marriage.

Suzuki, Shinichi. (1981). Ability Development From Age Zero. Warner Bros. Publications Inc. Florida. 96.
    -- Informative guidance for nurturing of young children through musical interest.

Wat Buddhavas of Houston. (1995). Typical Thai, The Best & Simple Thai Dishes. Postal and Printing Inc. TX. 170.
    -- A collection of favorite Thai recipes from the members of Thai temple in Houston, Texas.

Webmaster, Chinese Culture. [Onine] Available http://www.c-c-c. org/chineseculture/zodiac/Monkey.htm. 2006.
    -- The World Wide Web site contains information about Chinese and Chinese American art, history, and culture in the United States.

Webmaster, Thai Culture. [Online] Available http://frangipani.com/ huahin/tips.htm, January, 16, 1996.
    --The World Wide Web site contains information about Thai Culture and interesting things about Thailand.

Webmaster, FamilyMatters.tv (Online) Available http://www. familymatters.tv/level_4/parenting/positivedevelopment. htm, 2004.

    -- The World Wide Web site contains useful information for family fun and travel information

Wheat, Ed, M.D. (1980). Love Life For Every Married Couple. Zondervan Publishing House. Michigan.251.
    -- A certified sex therapist's guidance that helped many troubled couples improve their love lives and build happier marriages.